Down, Out, and Under Arrest

Down, Out, and Under Arrest

Policing and Everyday Life in Skid Row

Forrest Stuart

THE UNIVERSITY OF CHICAGO PRESS | CHICAGO AND LONDON

Forrest Stuart is assistant professor of sociology at the University of Chicago.

The University of Chicago Press, Chicago 60637
The University of Chicago Press, Ltd., London
© 2016 by The University of Chicago
All rights reserved. Published 2016.
Printed in the United States of America

25 24 23 22 21 20 19 18 17 16 1 2 3 4 5

ISBN-13: 978-0-226-37081-1   (cloth)
ISBN-13: 978-0-226-37095-8   (e-book)
DOI: 10.7208/chicago/9780226370958.001.0001

Library of Congress Cataloging-in-Publication Data

Names: Stuart, Forrest, author.
Title: Down, out, and under arrest : policing and everyday life in skid row / Forrest Stuart.
Description: Chicago ; London : The University of Chicago Press, 2016. | Includes bibliographical references and index.
Identifiers: LCCN 2015046039 | ISBN 9780226370811 (cloth : alk. paper) | ISBN 9780226370958 (e-book).
Subjects: LCSH: Police-community relations—United States. | Urban poor—United States.
Classification: LCC HV7936.P8 S78 2016 | DDC 363.2/320869420979494—dc23 LC record available at http://lccn.loc.gov/2015046039

For Bobbi

Contents

Preface

In my first year working in Los Angeles's Skid Row, I was questioned by police fourteen times. For merely standing on the corner.

And that's nothing. Juliette, a woman I met during that time, has been stopped by police well over a hundred times. She has been arrested upward of sixty times. Add it all up, and she's given up more than a year of her life serving weeklong jail sentences. Her most common crime? Simply sitting on the sidewalk—an arrestable offense in LA.

For most Americans, the sight of this proud grandmother sitting on the concrete handcuffed and sobbing is unfathomable. For those who live and work in Skid Row, it's just another Tuesday morning. But as Juliette's tear-soaked shirt attests, the fortieth arrest is as traumatic as the first.

As the officers lifted Juliette to her feet, she repeated a single question: Why? It's a question we should all be asking. What purpose does this treatment serve, for our society or for Juliette? How did we reach a point where we've cut direct and indirect support for our poorest citizens yet are spending over six million dollars on additional policing for the square mile of Skid Row alone? What does this move mean for those caught in the bowels of our society? What does it tell us, more generally, about justice, equality, and opportunity in America?

This book is my attempt to answer these questions. To answer Juliette's question. It's my attempt to describe and explain the mounting criminalization of our lowliest neighbors. The answers, it turns out, are complicated, at times even counterintuitive. As though a Greek tragedy, it is a story built more on mistakes and misplaced priorities than on heroes and villains. We have created a situation where people on the many sides of this issue are genuinely trying to do the right thing, yet often come up short. Sometimes in ways that do serious harm.

To find answers, I spent five years working in Skid Row, seeing things from the perspective of the men and women who—reluctantly, in most cases—made it their home. Together, we walked the streets. We hung out on corners. We shared meals at homeless shelters. I lounged in their flophouse hotels, I met cousins and ex-lovers, I sat with them through court hearings. I watched them disappear into the backs of squad cars and cycle through the criminal justice system. I listened to their worries as they lost jobs, housing, and hope along the way. Their recurring interactions with the police felt so heavy that I knew I couldn't stop there. So I devoted serious time to the police. I sat with officers in the station between shifts, and I shadowed them out on patrol. I got to know them on a personal level. We shared beers, bemoaned the Dodgers, and complained about girlfriends.

As I began to get a feel for the passions and grievances of the residents and of the police, I was struck by the realization that these voices are seldom heard in the public discourse about policing and poverty. We hear a lot of smart people talking about the constant, sometimes fatal tension between police officers and the poor, but few of those experts have taken the time to speak with members of either group, to hear their stories or, perhaps more crucially, listen to what they have to say about each other. Turn on the evening news and you'll see plenty of high-ranking talking heads—police chiefs, lawyers, media pundits. They will rattle off their opinions about what they think is going on. But will you hear from those who live and breathe this reality every day? Not likely. For too long we've silenced the exact people who are pitted against each another on America's streets.

I wrote this book to fill that gap. Throughout, I rely on the voices of residents and officers I met in Skid Row. I draw on archives and records to put these stories into historical context. And, as a sociologist, I consult previous research to understand how each police stop, ticket, or arrest—no matter how surprising or unique—is part of a larger system.

The result is a close-up portrait of our current approach to policing America's most disadvantaged. Rather than offer the poor a hand up, we brandish a fist and threaten to knock them back down if they misstep. In the process, we create a new brand of inequality. Fear of police and the desire to stay out of handcuffs ripples across entire communities, seeping into relationships among friends and family members. Some turn on each another. Others retreat deeper into the shadows. But within this turmoil we also see glimmers of hope, sometimes from the least likely of sources. I don't think I'm being overly optimistic when I say that a movement is building, and we need to take note.

If I've done my job well, the following pages will help people understand what's being done in our name, and why. More importantly, these pages will help us see what the first steps might be toward changing things, and pushing for reforms designed to foster positive change in the lives of America's poorest, most disenfranchised citizens.

As you read this book, I ask you to suspend some of your assumptions about who the poor are, who the police are, and why they do what they do. Understanding our current situation and building a more equitable world requires us to come at the problem from a new angle. Let's face it. What we're doing now simply isn't working, so we have to start scrutinizing it in a new light. This book is my effort to do just that.

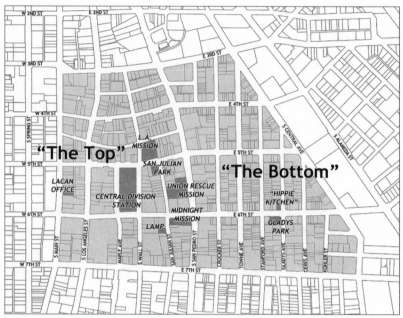

Map of Skid Row

Introduction

Darryl Watkins is a balding black man in his midfifties. His slight limp and callused hands tell of a life of manual labor. A veteran of the first Gulf war, Darryl suffers from partial hearing loss and recurring symptoms of post-traumatic stress disorder (PTSD). For the three years before we met, Darryl had held a part-time, off-the-books job stocking shelves and mopping the floors of a small convenience store in South Central Los Angeles. To make ends meet, he combined the $150 in cash he took home each week with his monthly General Relief check of $221. This meager income allowed Darryl to rent a small studio apartment a few blocks from the store. One day, without warning, Darryl's life took a turn for the worse. His employer sold the shop and let Darryl go. Without consistent income, Darryl was soon evicted from his apartment. As part of his search for a new place to live, he made the two-hour bus ride to the Veterans Affairs benefits office to ask for assistance. The VA could offer no immediate help. Instead, they handed Darryl a list of cheap single-room-occupancy (SRO) hotels located across town, in Los Angeles's Skid Row district.

Known locally as "the Nickel," Skid Row is a fifty-block neighborhood on the eastern flank of the city's rapidly redeveloping downtown. Despite their geographic proximity, the two areas are worlds apart. Mere blocks from LA's iconic city hall, revitalized central business district, and hippest new coffee shops sits one of the rawest expressions of structural violence and urban marginality found anywhere in America. Described by historian Mike Davis as "the inner circle of Dante's inferno," the Nickel is home to some thirteen thousand residents living in extreme poverty.[1] Over the last three decades, the neighborhood has become a community of last resort for those hit hardest by deindustrialization and welfare cutbacks. As job opportunities and social supports continue to dry up, denizens from across the United States are migrating to LA's Skid Row in search of emergency resources and low-cost housing. The population is overwhelmingly made up of black, undereducated, working-age men, many of whom have problems associated with physical disabilities, mental illness, and addiction.[2] With one-third of Skid Row's residents living on the streets, in shelters, or in temporary housing, the neighborhood is widely considered the homeless capital of America.

Despite having lived in Los Angeles most of his life, Darryl had never set foot in Skid Row until the VA suggested he live there. Still, he was well aware of its reputation as a place of exile. "It hit me like a ton of bricks," he recalled of learning about his "housing options." "I got a big ol' knot in my stomach as soon as the lady on the desk said those two words: Skid Row. I guess that's when it finally sunk in. I was finally at the end of the road. Rock bottom."

Having exhausted all other options, Darryl reluctantly slung his duffel bag on his back and boarded a bus for Skid Row, where he used his remaining savings to rent a room in an SRO hotel. Despite the spartan accommodations, with their faint odor and shared toilet, he forced himself to hold on to hope. To make his rent, he joined the fleet of residents who spend their days scavenging nearby alleys, pushing rickety shopping carts in search of cardboard boxes, aluminum cans, small electronics, and anything else that can be converted into cash. When the hauls were good, Darryl was able to afford his room. When times were lean, he resorted to sleeping on the streets or in a shelter.

Darryl and I met shortly after his arrival. We bonded over a heated game of dominoes in one of Skid Row's small parks. Like Darryl, I was a relative newcomer to the neighborhood. Yet our paths to this place could not have been more different. At the time, I was a graduate student at UCLA interested in writing a book on the daily survival strategies of those relegated to the very bottom of the social hierarchy. Darryl was one of a number of Skid Row residents who graciously invited me into their lives, and I began trekking out with him most mornings to help him dumpster dive. It was difficult and dirty work, and Darryl seemed happy to have a curious and unpaid "apprentice" to hold open dumpster lids and help him haggle for better prices at the recycling center.

I was consistently impressed by Darryl's optimism in the face of such stark conditions. He greeted me in the mornings with a wide, gap-toothed smile and kept me laughing with stories about childhood sweethearts and boot-camp follies. Sometimes, however, after several hours sweating in the LA sun, his tone grew darker. "If you think about it," he complained once as we struggled to control his cumbersome cart, "I really shouldn't have to be doing any of this at all. I was there when America needed me. I had faith in my country, in my government. But where are they now, now that *I* need some help? I tried everywhere. DMH [Department of Mental Health], DPSS [Department of Public Social Services], the housing office, the VA. But it's the same broken record everywhere I go: 'We can't do anything for you, Mr. Watkins.' It's like they just used me up and left me out in the cold."

Darryl's words rang in my head for some time. Yet he was far from alone in this sentiment. From my first days in the neighborhood, I consistently heard newcomers tell me that they had "paid their dues"— whether by serving in the military, paying taxes, working diligently, or simply "keeping their nose clean" in impoverished, often violent conditions—only to be abandoned by the state in their most desperate moment. They quickly learned, however, that the abandonment was not complete. Rather, state intervention had been reorganized and reinserted in the form of aggressive policing. On the streets of the Nickel, the Los Angeles Police Department was intent on solving residents' problems and bringing them back into the fold, whether residents wanted this help or not.

For Darryl, this lesson came within weeks of his arrival. On an otherwise unremarkable morning, he sat alone on a curb next to his overflowing cart, resting his feet after a particularly tiring haul. Without warning, two LAPD squad cars slammed to a halt only feet away. The officers were on top of him before Darryl had time to react. They pushed him against a nearby wall and slapped handcuffs on his wrists. After searching him and running his name through a warrant database, they arrested him for sitting on the sidewalk—a misdemeanor and an arrestable offense in Los Angeles. But for Darryl, the suddenness of the arrest was quickly overshadowed by the curious nature of the booking process. At the station, the officers gave him an unexpected ultimatum: they would drop the charges if he enrolled in a twenty-one-day residential rehabilitation program. Darryl accepted the offer. Twenty minutes later, a caseworker escorted him and five other arrestees out of the station and two blocks east to the Union Rescue Mission (URM)—the largest shelter and nonprofit service provider in the United States. Once inside, Darryl began his mandatory participation in the URM's flagship employment training and Bible study classes.

I ran into Darryl the following week in the park. He recounted his arrest and explained that he had absconded from the program after only four days. Conditions inside the facility—particularly the mandatory lights-out and early bedtime—seemed to amplify his PTSD. Instead of sleeping, he told me, he spent those few evenings wrestling with insomnia and panic attacks. The facility allowed him to leave during daylight hours but required him to report back every four hours, for classes or simply to account for his whereabouts. This schedule made it virtually impossible to return to recycling, his usual means of generating income. The program also mandated that Darryl attend drug counseling and submit to random drug tests. The final straw came when the organization asked him to hand over his monthly General Relief check, insisting that doing so would teach him the merits of saving.

While Darryl was able to cut ties with the program quickly, avoiding contact with police proved far more difficult. Less than a week later, officers detained, handcuffed, and searched him and several other men as they stood in line for free sandwiches being distributed by an out-of-town church group. "The cops wouldn't let us get our food," he told me the next morning. "They said that instead of standing around waiting for handouts, we needed to be spending our time looking for jobs." Darryl pleaded with the officers, insisting that he had been unsuccessful in landing decent-paying work after his recent layoff. The officers responded by issuing him a littering ticket (for flicking his cigarette ash into the breeze). They instructed him to take it to the URM, where four hours of job counseling would eliminate the $174 fine. "They acted like they were doing me a favor," he said with frustration. But Darryl was determined not to return to the URM, even for four hours. Over time, the unpaid fine increased to over $500, his driver's license was suspended, and a warrant was issued for his arrest.

Several weeks later, officers detained Darryl again for sitting on the sidewalk near the URM. Instead of arresting him, these officers presented him with the now familiar ultimatum right there on the spot: they would take Darryl to jail unless he walked back into the facility and enrolled in one of its rehabilitation programs. Once more, Darryl opted for the latter choice. The officers watched closely as he made his way inside. Resolved not to reenter the program, he sat in the lobby for several hours, leaving only when he felt confident that the officers' shift had ended. So began a recurring cycle. Over the next four months, the police stopped Darryl three more times, resulting in an additional citation, a second arrest, a three-week jail sentence, and another mandated stay in a rehabilitation program. I kept up with Darryl throughout this period. His optimism and magnetic personality had begun to dull as his deepening entanglements with the criminal justice system made it harder for him to get back on his feet, let alone scrape up enough money to support himself.

||||||||||||||

Police encounters like Darryl's have become a daily, if not hourly, occurrence in Skid Row. In September 2006, just before Darryl and I arrived in the area, the LAPD had launched the Safer Cities Initiative (SCI), one of the most intense policing campaigns ever seen. At an annual price tag of six million dollars, SCI saturated the neighborhood's 0.85 square miles with eighty *additional* officers, making LA's Skid Row home to arguably the densest concentration of standing police forces anywhere in the United States.[3] Adhering to the "zero tolerance" model of law enforcement, officers made nine thousand arrests and issued twelve thousand citations in the initiative's first year alone.

Over the course of five years, I spent time with hundreds of Skid Row residents for whom the police were a constant concern. I witnessed and heard about repeated detainments, interrogations, citations, arrests, and incarceration at the hands of the LAPD. I quickly realized that understanding the daily realities of America's most disadvantaged—the dilemmas that complicate securing an income, obtaining housing, or merely acquiring a meal—requires that we consider the pervasive role and impact of the police. *Down, Out, and Under Arrest* is the result. This book builds outward from thousands of police interactions and experiences like Darryl's to show how policing is reshaping urban poverty and marginality in the twenty-first century.

This book makes two central assertions. The first is that zero-tolerance policing campaigns like the Safer Cities Initiative represent a profound shift in contemporary poverty governance. As federal, state, and local governments continue to purge welfare rolls, eliminate housing programs, and privatize service provision, the police are increasingly tasked with day-to-day management of the growing number of citizens falling through the holes in the threadbare social safety net. Contrary to many of our assumptions about policing, these interventions are not simply intended to lock up the poor and throw away the key. Rather, they reflect what I term *therapeutic policing*—a paternalistic brand of spatial, behavioral, and moral discipline designed to "cure" those at the bottom of the social hierarchy of the individual pathologies deemed responsible for their abject circumstances.

The second major contention is that this interventionist mode of social control has reshaped the cultural contexts of poor neighborhoods. In their efforts to cope with omnipresent regulation and surveillance, residents develop a shared cognitive framework—what I call *cop wisdom*—that becomes a guide for processing information, perceiving available options, and making moral sense of experiences, even when police officers are not (yet) physically present. Cop wisdom also provides the foundation for residents' efforts to evade, deflect, and otherwise contest unwanted police contact. Through this process, policing has become intimately woven into the social fabric of everyday life, restructuring how those relegated to the bottom of the social order come to understand their peers, their communities, and themselves.

Taken together, these developments reflect a dramatic transformation in relations between the state and the urban poor. Throughout the latter half of the twentieth century, our most impoverished communities faced an era of "malign neglect" on the part of a state that was unwilling to provide adequate economic, social, and physical protections.[4] While the down-and-out have received neither respite from market insecurities nor meaningful increases in financial support, they confront a new set of challenges to mere survival. The malign neglect of the past is increasingly supplanted by an era of "malign attention." A reorganized, interventionist state reaches even deeper into the lives of the urban poor to exert strict control over their most mundane and commonplace behaviors.

Policing the Poor

Poverty governance—the supervision, regulation, and integration of impoverished populations into civil society and the market—is a perennial state concern. Generations of social thinkers, from Karl Marx to Michel Foucault, have called attention to the fact that the police, the courts, and prison constitute a primary means by which the state accomplishes this task. Criminal justice policies operate in tandem with social welfare policies to ensure the cooperation, contribution, and quiescence of those living on society's margins.[5] In sociologist Loïc Wacquant's recent formulation, the poor are "doubly regulated" by the feminine "left hand" of the state, represented by social assistance programs, labor laws, and education, and by the masculine "right hand" of the state, embodied in criminal justice institutions.[6]

The history of American social welfare and criminal justice reveals a symbiotic relation between these twin institutions, which often come to reflect the same ideologies regarding the state's responsibilities to its citizens. Beginning in the early twentieth century, social welfare policies embraced Keynesian principles that sought to counter the recessive cycles of the economy, protect vulnerable populations, and curb inequalities, largely by offering the poor a partial but significant reprieve from market pressures. The best known of such policies was Aid to Families with Dependent Children (AFDC), which provided supplemental income for poor single mothers. This commitment to social citizenship found its double in the criminal justice approach known as "penal-welfarism."[7] Reflecting a commitment to rehabilitation and reintegration, penal-welfarist policies embraced social work with offenders and their families, indeterminate sentences linked to early release and parole, and social inquiry and psychiatric reports. Criminal offending was often viewed as a result of poverty and deprivation, while crime reduction depended on the expansion of economic and social opportunity.[8] From this perspective, prison sentences were often seen as counterproductive to the larger process of integration and correction.

Beginning in the 1960s, however, the suppositions and goals of the Keynesian activist state came under serious attack by a new intellectual and political movement: neoliberalism. Theorized most famously by economists Friedrich Hayek and Milton Friedman, and implemented by Presidents Ronald Reagan and Bill Clinton, neoliberalism emphasizes the need to mobilize the state on behalf of the market while embracing market logics—such as supply and demand—as the optimal device for organizing human activities and distributing goods and services.[9] Whereas Keynesian policies use state power to protect citizens against the vagaries of unfettered capitalism, neoliberal policies ease state regulation over the market to increase competition, free trade, and entrepreneurialism.[10]

Neoliberal reforms have resulted in a sizable reorganization and reprioritization of social welfare policy. Contrary to the common academic and public narrative, welfare expenditures have actually *increased* over the last six decades. This expansion, however, has been steadily funneled away from the most destitute.[11] Support to the so-called undeserving poor—able-bodied, unemployed, unmarried, non-elderly—has been slashed as part of an ideological agenda to incentivize more "acceptable" market behaviors. Changes to AFDC are a prime example. Between 1979 and 1990, the median value of monthly AFDC support payments decreased by 40 percent, from $606 to $364 for a family of three—a level of support that comes to about half the federal poverty level.[12] In 1996, the Clinton administration abolished AFDC and replaced it with Temporary Aid for Needy Families (TANF), a program that ties receipt of aid to a number of strict stipulations, including satisfactory participation in the formal labor market. The result was a 20 percent decline in state transfers to single mothers between 1983 and 2004. Services for the poor have also been increasingly outsourced from the government to nonprofit, voluntary, and commercial agencies. By 2002, all but one state had contracted its TANF obligations to private entities.[13] The federal government similarly devolved its previous responsibilities for the provision of affordable housing to the private sector. Rather than meet increasing demand by constructing or subsidizing public housing, it turned to vouchers that require the poor to enter the private market to secure housing. These reforms, combined with the massive de-institutionalization of mentally ill individuals, contributed to an alarming upswing in homelessness in the latter half of the twentieth century.[14]

The rollback of welfare state protections for the most downtrodden was accompanied by the rollout of a vastly enlarged police and penal state to manage the ensuing spike in social and economic insecurity.[15] The result has been a historic rise in arrests, which peaked at over fifteen million in 1997. Over the last three decades, the incarceration rate in the United States has increased sevenfold, with 2.3 million people currently sitting in prisons and jails and an additional 5 million on probation or parole.[16] Scholars in a number of disciplines have interpreted these trends as a "punitive turn" in criminal justice, in which the once-dominant ideals of rehabilitation and reintegration have been supplanted by the more repressive aims of containment and exclusion.[17] In *Punishing the Poor*, arguably the most comprehensive analysis of this shift, Wacquant asserts that rather than attempt to reform, assist, or bring marginal populations back into the social fold, police, courts, and prisons now work primarily toward the *"invisibilization* of the social 'problems' that the state . . . no longer can or cares to treat at its roots."[18] In stark contrast to penal-welfarism, Wacquant writes, the contemporary criminal justice system is dedicated to "forcibly 'disappearing' the most disruptive of [the poor] . . . into the swelling dungeons . . . geared toward brute neutralization, rote retribution, and simple warehousing."[19]

Observers similarly find evidence of the punitive turn in policing policies that expel marginal populations from downtown areas to more peripheral and abandoned districts in order to make way for redevelopment and gentrification.[20] Neoliberal economic policies, through market deregulation, have created intense competition between cities to lure increasingly footloose investment dollars. Yet the growing visibility of poverty and the presence of homelessness, begging, prostitution, and people with mental and physical disabilities threaten municipal aspirations for reinvigorating the urban core as a viable site for capital accumulation.

In response, cities across the United States have adopted zero-tolerance policing policies inspired by James Q. Wilson and George Kelling's "broken windows" theory of crime.[21] According to this theory, cities can most effectively reduce serious crime and improve quality of life by aggressively targeting minor forms of disorderly behavior, such as "panhandling, street prostitution, drunkenness . . . obstruction of streets and public spaces . . . unlicensed vending and peddling . . . and other such acts."[22] The broken windows theory calls for a fundamental reorientation of law enforcement priorities away from a narrow focus on felony offenses and toward the constant and unyielding punishment of public behaviors deemed "offensive." Cities have simultaneously drafted stringent municipal ordinances, sometimes referred to as "quality-of-life laws" or "civility laws," that effectively criminalize poverty. These ordinances prohibit a range of formerly legal public behaviors associated with poverty and informal economic behavior, including sitting or lying on sidewalks, placing one's personal possessions on public property for more than a short period of time, or selling newspapers and other written material in public spaces.[23] For most commentators, zero-tolerance policing forms the cornerstone of what geographer Neil Smith calls "a vengeful and reactionary viciousness against various populations accused of 'stealing' the city from the white upper classes."[24]

The punitive turn has become an obligatory point of departure for discussions of urban poverty and poverty governance.[25] Throughout my time in Skid Row, I continually compared this narrative with my own observations. At first glance, police encounters like Darryl's appeared to confirm the arrival of this so-called new punitiveness. Indeed, Darryl's mere physical presence in public space activated constant and harsh penalties as the police subjected him to repeated detainments, insurmountable fines, and jail time for such unremarkable behaviors as sitting to catch his breath, smoking a cigarette, or waiting in line for a free meal. From this angle, the police seemed to be creating what legal geographer Don Mitchell describes as "a world in which a whole class of people simply cannot be, entirely because they have no place to be."[26]

Appearances can be deceiving, however. The more closely I examined the concrete, street-level interactions between officers and residents, the less these encounters looked like a turn toward brute retribution. My doubts continued to grow as I spent time alongside the officers charged with patrolling Skid Row's streets. I observed interactions like those described by Darryl, but from the opposite side of the badge. Among those I met, Officer Chris Mendez was one of the most proactive. He was especially aggressive in preventing residents from forming lines along the sidewalks in anticipation of food giveaways. I watched one morning as he and his partner detained, interrogated, and ultimately disbanded a group of men who stood waiting for free oatmeal and coffee. The men were clearly frustrated that the officers had interfered with their breakfasts, and they initially challenged the orders to vacate the area. They fell quiet, however, when Officer Mendez reached for his handcuffs and threatened to arrest them all for loitering. Mendez filled the subsequent silence with an impromptu lecture on self-responsibility and hard work. Although several of the men were clearly older than the officer (perhaps old enough to be his father), he spoke with the stern tone of a disappointed parent:

> Actions speak louder than words, gentlemen. And right now, all I hear is a whole lot of words and not much action. You say you want me to leave you guys alone? Then you know what you gotta do. All this time you're spending taking things from other people, you could be buying that stuff with your *own* money. Every minute you spend down here just standing around is a minute you could be out there working, earning your *own* keep. I'm being hard on you because you're not being hard enough on yourselves.

In a move that simultaneously communicated his paternalist concern for the men and his tight control over their immediate fates, Officer Mendez concluded his lecture by dismissing them without arrest or citation. He said would give them a pass. This time. However, he promised that he would not hesitate to arrest them if he spotted them milling about idly at any point in the remainder of his shift. Later, when Officer Mendez and I discussed the interaction, he confidently explained that one of the most important components of his job was to, as he put it, "cut through the excuses." "By staying on top of them, they start to learn that all those excuses don't do anything but get them in trouble. Every time we come down on them, they learn they're going to have to start doing something better with their lives."

Darryl's experiences and Officer Mendez's actions demonstrate that while Los Angeles's zero-tolerance policies and quality-of-life laws grant police the power to arrest individuals like Darryl during virtually any interaction, officers do not do so in any sort of automatic fashion. Rather than systematically "disappear" Skid Row denizens from the urban landscape, officers repeatedly allow them to remain in the neighborhood, so long as they demonstrate a willingness to engage in approved, productive behaviors. Furthermore, even when officers do decide to arrest residents, they do not summarily ship them off to be warehoused in jail or prison. Whether on the streets or at the station, officers use the threat of citation and arrest to compel these individuals to take steps to better themselves and their circumstances. This all means that while the police are undoubtedly punitive, their punitiveness does not necessarily operate in place of, or in opposition to, rehabilitation and reintegration. Rather, punitiveness routinely proceeds on behalf of these aims.

Velvet Fist in Iron Glove

These encounters reflect an alternate, though reciprocal, dimension of our current mode of neoliberal poverty governance: one that centers on a therapeutic program for "improving poor people."[27] As defined by political scientist Andrew Polsky, a therapeutic approach "begins with the premise that some people are unable to adjust to the demands of everyday life or function according to the rules by which most of us operate."[28] These people are seen as requiring expert help if they are to acquire the skills and habits necessary for full and productive citizenship. Therapeutic interventions, then, are intended to reintegrate marginal citizens back into the mainstream by fostering new behaviors, instilling proper values, and ensuring profound changes in the intimate spheres of life.[29]

The neoliberal state not only looks to enhance market operations but seeks to produce citizens who are more willing and capable of entering into the market.[30] As social problems are increasingly redefined as the result of personal choices (rather than the result of structural inadequacies or political failings), the poor are envisioned as lacking the necessary levels of competence, intention, and willpower to responsibly manage their daily (market) activities. As James Q. Wilson, one of the most prominent spokesmen for this approach, has put it, those who live in poverty, particularly those who are "homeless, criminals, [and] drug addicts," "have by their behavior indicated that they do not display the minimal level of self-control expected of decent citizens."[31] According to this formulation, if the poor are too irresponsible to act in their own interests, then the state has an obligation to step in for their own good. The state must assume a paternal role, supervising and directing the poor until they can govern themselves in the desired ways.[32]

This paternalistic and disciplinary enterprise is clearly visible in recent social welfare reforms. The quantitative rollback and outsourcing of entitlements and services since the 1970s has been coupled with qualitative shifts in the underlying function of welfare provision more broadly.[33] Whereas previous needs-based relief policies worked to *de*commodify the lives of disadvantaged citizens by making daily survival less contingent on selling their labor on the market, contemporary relief agencies and private welfare organizations strive to *re*commodify this labor and furnish employers with self-regulating, prudent, and obedient employees. By making the receipt of aid contingent on behavioral modification classes, responsibility contracts, drug testing, fingerprinting, and paternity tests, welfare programs seek to teach the poor to reconsider their past choices and to "empower" them to make better future decisions. These programs treat poverty not as an economic condition but as a quasi-medical one, akin to addiction or dependence. Following this logic, they frequently adopt the twelve-step recovery model made famous by Alcoholics Anonymous to solve a host of personal problems.[34] As welfare scholar Robert Fairbanks notes, the quintessential loss to be recovered, reclaimed, and reinstated in such programs is the capacity for self-governance.[35]

In this book I make the case that policing constitutes an additional technique for "conducting the conduct" of the poor, operating alongside and in collaboration with this new breed of welfare programming.[36] The police thus constitute an important, though surprisingly overlooked, pathway by which neoliberalism's disciplinary enterprise breaches the walls of welfare organizations and suffuses the streets and sidewalks of marginalized communities. Therapeutic policing operates as a form of outreach social work that aims to transform and reintegrate residents as productive, self-governing citizens. Equipped with new legal tools and expanded discretionary authority, officers use coercive ultimatums—enter a rehabilitative program or go to jail, look for employment or suffer monetary fines—to instill residents with new habits, attitudes, and dispositions. Deployed as "tough love" for residents' own good, this street-level mode of poverty governance legitimates elevated levels of repression while widening the net of coercive control.[37] As a result, additional (and previously noncriminal) behaviors and populations are subjected to ubiquitous surveillance and intrusive regulation.

Understanding this disciplinary process requires that we pull back from current narratives that see punitiveness as the alpha and omega of contemporary policing. As Foucault reminds us, "Punitive measures are not simply 'negative' mechanisms that make it possible to repress, to prevent, to eliminate"; rather, "they are linked to a whole series of positive and useful effects which it is their task to support."[38] In other words, such punitive measures as citation, arrest, and incarceration must be seen not merely as *ends*, but also as *means*. They provide the coercive "stick" with which officers attempt to incentivize personal development and persuade residents like Darryl to make different personal choices. Punitive measures make therapeutic ultimatums possible.

A View from the Bottom

Sketching a complete picture of policing—or any state intervention—requires asking how it affects those individuals, groups, and communities who are its targets.[39] A conventional evaluation of the Safer Cities Initiative would typically begin (and likely conclude) by asking how effective it has been in reducing crime. Has the initiative made Skid Row any safer for its already vulnerable population? In this regard, SCI has come up short. Comparisons of crime rates between Skid Row and other parts of Los Angeles (where SCI was not operating), both before and after the launch of the initiative, indicate that, while crime did in fact decline following the launch of SCI—a reduction the city was more than happy to publicize—this trend had actually begun earlier and was experienced even in areas where SCI was not implemented.[40] It appears that crime fell at roughly the same rate across the city, largely irrespective of the police policy in place.

That the Safer Cities Initiative has not significantly reduced crime does not mean that it has had no impact. To focus merely on the ability (or inability) of the police to reduce crime is to continue to neglect the "positive" effects of policing, to overlook how policing "moulds, trains, builds up, and creates subjects."[41] One of the main arguments I make in this book is that policing operates as a powerful *cultural agent*—that is, it actively generates and regenerates the cultural context of impoverished neighborhoods.[42] In sociological terms, "culture" refers to the shared outlooks, schemas, and cognitive frameworks by which neighborhood residents make sense of their social world.[43] Cultural contexts influence behavior, supply "strategies of action," and provide the interpretive grids through which individuals and groups evaluate events, judge conduct, and understand each other and themselves.[44]

The cultural contexts of poor neighborhoods, particularly of Skid Row districts, have long been an object of sociological study.[45] Throughout the twentieth century, ethnographers provided up-close portraits of the daily travails and social relations that emerged amid deleterious urban conditions. Prior to the spread of zero-tolerance policing in the 1990s, these communities were beset by a systematic lack of police vigilance—a glaring deficiency of protection when residents required it most.[46] In his classic study of police behavior in Skid Row districts in the 1960s, sociologist Egon Bittner found that officers merely attempted to keep problematic behaviors at "acceptable" and "normal" levels rather than meaningfully addressing crime.[47] Similarly, Terry Williams documented a virtual abandonment of New York City's poorest neighborhoods throughout the 1980s, even at the height of the crack epidemic.[48] Williams reported that "the police have firm knowledge about [crack] selling spots, but they usually ignore the spots. . . . For the most part the police stay away."[49] In a review of twentieth-century ethnographies of poor neighborhoods, Alice Goffman laments the virtual absence of the police in these accounts.[50]

Despite this absence, however, I contend that we can (and should) reread these accounts *as* studies of policing and its cultural effects. What these works provide is an analysis of the kinds of cultural dispositions and patterned social practices that develop amid a lack of police vigilance. These accounts underscore that even in its relative absence, policing plays a central role in structuring community dynamics. For instance, in his iconic description of the 1960s ghetto, sociologist Kenneth Clark wrote that "the lowering of police vigilance and efficiency" led to the "unstated and sometimes stated acceptance of crime and violence as normal."[51] In a column aptly titled "Well That's Just Skid Row," the *Los Angeles Times* reported that Skid Row's residents were so "inured to street violence" during the 1980s that "the brutal slayings of two people within two blocks of each other the night before drew far less attention than the taping of an episode of the television show, 'Beauty and the Beast.'"[52] Unsurprisingly, these conditions gave rise to a "wholesale restructuring of the social, temporal, and spatial organization of everyday life" in which "simply maneuvering one's way through the streets [was] a major dilemma . . . that cannot but affect all aspects of neighbor-hood life."⁵³

Lack of adequate police protection forced residents to take safety into their own hands. To do so, they cultivated and refined a sophisti-cated form of what urban sociologist Elijah Anderson calls *street wis-dom*—a cognitive framework that "allows one to 'see through' public situations, to anticipate what is about to happen based on cues and signals from those one encounters."⁵⁴ Equipped with this framework, streetwise residents engaged in what we might call a *folk criminology*, in which they reinterpreted the world through the eyes of hypothet-ical criminals. By reclassifying public spaces and their occupants in this manner, residents were better able to outwit potential assailants and thus ensure safe passage to their destinations. Deploying ade-quate street wisdom was a serious social game, for failing to do so could mean loss of property, injury, or even death.

The consequences of this cultural context extended well beyond the realm of physical protection. By sowing distrust and suspicion of fellow inhabitants, it eroded social solidarity, prompting residents to internalize and reproduce the negative stereotypes, or "territorial stigma," placed on those living in neighborhoods seen as "dumping grounds" for deviant and defamed populations.⁵⁵ As the "single most protrusive feature of the lived experience of those trapped in these sulfuric zones," territorial stigma stimulates those who live within a stigmatized area to differentiate themselves from their neighbors by any means possible.⁵⁶ This socially corrosive practice is particu-larly pronounced in Skid Row districts. As Howard Bahr explains, a Skid Row resident "may stress little things which set him apart from other men, or continually remind that his past was different, that he is not a 'bum' like many of those around him."⁵⁷ As residents construct rigid moral dichotomies between themselves and their neighbors— "respectable" versus "shady," "decent" versus "street," or "good" versus "ghetto"—territorial stigma undercuts the informal modes of social control, collective action, and community building that might other-wise improve neighborhood conditions.⁵⁸

Becoming Copwise

America's most impoverished neighborhoods have undergone a dramatic about-face in recent years. Most notably, police officers now saturate many of the neighborhoods and spaces where they were once neglectful. As a result, criminal assailants no longer represent the sole threat to property and life. In Skid Row, the police have become a ubiquitous and highly disruptive presence in residents' struggle for daily survival. Police interactions are so frequent that one of the residents I befriended, a middle-aged black woman named Diane, described them as "almost like bathing."

Hard numbers on the ubiquity of police in Skid Row are difficult to come by. Official citation and arrest numbers gloss over the thousands of instances in which officers detain, interrogate, search, and make demands of inhabitants without activating the formal criminal justice process. One of the only existing estimates comes from a pilot study conducted by a local community organization in 2010. In surveys and interviews, residents reported an average of 5.3 pedestrian stops over the course of the previous year. Residents reported being handcuffed, searched, and having their names run through a warrant database during almost three-quarters of these stops. Just under half reported verbal or physical abuse on the part of the officers involved. Stops that ended in citation or arrest created new and lasting obstacles: more than half of respondents reported loss of housing, one in three loss of access to social services, and one in six loss of employment or income as a result of such encounters.[59]

For those on the receiving end, therapeutic policing feels less like helpful guidance and more like abuse. More tough than love. The kinds of self-improvements, "free" choices, and new behaviors demanded by officers are largely incongruent with the biographies, material needs, and social organization of Skid Row and its inhabitants. Therapeutic policing tells residents to "get a real job," even as stable and decently paying employment continues to dwindle. It tells them to "get off the streets," despite the declining availability of affordable housing. It tells them to "get clean and sober," despite the continued defunding and privatization of health and rehabilitative services.

In the end, therapeutic policing can cause more problems than it cures. Such relentless police contact destabilizes the already precarious lives of those caught in its crosshairs. And because therapeutic policing views the urban poor as irresponsible and self-destructive, it actively delegitimizes and criminalizes indigenous, self-directed attempts at rehabilitation and upward mobility that may resonate more harmoniously with residents' personal circumstances than the regimes of recovery dictated from above.

While residents may not necessarily conform to police demands, they nonetheless learn valuable lessons from their repeated run-ins with officers. They learn that wholly refraining from criminal activity is not sufficient to eliminate the persistence of, and injury caused by, unwanted (and largely unwarranted) police contact. Additional measures are necessary. After Darryl's third unexpected run-in with officers, the two of us sat talking at a cement picnic table in the park. It was late in the afternoon, and Darryl had just come down from his stuffy SRO room, where he had locked himself away for most of the day. Observing that his recent encounters with police had all occurred in the daytime, he had made the decision to limit his movements through the neighborhood to the evenings, when he knew patrols were lighter. Realizing that his detainments had taken place on the sidewalks adjacent to rehabilitation facilities, he had begun avoiding these locations. He had also resolved to steer clear of large, unfamiliar groups of pedestrians.

"The cops thought I was just hanging out with those guys who spend all day kicking it outside of the Union [Rescue Mission]," Darryl told me, recapping his first citation. "They thought I was one of them. But I ain't *nothing* like them. Those fools actually *like* being down here. They're looking for handouts so they can keep on drinking all day. But me, I'm only trying to get some cheap lunch so I can save up and rent a real crib as far away from this hell-hole as possible."

In addition to cataloging particular times of day, geographic locations, and social groups that drew elevated scrutiny from officers, Darryl made the (admittedly impulsive) decision to throw away his driver's license. He had noticed that officers were sometimes in too much of a hurry to run further background checks on pedestrians who did not carry identification. In future interactions with officers, Darryl planned to impersonate his cousin, who did not have Darryl's quickly growing record of citations, fines, and arrests.

Like others I met during my fieldwork, Darryl responded to the ambient threat of policing by developing the cognitive framework of cop wisdom. Like streetwise residents in underpoliced neighborhoods, copwise individuals learn to reinterpret the mundane scenarios, spaces, and people found in the neighborhood. They do so not to avoid potential criminal victimization, as a streetwise resident might, but to reduce the probability of detrimental police contact. To make police behaviors and interventions more legible, copwise residents engage in what I refer to as a *folk ethnography of policing*. By reimagining their world through the eyes of officers, they attempt to discern and manipulate the various considerations that motivate officers' typical patrol behaviors. On the streets of Skid Row, where therapeutic policing leverages coercive law enforcement powers to transform "undisciplined" citizens into self-regulating, sober, and productive ones, residents mobilize their folk analyses of policing to convince officers that they number among the latter.

By providing a common platform from which residents proactively evade, deflect, and subvert officers' paternalistic interventions, cop wisdom constitutes a cultural foundation for what anthropologist James Scott calls "everyday forms of resistance."[60] These are "the ordinary weapons of relatively powerless groups: foot dragging, dissimulation, false compliance, pilfering, feigned ignorance, slander, arson, sabotage, and so forth."[61] Like the assembly-line worker who intentionally slows production output, or the welfare recipient who hides additional sources of income, copwise residents find creative ways of exploiting the blind spots of surveillance and regulation to satisfy daily needs and secure a modicum of autonomous personal dignity.[62] Residents rely on their cop wisdom to develop and defend indigenous forms of self-help and to construct a supportive milieu outside of the spaces and processes demanded by the police.

However much it relieves the pressure of ubiquitous policing, cop wisdom is by no means a panacea, and we should take care not to unduly romanticize the resistance it engenders. Everyday forms of resistance are akin to what social thinker Michel de Certeau refers to as "tactics."[63] In contrast to "strategies," which are collective, organized, and aggressive, tactics are defensive and individualistic. Thus, while everyday forms of resistance may temporarily divert or forestall repression by the powerful, they do not challenge the larger, structural political-economic situation in the way that more formalized and oppositional social movement strategies may. The "weapons of the weak" are unlikely to seriously affect the various forms of exploitation they confront.[64] Furthermore, the individualistic character of everyday resistance creates an inherent contradiction. As anthropologist Nancy Scheper-Hughes warns, everyday resistance often requires "a certain 'selfishness' that pits individuals against each other and that rewards those who take advantage of those even weaker."[65]

These limits and contradictions of everyday resistance ring true in Skid Row. While cop wisdom provides temporary relief from the ubiquitous threat of disruptive police contact, it often comes at the long-term expense of the neighborhood population as a whole, including even the most copwise residents. It especially amplifies the salience and sting of territorial stigma. When police contact looms as a constant threat, the stakes of identifying and distancing oneself from the "real" criminals and moral deviants of the neighborhood increase significantly. Residents are forced to double down on mutual avoidance and lateral denigration. These atomizing practices are no longer just a matter of carving out self-esteem; they become central to survival. If Skid Row residents fail to prove their decency—if they are ineffective in demonstrating that they are not like those who truly "deserve" police attention—they may quickly find themselves in handcuffs, in the back of a squad car, or in a jail cell. This predicament propels already marginalized residents to engage in a form of what political scientist Cathy Cohen calls "secondary marginalization" as they monitor and regulate their peers in ways that can perpetuate misery and alienation.[66]

Even so, in some contexts cop wisdom can provide residents with the knowledge and skills necessary for carrying out more collective, overt opposition to policing. For some residents, cop wisdom serves as a more altruistic tool for overcoming denigrated statuses, protecting fellow inhabitants, and ultimately undercutting the policies and practices on which therapeutic policing relies. A final intent of this book, then, is to shed light on the factors that lead residents to move from individualized tactics to collective strategies. As I will demonstrate, one of the most powerful among these factors is the manner in which residents come to perceive and manage the territorial stigma of their neighborhood. Those who reject externally imposed stereotypes and perceive a higher degree of commonality with their neighbors are those most likely to engage in organized forms of resistance that are capable of bringing about meaningful police reforms.

Studying Therapeutic Policing and Its Impacts in Skid Row

Ever since the early twentieth century, when the first Chicago School popularized urban sociology, Skid Row districts—much like "the ghetto" or "the slum"—have been considered a common, even "natural" feature of the urban ecology.[67] Throughout US history, Skid Row districts have been inhabited by the city's most maligned and marginalized populations. Seen by the academy and the public alike as "the natural habitat of people who lack the capacities and commitments to live 'normal' lives on a sustained basis," the districts provide an ideal setting to investigate how American society views and regulates those who are least willing or able to live up to dominant expectations and moral standards.[68]

The city of Los Angeles officially designates its Skid Row as the eastern section of downtown, located between Third and Seventh

Streets, bounded by Main Street on the west and Central Avenue to the east. Given the influx of new residents since the 1970s, as well as the high rates of mobility within the neighborhood, precise demographic statistics are difficult to come by.[69] By compiling various government sources, however, it is reasonable to estimate that the vast majority of residents are male (80 percent) and black (70–75 percent), with Latinos (20 percent) and whites (8 percent) making up the next largest racial/ethnic groups. While the concentration of homeless individuals has earned the neighborhood the title of homeless capital of the United States, the majority of residents (two-thirds of the population) are, in fact, housed. Indeed, with over nine thousand private, voucher-based, and subsidized SRO units in such a condensed area, Skid Row also qualifies as the affordable housing capital of the region, if not the country. The median income of these SRO residents hovers around $4,500, which places even the most stable members of the population far below the official threshold of "very low income." Roughly nine out of ten SRO residents are unemployed, and almost half (45 percent) report a physical disability or mental illness.

As a direct result of neoliberal reforms to both social welfare and criminal justice, Skid Row has become saturated by formal poverty governance organizations. The privatization of welfare services and their subsequent concentration within the neighborhood has made Skid Row into the social service hub of southern California, boasting an unrivaled density of large nonprofit, religious, and voluntary social service providers. The historical genesis and reach of the neighborhood's organizational landscape is detailed in chapter 1. For now, it is sufficient to note that Skid Row's service organizations provide over 40 percent of the county's shelter beds, despite the fact that the neighborhood comprises only 0.02 percent of the county's 4,060 square miles.[70] Skid Row also contains over 54 percent of the permanent housing, 37 percent of the transitional housing, and 43 percent of the emergency shelter housing funded by the county's primary homelessness and housing agency.[71]

The concentration of service organizations is matched only by the

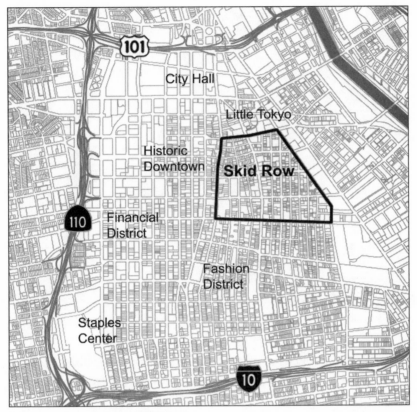

Downtown Los Angeles and Skid Row.

prevalence of the Los Angeles Police Department. Skid Row and the surrounding four miles of downtown fall under the jurisdiction of LAPD's Central Division, whose block-long, bunkerlike station is located in the epicenter of Skid Row, mere steps from the nation's largest service providers. With 329 total assigned officers, Central Division has more officers per square mile (73.1) and per thousand residents (8.2) than any other LAPD division.[72]

LA's Skid Row is clearly not your "typical" urban area. It does not resemble an average poor neighborhood, if such a place even exists.[73] Only a handful of neighborhoods—places like San Francisco's Tenderloin and Vancouver's Downtown Eastside—come close to replicating Skid Row's distinct constellation of conditions. Yet, this distinc-

Sixth and San Julian Streets: The heart of LA's Skid Row.

tiveness is precisely what makes Skid Row such an ideal and powerful case study. As sociologist Robert Zussman writes, "Successful case studies look at extremes, unusual circumstances, and analytically clear examples, all of which are important not because they are representative but because they show a process or a problem in particularly clear relief."[74] While the specific findings presented in this book may not appear in exactly the same way in all other contexts, the Skid Row case shows us generalizable social processes, as well as the particular conditions under which these processes are likely to arise.[75]

My investigation of these processes as manifested in Skid Row was primarily ethnographic. By definition, ethnography is "social research based on the close-up, on-the-ground observation of people and institutions in real time and space, in which the investigator embeds herself near (or within) the phenomenon so as to detect how and why agents on the scene act, think and feel the way they do."[76] As I noted earlier, this project did not begin as a study of policing, but ethnography's demand that researchers take their subjects' preoccupations, motivations, and resulting actions seriously made it nearly impossible for me to keep the issue of policing nestled quietly at the margins, as I had originally intended. More details on this necessary shift in focus, as well as a more comprehensive discussion of the dilemmas of conducting fieldwork in a heavily policed neighborhood and the practical concerns of my multiperspectival approach are laid out in the methodological appendix. But since every ethnographic project—from the questions asked to the data gathered to the final analysis—is inescapably colored by the personality, position, and entry point of the researcher, I offer a brief summary of my approach to the research here.

I carried out fieldwork over the course of five years—from 2007 through 2012—during which time I spent between ten and thirty hours per week engaged in participant observation. In the long tradition of urban ethnographies, I strove to immerse myself in the daily routines of those living and working in the neighborhood.[77] I spent a majority of my time in Skid Row's public spaces, though my research also took me into SROs, shelters, community organizations, and the Central Division station.

From my initial days of fieldwork, the ubiquitous presence of the police in everyday life became increasingly apparent. Most immediately, it created obstacles for establishing contact and building rapport with residents. Given my own appearance—specifically my short, military-style haircut, muscular build, and phenotypical attributes—residents routinely assumed that I was a plainclothes officer. As a mixed-race man—my father is black and my mother Mexican—my skin tone is noticeably lighter than that of the majority of the population, more closely resembling that of the predominantly white and Latino police force. Compounding this issue, some residents interpreted many of the standard fieldwork practices—idle presence in public space, unsolicited small talk with strangers, casual eavesdropping, and constant note-taking—as further indications that I might be an officer.

I gradually established friendships with a number of residents and

peer groups who "vouched" for my identity and intentions throughout the remainder of my research. The experiences of two of these
groups—a collection of men who gathered in one of Skid Row's parks,
and a group of street vendors who sold goods along its sidewalks—are
detailed in two of the later chapters. While I was initially interested
in documenting these men's daily survival strategies, their repeated
interactions with the police and deepening criminal justice entanglements constantly hummed in the background of my field notes. The
longer I spent in the neighborhood, the more firsthand experiences
I myself had with the police, making this topic even harder to quiet.

After a year of observations and focused conversations with residents about their ongoing interactions with Central Division officers,
I found myself increasingly uncomfortable with the portrait of policing that was emerging. I had compiled significant data on the *effects*
of Skid Row policing, but I knew very little about its *causes*. Residents'
diverse and sometimes contradictory opinions on the matter only
muddied the waters. While these kinds of bottom-up understand-
ings are vital for explaining the cultural contexts and behaviors that
develop among the targets of policing, they hardly count as accurate
or empirically based explanations for why officers engaged in such
frequent and intense interactions, or what exactly officers hoped to
achieve through the process. For that, I needed to talk to cops.

In 2008, I began conducting fieldwork alongside Central Division
officers. While my coplike appearance had made some residents
wary, it seemed to put officers at ease and allowed me to gain access
to Central Division relatively easily. I began with informal interviews
with patrol officers and leadership. During these meetings, I received
several invitations to participate in ride-alongs. I declined every invitation, however, since I planned to continue conducting fieldwork
alongside residents. If some residents had suspected me of being an
officer when I merely stood around in public, then seeing me rid-
ing in police cruisers would thoroughly sink my hopes of building
trust. Fortunately, a handful of officers helped me develop an alternative and informal means of observation—what they sarcastically

referred to as "walk-alongs." Skid Row's density and relatively small size made it possible for me to walk behind patrols—whether officers were on foot, bicycles, or horses, or even in cars—and thus observe their interactions with residents. I debriefed incidents with officers either on the scene, later in the day, or during subsequent shifts. I also observed officer training modules, and I participated in a range of Central Division's public forums. These included community policing meetings with residents and local stakeholder organizations, as well as public safety walks organized by social service providers and local businesses.

Seeking further diversity of perspectives, my fieldwork also incorporated the most vocal opponent of the Safer Cities Initiative—a grassroots organization called the Los Angeles Community Action Network (LACAN). Established in 1999, LACAN's membership is comprised almost exclusively of low-income, SRO-housed, and homeless Skid Row residents. After alleviating members' concerns that I was not in fact an undercover officer, LACAN allowed me to assist in a range of manual, clerical, and community outreach work in exchange for access. As part of this, I participated in the organization's "Community Watch" program. For multiple hours each day, the Community Watch team patrols the neighborhood videotaping police interactions. Participating in Community Watch provided me with additional opportunities to document police behavior, this time from the perspective of onlooking residents and suspects. Traveling the neighborhood alongside well-known residents also allowed me access to a greater range of individuals and groups than I would likely have had on my own.

My involvement with this varied set of neighborhood actors meant that my time in the field was often divided between multiple "subsites." I typically focused on one at a time, spending a few months of concentrated fieldwork in a subsite before rotating to the next. There were times, however, when I incorporated each subsite into a single outing. On one notable day in 2009, for example, I began fieldwork just before 9:00 a.m. at the LACAN office, where I attended a meeting with residents concerning recent evictions from SRO hotels. Afterward, I informally interviewed a resident who had recently joined Community Watch. Just before noon, I walked three blocks east to San Julian Park for a game of chess with one of the street vendors. Then the two of us sold homemade incense along the adjacent sidewalks. In the afternoon, I walked to the Central Division station to attend a community policing meeting. On my way, I paused to observe a detainment by two officers whom I knew; I spoke with them about the interaction after they released their suspects. A major advantage to this approach was that it allowed me to gain multiple perspectives on particular policing events and issues as they occurred.[78]

To place my ethnographic observations in historical context, I supplemented my fieldwork with archival research, interviews with individuals who had been involved in Skid Row's historical development, and over fifteen thousand pages of LAPD records obtained under the California Public Records Act.[79] These records included e-mail correspondence, meeting minutes, internal memoranda, administrative procedures, and financial records pertaining to Central Division, City Hall, and Skid Row's most prominent organizations. Beyond providing invaluable historical and organizational data, these backstage records and communications allowed me to better confirm the veracity of front-stage statements and actions.

Virtually all of the names used throughout this book are pseudonyms. This was a requirement of my university's human subjects protections and was also frequently requested by residents and officers. To further allay both groups' concerns, I have made occasional changes to intimate identifying details. Many residents had, and continue to have, tenuous legal entanglements, conflicts with the LAPD, and involvement in illicit activities. Many feared retaliation in the event that my research made them too readily identifiable. In recent years, police officers, like many other frontline public employees, face punishments (and at times, termination) for merely speaking candidly. Pseudonyms help ensure confidentiality and allow me to provide a more honest rendering of actions and statements by both the police and the policed. I make two exceptions to anonymity: first, for individuals whose names appear in mass publications like newspapers and city records, which I cite; and second, for public representatives of city agencies, businesses, and organizations.

Plan of the Book

What follows is an investigation into the objective underpinnings, real-time implementation, and subjective implications of policing in LA's Skid Row. The structure of the book reflects an effort to sketch these processes through the multiple and often conflicting perspectives of the various neighborhood actors involved. Part I provides a "top-down" view of policing, presented primarily from the standpoint of those charged with regulating Skid Row and its population. Chapter 1 draws on a combination of historical data and ethnographic fieldwork to excavate the historical origins of the Safer Cities Initiative. The chapter proceeds from an unanticipated observation: In the face of the purported death of rehabilitation and reintegration, Skid Row's highly punitive law enforcement policies were actually designed, legitimized, and enacted by therapeutically oriented private welfare organizations. The chapter demonstrates that the privatization of social welfare, combined with other neoliberal reforms of the late twentieth century, transformed the organizational dynamics of Skid Row. These transformations have allowed a collection of paternalistic and disciplinary organizations to convert Skid Row from an urban area designed to merely contain the urban poor into one that is explicitly designed to improve the poor. They have achieved this by enlisting the coercive power of the police.

Chapter 2 moves out into Skid Row's streets to illustrate how this therapeutic project manifests in officers' daily patrol practices and routine interactions with residents. The growing influence of the disciplinary organizations has fundamentally transformed the ways in which officers understand their work, the neighborhood, its inhabitants, and their problems. Whereas officers throughout most of the twentieth century intended their patrols and discretionary enforcement to merely quarantine the urban poor within Skid Row's boundaries, officers now work chiefly to "shepherd" wayward citizens toward more approved lifestyle choices and eventual reintegration into conventional society beyond Skid Row.

Part II reverses the perspective to reconsider policing from the standpoint of its targets. Employing a "bottom-up" view, it shows how Skid Row residents' attempts to negotiate omnipresent surveillance and regulation spill over into the cultural context of the neighborhood, transforming key sociological processes that have long been associated with urban poverty. Read in succession, each chapter in part II presents an additional technique by which residents mobilize their acquired cop wisdom. Each chapter captures the increasing intensity, reach, and formalization of resistance, and reveals how residents' individual biographies, daily concerns, and ideas about the neighborhood promote distinct ways of coping with the ever-present threat of police contact.

Chapter 3 follows the lives of a group of roughly thirteen black residents as they attempted to build their own, indigenous form of drug recovery and reintegration program in the face of officers' coercive mandates to enter formal treatment facilities. Pressed with the continual threat of arrest and (re)incarceration, the men drew on their collective cop wisdom to hone their skills at evading police contact, primarily by carving symbolic and physical distance between themselves and addicts, drug dealers, and other "typical" Skid Row residents. While their efforts often proved successful, they required the men to constrict their social networks, limit their daily round, and directly perpetuate territorial stigma.

Chapter 4 examines the cop wisdom and resistance strategies developed by a group of Skid Row's street vendors. Unlike the men profiled in chapter 3, who tried to avoid contact with fellow residents, the vendors mobilized their folk analyses of policing to actively intervene in others' lives, exerting a strict form of informal social control in their immediate vicinity. To reduce the probability of police contact, the vendors labored to regulate even the most mundane aspects of nearby street life in hopes of eliminating the "problematic" scenarios most likely to attract police attention. At times, this surrogate form of policing entailed keeping the area free of debris, drug activity, and crime. In other instances, however, it led the vendors to aggressively suppress noncriminal individuals and previously tolerated behaviors in a manner that undermined fellow residents' life chances while exacerbating neighborhood stereotypes in more indirect ways.

Chapter 5 moves away from the subversive tactics depicted in the previous chapters and toward a collective strategy of resistance. The residents involved with LACAN's Community Watch program mobilized their cop wisdom as part of a formal campaign to oppose the Safer Cities Initiative and mitigate negative images of Skid Row and its population. These residents leveraged their intimate knowledge of police behavior to "track" officers through the neighborhood and record unconstitutional patrol practices. By creating incriminating videos of police behaviors, LACAN devised a novel form of legal evidence that was able to overcome the organization's previous lack of credibility and neutralize core therapeutic policing techniques.

The conclusion reflects on the major lessons learned regarding the role of the police in monitoring, regulating, and shaping the lives of the urban poor. While this book focuses squarely on life within Skid Row, the processes and phenomena discussed are by no means limited to that single setting. Evidence from a range of cities indicates that therapeutic policing has become institutionalized as a matter of municipal policy. We can similarly observe cop wisdom operating beyond the boundaries of Skid Row. The fallout from a number of highly publicized police shootings suggest that a range of communities have been forced to become copwise as a matter of daily survival. Against this backdrop, this book provides the necessary framework for understanding life in criminalized communities throughout America and across the globe.

Part I

Fixing the Poor

CHAPTER ONE

The Rise of Therapeutic Policing

On a cool evening in 2009, roughly 150 people, including myself, assembled in front of the Midnight Mission in anticipation of the monthly Skid Row Safety Walk. Created four years earlier to serve as a public face of the Safer Cities Initiative, these walks are the product of a collaboration between the Los Angeles Police Department, Skid Row's largest social service organizations, and the Central City East Association (CCEA)—a business improvement district (BID) representing the fish warehouses and other storage companies located in the eastern section of the neighborhood.[1] The Safety Walk is one part public relations campaign and one part social service outreach program. Officially described as "a vehicle by which to educate government leaders, the public and the press about the dangers of life (and death) on Skid Row," the hour-long procession weaves its way through Skid Row's streets offering residents free transportation to a participating social service organization.[2]

Attendees at the night's walk included LA city attorney Carmen Trutanich, LAPD deputy chief Sergio Diaz, the Central Division lieutenant and sergeant who oversee SCI deployments, CCEA executive director Estela Lopez, four representatives from Skid Row's largest service facilities, and three outreach workers from the Los Angeles Homeless Services Authority (LAHSA). This month, they were joined by more than twenty city and district attorneys from municipalities across the United States, in town for a seminar hosted by Trutanich's office on how to institute law enforcement policies like the Safer Cities Initiative in their own jurisdictions. The Safety Walk capped off a day of classroom sessions and tours of downtown's criminal justice buildings. It was now time for the visitors to witness Skid Row and its policing program with their own eyes.

As was routine, Trutanich began the event by addressing the group. He stood tall in the back of a white CCEA pickup truck parked near the curb. With his arms outstretched, he invited the out-of-town guests to take in the scene. "See this," he began. "This is something that is not just happening in LA. This can happen in *your* city too!" He pointed up and down the street. "I come down here as much as I can to let the people down here know that I care about them. That I am committed to turning this place into a way station. A place for people to get their lives back on track and get out. And it's going to be a collaborative effort between me, the DA, my buddy, the city attorney's office, the sheriff, the Central City East Association, and the police." As he spoke, Trutanich signaled Deputy Chief Diaz to join him on his makeshift stage.

"It's a partnership," Diaz echoed. "The partnership that we've forged with organizations like the Midnight Mission and the CCEA is allowing us to change all of this. Our partnership is allowing us to help people and reduce crime at the same time."

After similar comments from the Safety Walk's other leaders, the group made its way through the neighborhood. Ten patrol officers formed a protective bubble around the attendees, while three LAPD squad cars traveled ahead of the procession with lights flashing, blocking off streets and ordering pedestrians to clear out of the area. When the leaders of the Safety Walk encountered the small number of residents who remained standing or sitting on the sidewalk despite earlier police orders, they asked these individuals if they were interested in climbing into one of the LAHSA vans that trailed behind the procession, to be transported to the Midnight Mission. By the conclusion of the night's walk, not a single resident had taken them up on their offer. At one point the group approached an elderly black woman, who declined their help with visible distrust and hostility.

Seeing this, a representative from one of the partner social service organizations grabbed the attention of a small group of us in the crowd.

"Let me tell you what just went on over there," he began, pointing
behind him to the elderly woman while shaking his head in disapproval. "We just offered to bring this lady, free of charge, mind you,
into an organization like mine. But she refused. You can see we're
clearly trying to help her. We deal with this day in and day out. It's
called 'service resistance.' These people know that if they go into one
of our programs, they have to go to sleep at a certain time, they have a
lights-out, they have rules that they have to follow. Out here there are
no rules. It's a lifestyle. That's exactly why we need Safer Cities and
our partners in law enforcement. To help these folks understand that
they can't live without rules anymore."

||||||||||||||||

The monthly Skid Row Safety Walk captures the core logic of therapeutic policing, which leverages the coercive power of the criminal
justice system in an explicit effort to correct the attitudes, behaviors,
and lifestyle choices of the urban poor. This chapter traces the origins
and development of this disciplinary model of social control from the
birth of LA's Skid Row district through the launch of SCI over a century and a half later. In contrast to the prevailing scholarly and public
narrative, which explains the recent upswing in police punitiveness
as a decline, if not death, of the rehabilitative approach, the history
of Skid Row policing reveals that it is better understood as reflecting
a *renewed* commitment to these ideals. Indeed, SCI represents the res-
urrection of law enforcement policies characteristic of the late nineteenth century that actively sought to cure the economic and moral
pathologies supposed to lie at the root of urban poverty. Then as now,
those interventions—while expressly rehabilitative—are also highly
punitive.

The history of Skid Row policing serves as a corrective to two additional assumptions about America's so-called punitive turn in criminal justice. First, as Joe Soss and his colleagues recently point out,

scholars' claims of a wholesale move toward retribution and exclusion tend to hinge on a kind of latent functionalism.[3] By portraying the upswing in punitiveness as somehow "necessitated" by larger social forces, this work inadvertently neglects the agency of the myriad political actors involved.[4] Second, the few accounts that do consider political agency focus narrowly on the profit-driven and "revanchist" actions of business interests, who purportedly enlist the police to purge the urban poor from areas slated for gentrification and redevelopment.[5] Here, too, agency takes a back seat to the larger "needs" of capitalism.

Events like the Safety Walk offer the possibility of a different interpretation. Policies like the Safer Cities Initiative can more accurately be understood, not as an inevitable result of late industrial capitalism, but as contingent outcomes resulting from the concrete demands that a multitude of local interests and partners place on the police. Notably, these partners include private social welfare organizations like the Midnight Mission. These social welfare organizations—surprisingly overlooked in most accounts of contemporary urban social control—have been instrumental in moderating the levels and ultimate aims of police punitiveness throughout Skid Row's history. Their impact is on par with and at times even surpasses that of business interests.

A more comprehensive understanding of recent transformations in policing therefore requires us to reexamine the role of the police within the larger "organizational field" of poverty governance.[6] Following the work of French sociologist Pierre Bourdieu, an organizational field can be defined as "a set of organizations linked together as competitors and collaborators within a social space devoted to a particular type of action."[7] The field of poverty governance encompasses all those agencies and organizations typically involved in regulating poor populations. This includes state welfare bureaucracies, city officials, and the municipal police department, as well as private welfare organizations and local businesses. Field-level outcomes—whether housing policies, employment policies, or in this case, policing policies—are the collective product of the interorganizational agreements made between the actors within the field.

The following historical account is separated into three major periods in the development of Skid Row, paying particular attention to the neighborhood's fluctuating interorganizational agreements and the resulting transitions in law enforcement. Just as the aggressive law enforcement currently in place is not singularly punitive, it is also not entirely new. In the nineteenth century, the organized charity movement and the LAPD forged a symbiotic relationship to reform the "dangerous class" that accumulated in the neighborhood. Acting as "moral entrepreneurs," charity organizations pressed the city to create stringent municipal ordinances and enforcement standards designed to eliminate pauperism and compel new ways of living.[8] This trend reversed in the New Deal era beginning in the 1930s; with the rise of the centralized welfare state came the collapse of the organized charity movement. A more oppositional and politically radical collection of organizations rose in its place, ultimately forcing the LAPD to institute a more lenient and less corrective approach to policing for most of the twentieth century. In the wake of welfare state retrenchment and privatization in the late twentieth century, however, paternalist and therapeutic organizations resurfaced in Skid Row. Attempting to rebrand the neighborhood as a "recovery zone"—what Trutanich described as a "way station . . . for people to get their lives back on track"—these organizations have revived the earlier disciplinary model of policing. In Skid Row, policing has been at its *most* punitive precisely during those historical periods when the police were most concerned with saving the urban poor from themselves.

Resocializing Paupers: 1850s–1930s

Throughout its early history, Los Angeles's Skid Row closely mirrored the "Main Stem" (or "Hobohemia") districts found in other urban centers during the late nineteenth and early twentieth centuries.[9] Proximity to the Los Angeles River and a flat topography made the areas surrounding LA's nascent downtown ideal for the development of the packing and shipping industries. When the first locomotive arrived in Los Angeles in 1881, it brought with it a swell of migratory labor seeking jobs in the seasonal agricultural, industrial, and transportation sectors. Between 1870 and 1900, the population of Los Angeles exploded from 5,782 to 102,000.[10] Single-room occupancy (SRO) hotels—providing small rooms and communal baths at affordable prices—sprang up in Skid Row to accommodate new arrivals and short-term residents. Earning the nickname "Hell's Half Acre," the district became synonymous with bars, pawnshops, brothels, dance halls, and other businesses catering to a single adult male population.

Charity, voluntary, and other private welfare organizations saturated Los Angeles's Skid Row, as they did most major American cities. From the establishment in 1854 of southern California's first voluntary organization, the Hebrew Benevolent Society, private welfare played a central role in shaping the city's physical and moral landscape. Prior to the completion of the intercontinental railroad, organizations clustered in a section of downtown appropriately named Charity Street (current-day Grand Avenue). As the Skid Row district swelled with migrants, however, these organizations moved closer to their patrons. Here they joined with more prominent social reform groups arriving from the east coast. In 1892, the Salvation Army constructed its first southern California facility on Fifth Street, in the heart of Skid Row. The following year, the Associated Charities and the Charity Organization Society (COS) established branches nearby, consolidating the majority of the city's social welfare efforts under the mantle of "scientific charity."

Scientific charity held as its foremost objective the repression of pauperism through resocialization. Amid rapid urbanization, reformers perceived an increase in the number, visibility, and audacity of able-bodied poor who, rather than seek legitimate employment, attempted to live off public and private bounty.[11] Explaining pauperism as the result of willful defiance, moral deficiency, and lack of restraint, organizations pursued two principal strategies to restore the pauper class to self-sufficiency. First, to inhibit subsistence outside of formal employment, they advocated for the prohibition of begging, along with the elimination of all forms of indiscriminate relief. In the words of Stephen Humphrey Gurteen, one of the founders of the COS in the United States, aid free of conditions "encourages idleness and unthriftiness and improvidence," while creating dense neighborhoods of dependence and vice.[12] In one of the major statements of American charity organization principles, Josephine Shaw Lowell asserted that rather than risk reproducing the pauper class through overgenerous handouts, poor relief should aim to "insure a distinct moral and physical improvement on the part of all those . . . forced to have recourse to it."[13] "Discipline and education," Lowell claimed, should be "inseparably associated with any system of relief."[14]

At the same time that private welfare organizations curtailed alternative means of survival, they directly engaged in moral reform. Salvation Army founder William Booth referred to this two-pronged tactic as the "Scheme of Social Salvation."[15] Booth designed his program to attract paupers into Salvation Army facilities using any means available, including food, shelter, music, and the lure of staff uniforms. Once inside, the organization provided "a stable institutional environment during an initial period of rehabilitation."[16] For those who proved pliant, the organization continued to instill regular work habits, sobriety, and responsibility through temporary employment in one of its retail stores. For those who proved otherwise, the Salvation Army reserved more punitive options. Reclassifying the poor as "worthy" or "unworthy" according to their willingness to reform, organizations banished the latter to the rural farm colonies established outside of Los Angeles throughout the 1890s. Adopting the language of contagion, the Salvation Army and other organizations sought to incapacitate the morally incorrigible so they could no longer "infect their fellows, prey upon society, and multiply their kind."[17]

To give teeth to their coercive measures, private welfare organizations turned to the most authoritative local government agency of the time: the municipal police department. In the late nineteenth century, the middle and upper classes, fearful of the deleterious effects of rapid urbanization and industrialization, pressured civic authorities to create centralized police departments to provide a means of controlling paupers and white ethnic immigrants.[18] Because these departments predated other specialized city agencies, in many cases the police were either formally charged with or quickly assumed the burden, not only of controlling crime, but also overseeing social welfare services.[19] These included taking censuses, regulating health standards, providing ambulances, and supplying overnight lodging in police stations—functions that provided broad and amorphous powers to deeply intervene in the daily lives of the urban poor.[20]

The nineteenth-century police role developed via a symbiotic relationship with private welfare organizations.[21] First, organizations used their political influence at the state and city levels to draft ordinances prohibiting vagrancy, loitering, begging, and drunkenness. These so-called civility laws were written with intentionally vague language to give the police broad power to control the growing number of idle and "masterless men."[22] Second, charity organizations demanded that members of police departments behave much like surrogate organization employees. Most notably, the COS enlisted the police to investigate the homes of anyone receiving relief, draw up central registers of the poor, conduct door-to-door fundraising, discover child abuse and neglect, and assist in finding lost children.[23] As the president of the New York Society for the Prevention of Cruelty to Children wrote in 1887, "The Law and Humanity go hand-in-hand. . . . And instead of the local police . . . being antagonistic to the efforts of the Society . . . as too often occurs in European countries, they are assisted in their official duties, strengthened in their efforts."[24] For its targets, this evolving partnership was obvious. Managers and customers of the district's vaudeville theaters quickly learned to keep "a weather eye open for the social worker, with policeman in tow, out to preserve the integrity of the American home."[25]

In Los Angeles, the influence of private welfare organizations on the police was most apparent in their collaborative suppression of beggars, the bête noire of scientific charity. By 1897, the Charity Organization Society had pressured the Los Angeles Police Department to establish a "mendicancy detail," which consisted of plainclothes officers who patrolled the streets in search of beggars. Officers arrested habitual and professional beggars, while referring first-time offenders and "unfortunate cases" to the COS office.[26] Over the following two decades, charity organizations intensified their demands that the LAPD make the city inhospitable to begging. At the 1901 annual meeting of the Associated Charities, organization president H. W. Frank declared that Los Angeles had been overrun by "fake mendicants" who feigned infirmities and disabilities.[27] The next day, Los Angeles mayor Meredith Snyder responded by ordering a crackdown. As the *Los Angeles Times* reported, the LAPD expelled and arrested a mass of mendicants "who were pretending to be cripples."[28] Downtown's Spring Street, which had previously been lined with panhandlers, was virtually emptied, demonstrating that those "who depend on a sympathetic public for a living can be kept in check and so discouraged as to compel them to turn to honest toil."[29] When city officials informed charity organizations that existing begging laws limited further enforcement, these groups collectively lobbied the city council to pass an emergency begging ordinance. Whereas the previous law had allowed the police only to prohibit able-bodied individuals from begging, the new ordinance extended the ban to handicapped individuals as well. The ordinance also increased punishments. As a misdemeanor, begging was now punishable by up to fifty days in jail and a fine of $50.[30]

Los Angeles's crackdown on begging helps to illustrate the somewhat counterintuitive process whereby increased police involvement in social welfare functions actually *decreased* police tolerance for disorderly behaviors. Comparing arrest rates in twenty-three US cities between 1860 and 1920, police historian Eric Monkkonen finds that the more responsibility the police held over the management of the dangerous class, the more arrests they made for begging, public drunkenness, vagrancy, "corner lounging," and other minor public order offenses.[31] This decrease in tolerance is less surprising once we acknowledge the influence of private welfare organizations on the criminological thinking of the time. Police leaders adopted the core premises of scientific charity, which sought to *prevent* crime by altering the poor's improper thoughts and habits before they spiraled into outward criminality.

In the early twentieth century, there was no more vocal an advocate of this "pre-crime," social work role than August Vollmer. As consultant to the LAPD and president of the International Association of Chiefs of Police (IACP), Vollmer stressed the pointlessness of arresting offenders only after they had committed serious crimes. By that time, he argued, an individual's attitudes and behavior patterns had already been hardened. In his 1918 IACP address titled "The Policeman as a Social Worker," Vollmer argued that, if a police officer wished to reduce offending, "he must go up the stream a little further and dam it at its source."[32] In the words of another IACP president of the time, Joseph M. Quigley, "The police chief should be the moral physician of the community."[33] By adopting these ideas, the LAPD led the nation in creating programs and subdivisions explicitly aimed at moral reform, including a "matrons' division" focused on deterring delinquent girls and women before they turned to crime. In their early years, policewomen were recruited directly from charity organizations and trained in schools of social work.[34]

Skid Row policing was thus founded on the task of regulating both the economic activity and the morality of the urban poor. Police officers and organized charity workers, often indistinguishable in their actions, pursued a disciplinary model of social control that blended benevolent and punitive functions. Together, they sought to restore self-sufficiency, work ethic, and moral health by redirecting the intimate details of clients' lives. Famed charity activist Jacob Riis captured this coercive brand of paternalism, declaring that "it is a dreary old truth that those who would fight for the poor must fight the poor to do it."[35] In a short time, however, Riis's truth would come into serious question. New developments in America's economy and administration served to decouple police work from social work, thereby altering the roles of police officers in the everyday lives of the poor.

Containment and Quarantine: 1930s–1990s

The 1930s marked the beginning of profound transformations in Skid Row's demographics, infrastructure, and organizations—all of which led to a reconfiguration of Skid Row policing. The election of Franklin D. Roosevelt to the presidency in 1932 came at the beginning of the worst winter of the Great Depression. Historic levels of unemployment (25 percent) and dislocation were immediately visible on Skid Row streets, where the traditional, maligned population was now joined by what Nels Anderson once referred to as "novices of the road."[36] White-collar workers, skilled laborers, single women, and families with nowhere else to go flocked to the neighborhood.[37] As millions of workers lost their jobs, the highly moralizing view of the poor propagated by charity organizations gave way to more sympathetic characterizations of the poor as victims of social disorder who needed to be given the means for a settled, more secure existence.[38]

Over the next two decades, a series of government interventions would lift much of the area's population—newcomers and the former disreputable poor alike—out of Skid Row. New Deal programs, particularly the Federal Emergency Relief Administration (FERA), the Works Progress Administration (WPA), and the Civilian Conservation Corps (CCC), created new jobs and provided an unprecedented safety net. As one of the largest states in the union, California was fifth among all states in WPA spending ($750 million) and received over $580 million in federal relief grants.[39] Later, during World War II, military service and domestic wartime industries absorbed many of those who remained in Skid Row. In the postwar years, federal veterans' benefits allowed many of those returning home to secure stable employment and housing, and to avoid returning to their former conditions.[40] As a result, the Skid Row population was winnowed of all but the worst off. The district became, in effect, a "retirement community" for elderly, poor, white men suffering from chronic illnesses, disabilities, and alcoholism.[41] Population decline led to the closing of businesses, the rise of abandoned property, and the prevalence of urban blight. It was during this time that such districts first earned the generic and pejorative label "Skid Row."

These years also redefined the role of the voluntary sector in caring for the needs of the unemployed and destitute. While the charge of social welfare rested squarely in the hands of charity organizations throughout the nineteenth century, the intractability of poverty during the early 1900s, particularly during the Great Depression, underscored the limits of voluntarism and the necessity for centralized government action. As early as 1913, states and localities had created welfare departments to take over the task of poor relief. According to welfare historian Michael Katz, as charity organizations gave way to government bureaucracies, "relief became public welfare; almshouses became county, city, or town homes; superintendents of the poor, county commissioners of public welfare; overseers of the poor, public welfare officers; the State Board of Charities, the State Board of Welfare."[42] The creation of FERA during the early New Deal years thrust the federal government into the business of poor relief for the first time in history. From 1933 to 1936, FERA spent over $3 billion in public welfare benefits. More importantly, FERA stimulated the growth of the public welfare sector by granting money solely to public agencies, while stipulating that they further improve their administrative practices. Whereas public aid accounted for merely 1 percent of government spending in 1923, by 1939 it had grown to 27.1 percent. The New Deal effectively tipped the balance between private and public welfare provision in favor of the latter, relegating charity organizations to the margins of the emerging welfare state. At the organizational level, many of the leaders and members of the charity movement were drafted into the ranks of a budding public social work profession.[43]

The collapse of the organized charity movement left the management of Skid Row in the hands of a very different set of actors. Smaller organizations embracing more "accommodative" and, at times, politically radical approaches now dominated the neighborhood's organizational landscape.[44] Both the collection of small religious soup kitchens that provided day-to-day necessities of food, shelter, and prayer and the activist Catholic Worker organization, which supplemented emergency aid with civil rights, labor union, and antiwar campaigns, subscribed to a "systemic" explanation of poverty.[45] Whereas Skid Row's previous organizations had tended to treat poverty as the result of moral laxity, the remaining organizations took up the New Deal discourse that reconstructed the poor as dispossessed, often faultless victims of market and political vagaries.[46] One of the most apparent signs of this discursive shift came in the language used to describe Skid Row's residents. Instead of referring to "vagrants" or "transients," organizations like the Catholic Worker strategically coined the term "homeless." In doing so, they aimed to highlight a lack of housing as the only thing that separated the most severely impoverished population from more sympathetic groups.

At the same time that a discursive shift was occurring in the realm of social welfare, urban redevelopment advocates took a new interest in Skid Row. In the postwar years, Los Angeles's downtown had become a secondary and declining commercial zone. A height-limit ordinance, which prohibited the construction of buildings over thirteen stories (150 feet), hampered the development of an iconic skyline like those that characterized rival urban centers. In 1959, however, the city lifted the height restrictions, propelling downtown into an era of accelerated growth. As an archetype of postwar urban restructuring, downtown Los Angeles became one of the top destinations for multinational corporations. In just ten years, it rose from ninth to fifth on the list of corporate headquarter cities.[47]

With a new proprietary stake in luring mobile capital to LA, financial interests joined with downtown merchants to form the Downtown Business Men's Association—later renamed the Central City Association (CCA)—to exert influence over the built environment.

Singling out the easternmost section of downtown (the portion containing Skid Row) as the foremost obstacle to revitalization, the group set its sights on wholesale redevelopment. Throughout the 1950s and 1960s, business associations in cities across the United States orchestrated massive urban development projects that wiped many of America's largest Skid Row districts off the map. In LA, however, this effort unfolded more slowly and in more piecemeal fashion, providing key openings for opposition groups to vocalize their concerns and ultimately preserve Skid Row.

First, the CCA successfully lobbied the city to shut down the area's most problematic bars. Razing buildings that violated the seismic code, the CCA effectively eliminated 20 percent of the low-rent housing stock.[48] In 1972, the CCA produced a more comprehensive redevelopment strategy called the "Silverbook Plan" (a name derived from its metallic-colored cover). The plan slated eastern downtown for complete demolition, to be rebuilt and renamed "Central City East"—home to a regional university center, a central library, a metropolitan police station, massive parking garages, and a monorail.[49] The project was to be administered by the Los Angeles Community Redevelopment Agency (CRA) and funded through a "tax increment financing" arrangement, in which the area's tax revenues would be diverted directly to the CRA redevelopment budget.

Despite the CCA's overwhelming support in City Hall, a collection of Skid Row's remaining organizations defeated the Silverbook Plan. Soon after its drafting, the plan was discovered by Jeff Dietrich and Catherine Morris, two of the founding members of the LA Catholic Worker. Seeing that the design would eliminate their small soup kitchen—known locally as the "Hippie Kitchen"—as well as displace their patrons, Dietrich and Morris formed a coalition to author an alternative proposal. The coalition included the Legal Aid Foundation of Los Angeles (LAFLA), an organization providing civil legal services to low-income citizens; the Los Angeles Community Design Center (LACDC), a progressive organization that designs, develops, and preserves affordable housing; and several sympathetic philanthropists.

The Catholic Worker counterproposal—referred to as the "Community Plan" or "Bluebook"—proposed an opposite fate for Skid Row. Rather than demolish the neighborhood, the Community Plan called on the city to take steps to stabilize affordable housing and social services in the area. The goal was to reenvision and redesign Skid Row as a viable, albeit low-income, residential neighborhood. To this end, the coalition devised a rather unorthodox strategy. First, they explicitly delineated what had previously been rather amorphous neighborhood boundaries. According to Dietrich, "If you had asked someone in the 1970s to point on a map and show you 'Skid Row,' they would have probably just said 'All of downtown!' It definitely had a more spread-out feeling. So we decided to sit down and just draw it on a map, and really highlight it." Second, they elected to *embrace* the district's infamous reputation. In Dietrich's words:

> Our thinking was that the more we called one particular area "Skid Row," the better it would be for us. At the same time, we also wanted to really play on this ugly image that everyone had of Skid Row. We wanted to keep Skid Row scary. When it's scary, middle-class white people don't really show much interest in it anymore. They just don't want to be around it. Developers won't want it as much. When it's scary it's not as contested of a space.

Third, they took advantage of city council members' strong not-in-my-backyard sentiments by warning that the Silverbook Plan would displace Skid Row's population into the surrounding areas, reducing property values and angering constituents. As Dietrich recounts, "We started meeting with people and saying, 'Look what would happen if you try to clear this out. Look what would happen to downtown.'"[50]

Swayed by the activists' scare tactics, mayor Tom Bradley appointed a Blue Ribbon Citizens' Advisory Committee to incorporate the coalition's ideas into a new blueprint for eastern downtown. Finalized as the "1976 Containment Plan," the new design provided a compromise that satisfied each of the major parties involved. For the Catholic

Worker coalition, the city officially designated the fifty blocks they had marked off as Los Angeles's Skid Row. The plan concentrated and improved low-income housing within these boundaries through deliberate control of the housing stock. It also instructed the city to build or relocate social services, including shelters, rescue missions, and soup kitchens, as well as such amenities as new restrooms, parks, benches, recreation centers, and reading rooms, into the space.

Business and city leaders were equally attracted to the idea that Skid Row would act as a "magnet" that would pull impoverished and problematic populations out of neighboring districts. To enhance its magnetism, the Containment Plan discouraged the construction of low-income housing outside of Skid Row and encouraged the construction of "buffers" of light industrial buildings to "reinforce the edges between Skid Row and other land uses."[51] Social engineering is explicit in the plan: "When the Skid Row resident enters the buffer the psychological discomfort of the familiar Skid Row environment will be lost; he will not be inclined to travel far from the area of containment."[52] Skid Row would thus remain intact, but its visibility and "area of influence" would be significantly decreased.

Almost overnight, the Catholic Worker coalition converted Skid Row from a geographically blurred area into a clearly defined, officially recognized neighborhood—described in the Containment Plan as "a place where the Skid Row resident can call 'home.'"[53] In subsequent years, coalition members undertook a number of strategies to protect Skid Row against future demolition and redevelopment. First, they formed (and strategically named) several organizations to accelerate recognition of the neighborhood's new identity. In 1978, the group formed the Skid Row Development Corporation (SRDC), a nonprofit corporation funded by the CRA, to become the official "developer-protector" of the neighborhood.[54] Under Catholic Worker leadership, the SRDC obtained over $3 million in local and federal grants in its first three years to construct new low-income housing. This momentum led to the creation of two additional housing development organizations: the Single Room Occupancy Corporation in

1984 and the Skid Row Housing Trust in 1989. Also funded by the CRA, these organizations converted the area's crumbling flophouses into permanent housing units. The organizations also built two "pocket parks" and an elderly housing project. By 1987, only ten years after the publication of the containment strategy, the CRA had committed over $58 million to these endeavors.[55]

In addition to expanding the neighborhood's housing stock and amenities, the coalition established new social service organizations. Lamp, the most notable of these, aimed to improve the larger neighborhood setting as well as to provide supportive services.[56] In the words of its founder and executive director, Mollie Lowery:

As dysfunctional as Skid Row was, it was the only place people knew as adults. Once Lamp was created, it became a real safe haven for them, where they were really accepted. You know, everything was working, so I realized that what we needed to do was invest in making Skid Row a higher quality area to live, to not just have what people needed to survive, but to create a way to have people really thrive down here. . . . We weren't just service providers, we were advocates; advocates for system change.[57]

To further cement the idea and reality of Skid Row as a stable home for the extremely poor, Lamp established a market, laundromat, and other institutions found in more conventional neighborhoods. And to distance themselves from the earlier private welfare organizations, Lamp and other coalition organizations stopped referring to those in Skid Row as "clients." Instead, they spoke of "neighborhood residents" and "community members."

The historical significance of the Catholic Worker coalition's actions cannot be overstated. While other major US cities eliminated their Skid Row districts from the urban landscape, the Containment Plan ensured that LA's Skid Row will remain long into the future. In doing so, the Catholic Worker and its allies adopted a new vision of the neighborhood that acknowledged its residents' right to exist. Like

earlier welfare organizations, they specified a role for the police in realizing their vision. This time, however, the organizations demanded
a far more tolerant, "hands off," or even absent brand of policing.

As the model for social welfare delivery changed from private organizations toward centralized, bureaucratic, and specialized government agencies, so too did the role of municipal police departments.
The police no longer acted as preventive social workers; instead, they
became reactive and legalistic "crime-fighters" who focused on the
apprehension of serious criminals.[58] Examining arrest rates over
time, Monkkonen finds that US police departments made significantly fewer arrests in the early twentieth century for behaviors like
begging, vagrancy, and drunkenness, despite having grown in size.[59]
Instead, arrests for offenses against persons and property became the
chief priority of police work.

Geographically, police departments redirected their resources,
away from the aging populations in Skid Rows and toward immigrant and black neighborhoods associated with organized crime,
gang activity, and civil unrest.[60] In Los Angeles, the department disbanded the mendicancy detail and established the "intelligence detail" (known locally as the "gangster squad") in 1945. In the wake of
civil unrest in the 1960s, the LAPD intensified its crime-fighting and
intelligence-gathering roles by creating a number of new programs
and divisions. These included the Public Disorder and Intelligence Division (PDID), to monitor and infiltrate criminal enterprises; Community Resources against Hoodlums (CRASH), to combat gang- and
drug-related crime; Special Order 40, to interrogate individuals suspected of unauthorized immigration; and Special Weapons and Tactics (SWAT), to confront heavily armed suspects.

While the LAPD grew more aggressive in other parts of the city,
it policed Skid Row with a deliberately light touch. This treatment
resulted not only from the ongoing reconfiguration of priorities
within the department, but also from pressure from the Catholic
Worker coalition, which emerged as the most influential of the various downtown interests. The coalition's influence over LAPD behavior

first became apparent in the 1976 Containment Plan, which stated, "If anything beneficial is to be accomplished on Skid Row, the full cooperation of the Los Angeles Police Department is essential in an integrated program of 'protection and service' to the Skid Row person."[61] Calling for greater leniency for Skid Row residents, the plan mandated that the LAPD pursue a "protective approach rather than a suppressive approach."[62]

The Catholic Worker joined with other progressive organizations across the country to further de-escalate Skid Row policing by way of court orders. Throughout the 1960s and 1970s, these groups successfully challenged the constitutionality of nineteenth-century civility laws. In the best-known US Supreme Court case, *Papachristou v. City of Jacksonville* (1972), the court unanimously struck down a longstanding Florida loitering law. The decision stated that the law "furnishes a convenient tool for harsh and discriminatory enforcement by displeasure. It results in a regime in which the poor and unpopular are permitted to stand on a public sidewalk only at the whim of any police officer."[63]

Four years following *Papachristou*, the Catholic Worker and an ally organization, the Center for Law in the Public Interest, sought a similar decision in Skid Row. The organizations filed a class-action lawsuit against the LAPD, the city, and the county on behalf of three Skid Row inhabitants claiming improper and discriminatory treatment. The lead plaintiff, a forty-nine-year-old Oglala Sioux man named Robert Sundance, was a frequent patron of the Hippie Kitchen and close friend of Dietrich, Morris, and other members of the coalition. Over the fifteen years he had been living in Skid Row, Sundance was arrested more than two hundred times for public drunkenness, amassing over six years of time spent behind bars.[64] It was a clear violation of the principles laid out in the Containment Plan. As Morris recounts, "Whenever Robert was going to binge, he would stop by the kitchen and bring Jeff [Dietrich] this box with all of his things. He dropped it off because he knew that the cops were always going to come by and arrest him."[65] In addition to arguing that these arrests were overly punitive, the suit accused the LAPD of inhumane treatment when they transported arrestees. According to Morris, "They would pile all the guys on top of each other into this god-awful paddy wagon. Whenever they would turn a corner, these guys would literally roll around the back, hitting their heads and getting really hurt."[66]

After an eight-week trial, the US District Court handed down a decision decriminalizing public drunkenness. Ruling that "public drunks on Skid Row should be treated the same as anyone else arrested for a misdemeanor," the decision reinforced the coalition's long-standing mission to reenvision Skid Row as a viable residential neighborhood.[67] The court ordered that those arrested while intoxicated be taken to a detoxification center rather than jail. The decision also directed that the police vans be padded, equipped with seatbelts, and carry no more than ten passengers at a time. Reflecting on the watershed decision, Morris says, "You wouldn't believe how much it changed the way they treated the guys around here. They really stopped picking guys up. And if they picked them up they would just have to sit with them and wait until they sobered up. It was . . . a lot more humane."[68]

The coalition continued to ensure Skid Row's relaxed policing style by consistently defeating business, city, and LAPD efforts to intensify enforcement. This process is well illustrated in the back-and-forth that ensued over a series of LAPD "homeless sweeps" in the 1980s. In 1985, property and business owners along the Central Avenue Corridor formed the Central City East Association (CCEA), a business improvement district that currently encompasses the eastern, industrial section of the Skid Row neighborhood. One of the CCEA's first actions—and indeed the primary impetus for its founding—was to aggressively lobby the LAPD to begin clearing homeless people from Skid Row sidewalks.[69] Beginning in February 1985, the LAPD responded to CCEA requests, walking through the neighborhood arresting homeless sleepers. City maintenance crews followed closely behind to sweep up the remaining "debris." The Catholic Worker quickly mobilized in response. According to Morris, "We would go out . . . and block the bulldozers. As soon as we showed up, the police would call their supervisors. It would turn into a big standstill. They wouldn't work, we wouldn't leave, and we started going to court."[70]

In the wake of the standoffs, LAFLA filed a series of lawsuits against the city. Mayor Tom Bradley immediately suspended the sweeps. When Bradley resumed the sweeps a week later, he required that the LAPD post notices at least twelve hours before any pending police action. Unsatisfied with Bradley's concessions, the coalition continued its protests and legal challenges, forcing the city to reverse course once again. The mayor's office designed new guidelines, mandating that the LAPD post a permanent sweep schedule.[71] In an effort at appeasement, the city agreed to provide a room in a nearby SRO hotel to individuals caught in police sweeps.[72] Bradley also ordered officers not to make arrests unless they were able to provide housing. The coalition continued its resistance, forcing the city to lease a twelve-acre lot on the eastern side of Skid Row for a "tent city." When fully operational, the lot, which stayed open for about two years, accommodated roughly five hundred individuals per night.[73]

The mid-twentieth century thus elevated a new, influential set of Skid Row organizations to prominence. These actors succeeded in replacing the earlier, disciplinary form of poverty governance with a model predicated upon accommodative services and market protections. In doing so, they overturned aggressive, paternalist policing in favor of a more tolerant, hands-off approach. However, as developments at the close of the century would prove, these actors would fall victim to their own success. In drawing elevated resources and services to Skid Row, the Catholic Worker coalition unwittingly opened the door to an opposing set of organizational actors that would eventually supplant the coalition and renew the coercive benevolence that characterized the earlier period of policing.

Enforcing Recovery and Eliminating Temptations: 1990s–Today

In the closing decades of the twentieth century, Skid Row's population density, organizational landscape, and prevailing model of policing developed a striking resemblance to those of the nineteenth century. This reversion stemmed from a combination of factors. First, economic restructuring and deindustrialization, beginning in the 1970s, led to a dramatic rise in poverty and a steady repopulation of Skid Row. By the recession of 1982, national unemployment had reached 10.7 percent (up from 5.9 percent only three years earlier). A total of 12 million workers were unemployed, with 1.2 million discouraged from seeking employment.[74] With a quarter of all employment in southern California concentrated in traditional manufacturing industries such as automobiles, oil, rubber, and defense, Los Angeles County lost seventy-five thousand jobs from plant closures alone between 1978 and 1982.[75] Disadvantaged by subpar schooling, outcompeted by recent Latino immigrants, and facing racial discrimination in the emerging service economy, impoverished black residents migrated out of the ghettos of South Central Los Angeles and into the downtown area, where the majority of the remaining manufacturing jobs and affordable housing were concentrated. As in the nineteenth century, Skid Row—now referred to as "the Nickel"—swelled with the socially maligned. Instead of paupers and white ethnic immigrants, however, today's Skid Row is disproportionately made up of single black males between the ages of thirty and fifty with sporadic employment records.[76]

A second set of causes had to do with the transfer of social welfare responsibility out of the hands of federal, state, and local governments and back into the private sphere.[77] The Reagan administration, having entered office at the height of the recession, made good on its vow to "get the government off the backs of the people" by reversing many of the core social policies of the New Deal and the War on Poverty. Between 1982 and 1985, the administration cut the annual amount of federal funding designated for the poor by $57 billion.[78] New welfare policies also shifted the emphasis in direct assistance away from entitlements and income maintenance and toward more disciplinary programs, designed to promote self-sufficiency and employment while discouraging indiscriminate aid (as had nineteenth-century interventions before them).[79] In his first year, Reagan introduced new eligibility standards that purged 408,000 people from the rolls of AFDC. The administration also cut $2 billion from the $12 billion food stamp budget and $1 billion from the $3.5 billion school lunch program budget.[80]

President Clinton's 1996 Personal Responsibility and Work Opportunity Act (PRWORA) brought more cuts. In response, every major American municipality either abolished or reduced income relief to indigent single adults. In the face of a 400 percent increase in general relief applications since 1976, Los Angeles County decreased benefits from $285 to $221 per month. The county imposed strict time limits, cut eligibility to five months per year, and denied benefits to individuals identified as having substance abuse problems unless they enrolled in treatment programs. The county also added bureaucratic hurdles to the application process, including employment requirements, vocational skills training, substance abuse screening, fingerprinting, and photographing.[81] Like other localities, LA County justified its actions by accusing welfare recipients of using cash assistance to purchase drugs, eschew necessary treatment, and evade legitimate work.[82]

In the realm of housing, the federal government retreated from the creation and provision of affordable accommodations for poor Americans. Whereas previous federal housing assistance had relied on the construction of public housing, the Reagan administration increasingly turned toward the use of Section 8 vouchers, which provide low-income tenants with subsidies to use in the private rental market. Between 1980 and 1988, the proportion of the federal housing budget allocated for building new public housing units fell from 80 percent to 4 percent, while the allocation for tenant subsidies grew from 20 percent to 96 percent.[83] In Los Angeles, the end of new public housing construction created such demand that the county was repeatedly forced to close the overflowing voucher waiting list. Amid this demand, many of Skid Row's SRO hotels were converted into Section 8 units, a move that further attracted the region's urban poor and made Skid Row into Los Angeles's largest de facto housing project.

By the 1990s, the welfare state bureaucracies molded during the New Deal years had given way to what geographer Jennifer Wolch terms the "shadow state."[84] This collection of private, quasi-public, nonprofit, and voluntary organizations now delivers the majority of human services once supplied directly by the government. Serving as contractors and service providers, American shadow state organizations received 40 percent of the money spent by governments on human services, with nonprofit operating expenses increasing from $18.4 billion in 1960 to just short of $500 billion in 1993. The "charitable choice" provision of the 1996 PRWORA legislation further enlarged the role of the private sector by encouraging states to employ faith-based organizations as providers of federally funded welfare services.[85]

Privatization was particularly pronounced in services for precariously housed citizens. According to sociologist Teresa Gowan, the American "homeless industry" grew from fifteen hundred voluntary organizations in the 1980s to more than fifteen thousand by the early 1990s.[86] In 1991, the state of Massachusetts transferred its homeless shelters to the Salvation Army. By 1997, New York City had contracted out thirty-three of its forty shelters for homeless adults to nonprofit organizations.[87] Although the homeless industry in Los Angeles has always been administered by nonprofits, the county made a similar commitment to the private sphere when it established the Los Angeles Homeless Services Authority in 1993. Each year, LAHSA distributes over $70 million in federal, state, county, and city funds, primarily in contracts and predominantly in Skid Row.[88]

As part of its effort to provide the services promised to Skid Row's poor in the Containment Plan, the city assisted in the construction of three of the country's largest privately run "mega-shelters" within the neighborhood's boundaries. The first of the "big three" was the Los Angeles Mission, which was relocated from the periphery of the containment zone in 1992. The mission's new four-story, 156,000-square-foot, 306-bed facility was more than triple its former size. Nicknamed "Megamission" by the *Los Angeles Times*, the Los

Angeles Mission's status as the largest mission in the nation lasted only two years, until the next mega-shelter was constructed in Skid Row. Referred to as the "supermarket of missions," the Union Rescue Mission (URM) was relocated from outside the containment zone to within steps of the LA Mission.[89] Its five-story, 235,000-square-foot, $29 million facility holds over a thousand beds and can serve up to three thousand meals per day. With an annual budget of over $15 million, the facility also boasts a library, computer learning center, full gymnasium, chapel, and 122 paid staff members. A third facility, the Midnight Mission, was built within a block of the others in 2003. Operating on a slightly smaller scale, the Midnight's $22 million, 123,000-square-foot building houses 360 beds and has seating for five hundred people during meal services.[90]

The introduction of the big three immediately made Skid Row the social service capital of the region.[91] The concentration of the majority of these services in only a handful of facilities significantly altered the organizational dynamics that had characterized Skid Row for much of the twentieth century. First, in stark contrast to the Catholic Worker coalition's antagonism toward redevelopment interests, the mega-shelters developed a mutually beneficial collaboration with business and city leaders. This began when downtown boosters supplied the bulk of financial resources for the missions' relocations and expansions. In return for moving, the Community Redevelopment Agency provided a $6.5 million relocation grant to the URM and paid $1.5 million for its former building. In its place, the CRA planned the construction of "Plaza St. Vibiana," a pedestrian plaza and complex containing a performing arts center, library, hotel, and commercial and residential units. The Midnight Mission similarly capitalized on appreciating downtown land values, selling its former property to a private development company for $12 million, which covered the construction costs of the organization's new Skid Row facility. Midnight Mission leaders publicly explained their decision as motivated by a desire to cease impeding the progress of downtown revitalization.[92] Retail and real estate owners celebrated the moves, imagining that with the rescue missions and their patrons removed to a safe (yet profitable) distance, they could more effectively market downtown as "*noir*, edgy, [and] frontier-like in order to attract the young urban pioneers."[93] With names like "The Down and Out" and "The Nickel Diner," businesses appropriated Skid Row's infamous reputation to attract middle- and upper-class clientele. By the turn of the century, the same redevelopment interests that had once scorned Skid Row's private welfare organizations now expressed excitement for what the *Los Angeles Times* described as a "new dynamic" of cooperation.[94]

The mega-shelters' newfound relationships allowed them to supplant the Catholic Worker coalition as the foremost public representatives of Skid Row and its population. As a result, the coalition soon found itself marginalized in Skid Row decision-making. Dietrich recalls his realization of the organization's diminished status:

> It felt like we suddenly started losing. Before . . . there wasn't really anyone [in Skid Row] opposing us in an outward, high-stakes way. . . . It used to be that if we called up the [*Los Angeles*] *Times* and told them we were having a demonstration in Skid Row, they would send somebody down. We would get a hit. And they would read it all in [city] council chambers. . . . We used to get an op-ed piece in the paper multiple times per year. In fact, they would call *us* to see what *we* had planned! . . . But now things are different. It's like suddenly we became regarded as the lunatic fringe. You know, essentially pariahs. Now we try to phone in a press release and they go, "Who is this?"[95]

As the new voice of the destitute, the mega-shelters offered a revised view of Skid Row's population and correspondingly different model of service provision. Following a neoliberal model that locates the ultimate roots of poverty in individual choices and deficiencies of the poor themselves, the big three emphasized the need to resocialize and reeducate Skid Row residents. This shift coincided with larger shifts in welfare policy. Most notably, the Clinton administration's

The Down and Out, located one block west of Skid Row.

1993 "Continuum of Care" legislation redirected funding, away from organizations providing accommodative services and basic emergency shelter and toward those addressing obstacles to self-sufficiency and employment, particularly substance abuse, mental illness, poor life skills, and inadequate workforce training.[96] In an effort to remain competitive for funding, private welfare organizations across the country reoriented their organizational philosophies and began to pursue a new organizational purpose: the administration of intensive, long-term rehabilitation programs.

The mega-shelters embraced this new rhetoric. Their leaders openly criticized the work of organizations like the Catholic Worker, warning that, while providing accommodative services might "stabilize" the lives of the poor in Skid Row, it ultimately served to keep these individuals stuck in a life of poverty. According to Reverend Mark Holsinger, the LA Mission's executive director at the time of the relocation, "Just feeding them and giving them a bed is not doing anything but letting them exist, like a vegetable."[97] Instead, the mega-shelters stressed the need to rehabilitate the poor, so that they could *exit* Skid Row to rejoin mainstream society as responsible, productive, and self-governing citizens. For Holsinger, this could only be achieved through "a rigorous schedule of job training, work duties, educational classes, spiritual counseling and biblical instruction" that allowed an individual to "find hope, a much healthier self-esteem, reuniting the family whenever possible, finding gainful employment, and going back out and making a contribution to the community."[98] In the words of URM president Warren Currie, "We consider ourselves to be reparenting."[99]

By announcing that they were no longer offering the traditional assistance of "three hots and a cot" as an end in and of itself, the mega-shelters effectively resuscitated key components of Booth's nineteenth-century Scheme of Social Salvation. In direct opposition to Lamp's service philosophy, the mega-shelters leveraged the provision of food and shelter as what the URM's Currie referred to as a "feeder"—a means to attract the poor into rehabilitative programs and a tool to hold them accountable for continued self-improvement.[100] Adhering to the Continuum of Care model, mega-shelter programs involve a number of stages that place escalating demands upon participants. In the case of the Midnight Mission, potential residents must sign a contract pledging abstinence from alcohol and narcotics before even being admitted to a rehabilitation program. Other facilities require proof of up to ninety days of sobriety prior to admission. The URM's twelve-month "sustained recovery program" begins by putting those receiving emergency services to work serving food in the cafeteria.

Currie stresses the importance of these initial acts of responsibility, as they allow staff to better observe "if the person is for real," or if he lacks the commitment necessary to proceed in the program.[101] Caseworkers give participants deemed ready a red badge and begin "developing structure and accountability and reinstituting work values."[102] After thirty days, participants receive a yellow badge and begin classes in the learning center. With continued progress, participants receive a green badge to signify their transformation. "It can take from six to nine months before we deem you ready for graduation," Currie remarks on this final stage, "when we return them to society."[103] Throughout this process, participants are subject to automatic thirty-day expulsion for a number of infractions, including verbal abuse, consumption of alcohol or drugs, possession of drug paraphernalia, failing to check in throughout the day, or leaving the dormitory any time after 8:00 p.m.[104]

With the majority of social services controlled by the big three, it has become increasingly difficult for those in Skid Row to secure even the most basic resources without submitting to the mega-shelters' mandates. In his analysis of the accessibility of emergency shelter in Skid Row, legal scholar Gary Blasi finds that there are approximately 1,674 individuals sleeping on the streets, in encampments, or in vehicles each night in Skid Row, but only eleven shelter beds available for those *not* currently enrolled in formal rehabilitation programs.[105] Provided almost exclusively on a per-night and first-come-first-served basis, this small inventory of beds draws long lines that often form as early as 3:00 p.m.[106] Blasi further reports that, while those turned away have few options besides sleeping on Skid Row's sidewalks, a substantial number of shelter beds remain vacant every night precisely because they are tied to funding purposes.[107] "Because of turnover in the programs and the vagaries of funding," Blasi explains, "there may often be beds that, while literally unoccupied, are not 'available' in any meaningful sense."[108]

The mega-shelters' new organizational model led them to devote significant attention and resources to regulating Skid Row's larger neighborhood environment. Unlike the Catholic Worker or Lamp before them, however, the big three labored to *eliminate* conditions that would allow for comfortable and prolonged residence. According to mega-shelter leaders like Currie, organizational success depends in large part on their ability to separate clients who are developing "new habits of life" from the "temptations" and "old negative pulls" of former peers and activities along nearby streets and sidewalks.[109]

Line for emergency shelter beds outside the Midnight Mission, at 3:30 p.m.

In an attempt to more systematically grasp the dynamics of the "outside obstacles" threatening their work, the Los Angeles Mission partnered with Gallup to conduct a poll of 665 men and women in Skid Row. The results, claimed the LA Mission, showed that Skid Row residents' "true" desires were for job training and drug recovery programs, *not* hand-outs or donations, which only enabled them to continue shirking rehabilitation.[110] Based on the poll results, the LA Mission embarked on a prolonged and multifaceted campaign to prohibit panhandling, loitering, and indiscriminate aid in Skid Row and across the downtown area. In January 1993, the LA Mission joined with the CCA to launch the Downtown Safe and Clean Program. The program called on businesses located along Skid Row's borders to hire private security guards to drive off panhandlers, street corner groups, and individuals giving donations. The program also instituted a "transient assistance" component, whereby security guards steered those they encountered toward the LA Mission.

Building on the Safe and Clean Program, the big three partnered with LA councilwoman Jan Perry to introduce a motion to in the city council to create a municipal ordinance banning charitable food giveaways within the boundaries of Skid Row. Given the fact that over 60 percent of both housed and homeless individuals in Skid Row report such charity as a regular source of food, concerted efforts to terminate these activities make daily survival in the area contingent on entering the mega-shelters.[111] At the time of its introduction, the motion proposed to make such donations a misdemeanor offense, punishable by a fine or jail time.[112] This meant that the Catholic Worker, which had been serving coffee, oatmeal, and other food along Skid Row streets for over forty years, would suddenly be subject to stiff penalties. Criticizing this kind of charity as unstructured, unsafe, and unhealthy, Perry offered blunt instruction for those wishing to care for the poor: "Contact the missions, some of the larger organizations, and volunteer your time."[113] She added, "If we leave people on the street and don't create ways to bring them in for treatment, the problem will continue."[114] Downtown business interests greeted the proposal with overwhelming support. As one business owner stated, "The reality is, there isn't any need for food down here. If you're living down here, you can get five meals a day from the various missions. . . . That's the one thing that we're not lacking down here."[115]

As of this writing, the big three and their partners in government and business have not been able to attract enough council votes to enact the so-called feeding ordinance as law, despite significant effort and support. Following a model developed more than a century earlier, however, the mega-shelters turned to the police to provide alternative methods for transforming the daily choices and behaviors of Skid Row's population. Signs of formal collaboration between the mega-shelters and the Central Division first became apparent in October 1999, when officers, armed with mega-shelter brochures, began concerted efforts to direct those they encountered while on patrol into rehabilitative programs.[116] According to media reports, officers swept through the neighborhood, issuing citations for blocking the sidewalk, jaywalking, and other public nuisances to those who refused to make their way into the mega-shelters. The sudden uptick in enforcement caught residents and observers by surprise.

Eliminating "temptations" outside the Los Angeles Mission.

The *Los Angeles Times* characterized the move as "breaking a decades-old, albeit uneasy, truce," effectively "declaring war" on the Skid Row population.[117]

As might be expected, the LAPD offered an alternative interpretation. According to Stuart Maislin, Central Division's captain at the time, the department's strict enforcement was carried out *on behalf* of those in Skid Row. He argued that the sweeps represented the first step in an innovative strategy designed to reduce serious crime and victimization while creating an environment conducive to rehabilitation.[118] This approach to law enforcement had grown increasingly popular among law enforcement professionals, advocates, and academics, who were beginning to insist that urban policing should return to its former emphasis on maintaining public order. For the architects of the now-ubiquitous broken windows thesis, James Q. Wilson and George Kelling, it seems obvious that cities must reinstitute their civility laws if they are to reduce disorder and the crime that inevitably follows.[119] Criticizing *Papachristou* and similar Supreme Court decisions of the 1960s and 1970s, Wilson and Kelling assert that "this wish to 'decriminalize' disreputable behavior that 'harms no one'—and thus remove the ultimate sanction the police can employ to maintain neighborhood order—is, we think, a mistake."[120]

Facing a historic spike in crime, cities across America in the early 1990s embraced Wilson and Kelling's proposals to *recriminalize* a host of common public behaviors.[121] By the mid-1990s, more than 75 percent of municipalities had passed laws prohibiting or restricting panhandling, and nearly 70 percent forbade loitering or sleeping in public.[122] New York City led the charge. Citing Wilson and Kelling's ideas as an inspiration, New York police commissioner William Bratton flooded poor minority neighborhoods with large numbers of police officers to conduct impromptu stop-and-frisk searches and strictly enforce laws against quality-of-life and other minor offenses.[123] The crackdowns were particularly aggressive toward homeless individuals, "squeegee men," and others subsisting in the informal economy.

Following suit, the LAPD began formulating its own set of broken windows–inspired policies to be applied in Skid Row. Internal memoranda indicate that Central Division leaders collaborated with city council members to craft municipal ordinances prohibiting sleeping in public, public urination, and public defecation. Next, Central Division advised the city attorney's office in developing strict guidelines for the prosecution of such offenses. Third, they created the "Eastside Detail"—a patrol squad made up of officers on horseback, bicycles, and motorized scooters. Effectively resurrecting the mendicancy detail from the LAPD's early years, Central Division leaders emphasized that the squad would be "solely devoted to the enforcement of quality of life crimes."[124]

Three weeks after the drafting of the policing strategy, the City of Los Angeles hired New York's William Bratton as LAPD chief. While he was not responsible for the initial design of the Skid Row policing plan, the arrival of such a noted practitioner of the broken windows approach greatly enhanced its scope and impact. Drawing on lessons from his tenure in New York, Bratton paired the LAPD's initial plan with a "community policing" component. Despite its varied applications, community policing is generally understood as "a set of policies and programs aimed at increasing interaction between the police and the community for the purposes of fostering joint ownership and responsibility for a defined set of community problems arising from local crime and disorder."[125] Bratton's introduction of community policing thus served to institutionalize the role of the big three as formal authors of LAPD policy.

With their position at the table formally ensured, the megashelters turned to the task of designing, legitimizing, and implementing intensive enforcement. The organizations' heightened influence began in earnest when Bratton hired George Kelling, one of the architects of broken windows policing, as a consultant. For a fee of approximately $556,000, Kelling began holding monthly community policing meetings with Skid Row's most prominent organizational stakeholders.[126] Over the next four years, Kelling convened a group that included Ralph Plumb (chief executive of the URM), Larry Adamson (president and CEO of the Midnight Mission), Tracey Lovejoy (executive director of the CCEA), and Central Division leadership to further materialize the department's existing efforts. With the Catholic Worker coalition and residents notably missing from these sessions, meeting minutes state that "the Union Rescue Mission indicated that there was a *new* coalition of service providers now willing to work with other agencies, in collaboration, to deal with [Skid Row's] problems."[127]

In an effort to protect Central Division's enhanced enforcement from future criticisms, Kelling enlisted the new coalition to help the department "get to the moral high ground" by developing "a coordinated strategy of communication to the press regarding the forthcoming effort in Skid Row." [128] This included drafting press releases and op-ed pieces designed to tap into various public sympathies. In an illustrative *Los Angeles Times* op-ed, titled "A New Perspective

Emerges along Skid Row," Los Angeles Mission president Marshall McNott attacked the previous tolerant approach, while coupling the work of the LAPD and the mega-shelters:

> No one deserves to live in degraded squalor and filth—and menace their neighbors. The community has the responsibility to provide safe streets, even for the people who choose no other place to go, even with available options. We have the responsibility to help the less fortunate find those options. A permissive approach, while perhaps appealing to the humaneness in all of us, does little to provide meaningful assistance to those so needing it; assistance such as food, beds, showers, and long-term programs . . . are so much more restorative. . . . We support the work of the Los Angeles Police Department as it continues to enforce the laws of our community built on a foundation of compassion and sensitivity.[129]

Kelling's group built on narratives like these to design a number of joint policing and social service collaborations, including the monthly Skid Row Safety Walks. A less publicly visible dimension of the collaboration included a joint program that used arrests as a form of intake for rehabilitation programs. Under the Streets or Services (SOS) program, those arrested within Skid Row's boundaries on quality-of-life and misdemeanor charges are screened by caseworkers during booking. Arrestees with no outstanding felonies or history of violent crime are presented with two options: proceed to court and likely to jail, or enroll in a rehabilitation program. If arrestees choose the latter, their charges are immediately dropped and a caseworker escorts them to one of the designated facilities. At the height of the program, a caseworker was present at the Central Division station five days a week from 7:00 a.m. to noon.

Given Central Division's move toward stricter enforcement, SOS brought a steady wave of new and previously unwilling participants into the mega-shelter system. According to Central Division leadership, SOS referred an average of thirty individuals per month into rehabilitation programs. Even as an alternative to jail time, however, the mega-shelters faced significant obstacles in keeping new participants enrolled in their programs. Fewer than 10 percent of individuals enrolled in SOS twenty-one-day programs ever graduate. The median stay is only three days, with nearly a third of participants absconding within the first twenty-four hours, at which time they receive a failure to appear charge and a warrant is issued for their arrest.[130] SOS coordinators interpreted the underlying reason for program attrition as obvious: "It's very difficult to keep people, especially when they're in or near Skid Row, because there are so many temptations. . . . We're trying to make it a less desirable option, but it's an area that keeps calling people back."[131]

This rationale prompted Kelling's group to embark on a second collective project. In February 2006, Kelling led twenty-five members of the new mega-shelter coalition on a "fact-finding mission" to New York City to learn how to better address the "temptations" that undermine clients' success in recovery programs.[132] In addition to his regular meeting attendees, Kelling's delegation included Midnight Mission director Orlando Ward, Councilwoman Perry, and CCA president Carol Schatz, as well as California State Assembly member Fabian Núñez and California state senator Gill Cedillo. The group toured New York's social service organizations, courts, and public parks. They also attended instructional sessions on the broken windows approach, where Kelling stressed the need for even closer collaboration between the police and social service delivery organizations.[133] Upon their return to Los Angeles, the group heeded Kelling's instructions, drafting state-level legislation to eliminate influences they claimed "ambushed" individuals on the path to rehabilitation.[134] Just days after the New York trip, Cedillo introduced Senate Bill 1318, which added sentencing enhancements for any individual caught selling drugs within a thousand feet of a rehabilitation facility or shelter. With Núñez backing the bill, Governor Schwarzenegger signed SB 1318 into law seven months later.

The Safer Cities Initiative and the Recovery Zone Injunction

The collaboration between the mega-shelters and the LAPD culminated in the launch of the Safer Cities Initiative in September 2006. Key tenets of the policy resulted directly from Kelling's meetings, including the redeployment of fifty more patrol officers to join the Eastside Detail in cracking down on minor offenses and the creation of two senior lead officers (SLO) to act as community liaisons. These officers would "develop and distribute Outreach Flyers" that "delineate shelter and service locations."[135] While remaining "actively involved in the development of the LA Safer City Initiative,"[136] the big three mega-shelters partnered with the LAPD on two additional programs intended to use police contact as an additional point of entry into rehabilitation programs. The first program, called Homeless Alternatives to Living on the Street (HALO), offers the thousands of individuals receiving citations each month the option to work off their fines by performing community service—typically basic janitorial or manual labor—in one of the mega-shelters. As one of the assistant city attorneys overseeing the HALO program told me, "The work isn't the primary issue. After all, people are just doing basic work with a broom or a mop. The overarching mission is to get people into services while they're there."

The second program, the Homeless Court (HC) program, provides a more lenient adjudication system for homeless arrestees. Held monthly at one of the mega-shelter facilities, HC may *only* be accessed by individuals who have participated in a rehabilitation program for at least ninety consecutive days and have not been rearrested or ticketed in the previous six months. Individuals wishing to access HC can do so only by obtaining a letter of support from a case manager at an approved facility detailing the applicant's positive rehabilitation progress.

In the years following the launch of SCI, the big three further consolidated their position as the primary authors of criminal justice policies in Skid Row. In April 2010, city attorney Carmen Trutanich filed an injunction designed by the executive director of the URM, Andy Bales, to officially redesignate Skid Row's fifty blocks as the "Central City Recovery Zone." Modeled after several of the city's long-standing gang injunctions, and extending the logic of SB 1318, the recovery zone injunction banned troublesome individuals—specifically those suspected of involvement in drug activity—from entering the zone. According to LAPD commander (and former Central Division captain) Blake Chow, the injunction was intended to provide "an additional tool in the police toolkit."[137] It did so by allowing officers to bypass probable cause and arrest any of three hundred specific individuals (as well as eight hundred "surrogates and associates" to be named at a later date) for their mere presence within Skid Row's boundaries.

The lowered threshold for police contact is evident in the injunction's lengthy descriptions of criminal behavior. Reviving the LAPD's early twentieth-century campaign against mendicants who feigned infirmities, the injunction accuses some in Skid Row of faking disabilities and misfortune as a cover for criminal behavior:

> Some street drug dealers . . . use the community around them to mask their behavior such as using a wheelchair or walker to conceal their supply of narcotics, while also looking disabled. This also serves as a deterrent to law enforcement as a disabled suspect requires additional legal safeguards and resources in the event of an arrest.[138]

The document includes several pages describing the prevalence of criminals "on public streets, sidewalks, in and around alcoves and entry ways of businesses and restaurants," who "trespass on private property such as bathrooms of the various shelters and hotels to conduct their illicit operations" while "walking multiple 'laps' around certain blocks as they sell narcotics in the process . . . in a 'drive by' mode of operation, blocking traffic and interfering with . . . the Central City Recovery Zone."[139]

The injunction states that its underlying purpose is to increase the effectiveness of the mega-shelters. Even if this were not stated out-right, it would be clear in its articulation of the acceptable reasons for which individuals may enter the newly restricted zone, which include the utilization of "recovery services" at one of the three mega-shelters, each of which is listed by name. According to the injunction's "hardship exemption," individuals may receive a one-year reprieve from the injunction by enrolling in an approved rehabilitation program. The injunction mandates that enrolled individuals obtain written proof of their participation, which must be carried at all times and presented to officers upon request.

IIIIIIIIIIIIII

The mega-shelters' integral role in designing, legitimizing, and ultimately intensifying Skid Row policing over the last three decades sheds fresh light on the foundations and functions of therapeutic policing. From the initial creation of the uniformed police in nineteenth-century America, the intensity of police intervention into the daily lives of the urban poor has stood in inverse relation to the robustness of the centralized welfare state. The regulation of commonplace and mundane behaviors has been a foremost policing concern at those times when the welfare state was either undeveloped, as in the late 1800s, or minimized through devolution and privatization, as is the case today. Conversely, when the welfare state was at its strongest, directly providing poor relief through specialized public agencies, the police adhered to a relatively hands-off approach to these same behaviors, ceding support functions to other state bureaucratic agencies. Contrary to reigning scholarly narratives, these shifts do not reflect some kind of self-correcting logic of the larger system. Rather, they have been propelled by private welfare organizations that place powerful demands upon the police.[140] More paternalist and therapeutic organizations have consistently filled the vacuum during times when the welfare state has been diminished. These actors have dominated the field of poverty governance and enlisted the coercive power of the police in a collaborative project to transform and improve the poor.

Given the historical influence of private welfare organizations over policing policies, their virtual absence from current attempts to explain the intensification of law enforcement is curious. Continuing to ignore the role of these social actors threatens to gravely mischaracterize recent policing trends. First, doing so presents the risk of misinterpreting the uptick in punitiveness as necessarily antithetical to rehabilitation. Consider, for example, the unprecedented number of misdemeanor arrests made in Skid Row in recent years—over twenty-five hundred in the first year of SCI alone.[141] Viewed in isolation or from afar, this unprecedented number of arrests, largely for minor violations, appears to exemplify a revanchist, postdisciplinary attempt to round up the poor and keep them behind bars. Enlarging the scope of analysis to incorporate the organizational field of poverty governance reveals a very different picture. These arrests are made in the direct service of local welfare organizations' myriad rehabilitative programs, which use police punishments, such as arrest, as key points of intake and program enrollment. Joint initiatives like SOS, HALO, and Homeless Court are explicitly designed to convert arrestees into clients.

Second, accounts that ignore therapeutic organizations risk overstating the power of entrepreneurial business interests to freely and single-handedly amplify criminalization.[142] While these actors have certainly exerted increasing influence over the regulation of urban space, their sway over policing policies is nonetheless mediated by private welfare organizations that have historically acted as representative voices of the urban poor. In the mid-twentieth century, for example, the Catholic Worker coalition provided a counterweight to local redevelopment interests, impeding criminalization by framing aggressive policing as detrimental to Skid Row denizens. Over the last three decades, however, Skid Row's mega-shelters have reversed this relationship. Working collaboratively with downtown boosters, they facilitate the intensification of law enforcement by reframing it as beneficial to its targets, carried out for their own good.

Studies conducted in other cities have shown private welfare organizations to be integral, if not necessary, for the development of some of the most stringent quality-of-life laws and most punitive enforcement policies. In both San Francisco and Berkeley, California, for example, private welfare organizations were among the most vocal supporters of proposed ordinances to prohibit sitting or lying on the sidewalk.[143] In Seattle, private welfare organizations have entered into contracts with the police department to carry out "trespass admonishments" that allow the police to ban "service resistant" and other disruptive individuals who refuse or obstruct rehabilitative programming.[144] Seattle's "exclusion orders" further benefit these organizations by stipulating that impoverished individuals may only enter certain parts of the city if they are actively seeking treatment and services. As in Skid Row, these individuals become subject to arrest if they attempt to socialize with former peers or engage in social contact that is deemed to undermine their own or others' self-improvement.

This chapter has focused primarily on how therapeutic policing manifests on the books, in municipal ordinances and official enforcement policies. This is an admittedly partial picture. For a more complete rendering, the next chapter turns its attention to how therapeutic policing unfolds on the streets, in the actions of individual patrol officers. As political scientist Michael Lipsky reminds us, patrol officers are quintessential examples of "street-level bureaucrats."[145] Like all frontline public employees, police officers possess a significant amount of autonomy and discretion to determine precisely when and how they will (or will not) enforce the law. These discretionary actions effectively "add up" to official policy as concretely experienced by citizens. On the streets of Skid Row, officers mobilize the law in the service of larger disciplinary aims.

CHAPTER TWO

From Rabble Management to Recovery Management

Officer Tom Morgan and I squeezed into his closet-size office on the second floor of the Central Division station. Two months earlier, Morgan had been assigned to help supervise a new task force implementing one of the city's reinvigorated quality-of-life laws, Los Angeles Municipal Code (LAMC) 41.59—a vague prohibition against "aggressive panhandling."[1] Morgan's team enforces the ordinance through "panhandling stings," in which plainclothes officers pose as "decoy pedestrians" to better observe and arrest individuals who beg for spare change in and around Skid Row. A week earlier, Morgan had invited me to observe the task force in action. We met today to review the logistics of the upcoming sting.

"You won't believe how much money these guys make in a day," Morgan said with a chuckle. "I mean, it's not enough to retire on, not even close, but it's enough to keep them all drunk and high all day. They'd rather do that than go out and look for a real job. The problem is, with them out there, the whole community suffers. Crime goes up, they piss on the buildings, and they set a bad example for other people down here who don't really wanna work."

After an hour of lighthearted conversation about the panhandlers and the task force, our discussion shifted to more personal topics. Morgan's new leadership role had brought him back to the neighborhood where he, like many rookie LAPD officers, had begun his career nearly two decades earlier. Morgan confessed that while the promotion was welcome and long overdue, he felt conflicted about his return to Central Division. Exuding his usual confidence, Morgan reclined in his chair until his back was resting on the concrete wall of his office. He pointed to the outdated paint scheme behind his head. "Same paint as when I left," he said with a smirk. "But I'll tell you what. This place was the best-kept secret in the department. This was the most fun division. It's gotten kind of boring now though." For Morgan, the creation of a task force for the sole purpose of arresting panhandlers symbolized the recent changes to Central Division's mandate and patrol practices. "We spend a lot of our time just responding to these people's gripes," he had complained on another occasion, following a meeting with a group of social service organizations. "They're calling us all the time. Always with the same thing: 'There's a bunch of guys out on the street doing this or that. They're over here causing problems, messing with the guys in the programs, selling drugs, getting drunk. Can you come and arrest these guys?' And they want us to go do it *right away*. Nowadays we've got everybody telling us how to do our jobs."

Morgan continued to reminisce about the autonomy and "fun" that came with working the Skid Row beat prior to the mega-shelters' escalating demands for aggressive and formal law enforcement. "I remember the first day I came down here as a rookie in the early nineties," he recalled nostalgically. "No squad cars. Just foot patrols. You would just walk out of the station with just your hat and your baton and your ticket book in your back pocket. And at the end of the day I would come home sore. My hands would be all cut up and scratched, and my uniform would be all torn up and ripped from spending the whole day breaking up fights. Back then, we wouldn't really arrest people. That wasn't what we were there for. We were just trying to keep people off of each other." Morgan sat upright in his chair, giving his next statement an added emphasis. "Back in the day, we wouldn't have *arrested* these guys. We would have just told them to move. And if they gave us any trouble? Well, we knew how to make them listen." He leaned back with a defiant smile, letting these last words hang in the air.[2]

||||||||||||||||

In chapter 1, I detailed the historical trajectory of Skid Row policing over the last century and a half. With the reinvigorated partnership between the LAPD and the area's therapeutically oriented organizations, Skid Row policing underwent a pronounced shift beginning in the 1990s. Since that time, Central Division has adopted an increasingly aggressive, zero-tolerance stance on behalf of the local megashelters, bent on resocializing Skid Row's poor. Sergeant Morgan's nostalgia indicates that the weight of these organizations' demands has not been lost on those working the beat. According to the twenty-plus-year veteran, the new directive to address problematic individuals and behaviors primarily through such formal legal sanctions as arrest and incarceration has dealt a significant blow to the discretionary powers previously held by officers. In Morgan's opinion, this one-size-fits-all enforcement approach has curtailed officers' ability to rely on their own professional knowledge, or "street sense," when responding to Skid Row's problems.

Officer Morgan is not alone in this view. Recent work on the so-called new punitiveness similarly bemoans the purported "death of discretion."[3] For example, in an emotive critique of the Safer Cities Initiative, criminal justice scholar Michael D. White argues that Central Division's zero-tolerance approach curtails officers' freedom to solve problems through informal and potentially more compassionate means.[4] For White and others, the Division's increased reliance on citations, arrests, and other punitive measures has eroded the essential "craft" of police work.[5] Others point to the proliferation of the zero-tolerance approach as prime evidence that "the therapeutic philosophy of 'rehabilitation' has been more or less supplanted by a managerialist approach," which levels blanket interventions at the urban poor to exclude and "invisibilize" them.[6]

This widely accepted characterization of zero-tolerance policing is only partially correct. While zero-tolerance approaches do require patrol officers to initiate formal legal sanctions at a higher rate, they have not stripped officers of their discretionary authority. To the contrary, when examined in practice, zero-tolerance policies *increase* officer discretion. As cities across the globe draft ordinances outlawing such ambiguous and commonplace behaviors as loitering, panhandling, and blocking the sidewalk, police officers have gained a new flexibility to conduct stops, interrogations, and searches where they might otherwise have lacked legal authority or probable cause.[7] Contemporary officers possess considerable latitude to determine for themselves exactly when and how they will issue citations and make arrests, and if they will do so at all.[8] Officers treat laws and enforcement policies not as rigid guides for behavior, but as flexible resources and strategic means for achieving larger, often extralegal ends.[9]

On the streets of Skid Row, officers routinely used the elevated discretionary authority granted by the zero-tolerance approach to accomplish distinctly therapeutic goals. These officers strategically mobilized punitive measures in an attempt to rehabilitate and transform those who had "fallen" to the neighborhood. Specifically, they leveraged constant (threats of) enforcement to "teach" Skid Row denizens to improve themselves through self-regulation and reasoned choices. Discretionary enforcement enabled officers to reconfigure the neighborhood's physical and social ecology so as to funnel individuals toward more approved behavioral and lifestyle options, most of which centered on admission to therapeutically oriented private welfare organizations. Thus, rather than signal the death of either discretion or rehabilitation, the aggressive zero-tolerance approach deployed in Skid Row has invigorated both.

In the pages that follow, I move from the historical approach employed in the last chapter to an ethnographic perspective that reveals how therapeutic policing unfolds on the streets. While the turn to ethnographic methods provides a much-needed account of "actually existing" policing, it does have a notable drawback.[10] Given the emphasis on documenting behaviors *in situ*, ethnographic observations are, by necessity, almost always limited to the contemporary moment. Without comparative data from the past, ethnographers have difficulty determining if they are in fact observing phenomena that are historically different or new. In this respect I am fortunate. The mid-twentieth century marked a period of immense scholarly interest in the social life of Skid Row, particularly in the daily patrol activities of police officers.[11] In fact, it is often said that scholars first "discovered" police discretion while conducting research on the streets of Skid Row.[12]

To place current patrols in their appropriate historical context, this chapter is structured as an "ethnographic revisit" to what is arguably the most influential twentieth-century ethnography of Skid Row policing, Egon Bittner's "The Police on Skid Row: A Study of Peacekeeping."[13] An ethnographic revisit is defined as "an intensive comparison of one's own fieldwork with a prior ethnography of the same site, usually conducted by someone else."[14] In contrast to replication, which seeks to identify similarities between different cases, a revisit looks to discover variation between the present and a former time period, pinpointing how local processes take on different forms and meanings. My own revisit demonstrates that officers' patrol behaviors and discretionary enforcement patterns were shaped by three primary factors: (1) officers' broader conceptions of the neighborhood; (2) officers' perceptions of the individuals, behaviors, and situations they encountered; and (3) officers' calculations of the most appropriate forms of intervention. As these factors have shifted, street-level policing has followed suit, taking on a distinctly disciplinary quality in the process.

Patrolling the Rabble Zone: Containment and Quarantine in the Twentieth Century

Police discretion is, first and foremost, contingent upon how officers conceive of the neighborhoods they patrol. Officers read situations, interpret citizen actions, and formulate their responses in light of the prevailing spatial order, or "normative geography," which delineates what is normal, just, and appropriate within a given location.[15]

Throughout most of the twentieth century, officers conceived of Skid Row as a "rabble zone"—that is, a literal "reservation" for those among the urban poor for whom "society at large has abandoned all hope . . . and has ceased to rehabilitate."[16] As a result, officers oriented their daily responsibilities around the modest and nonrehabilitative task of *rabble management*. Rabble management had two primary impera- tives. The first was what Bittner refers to as "containment."[17] Officers primarily attempted to prevent Skid Row's problems from spilling over into surrounding neighborhoods and thereby interfering with the lives of "decent citizens." In Los Angeles, the Containment Plan made this goal explicit. The second goal, which Bittner calls "preven- tive protection," was to prohibit residents from preying excessively upon one another or on the "reputable" persons who might pass through the area.[18]

Rabble management was intended neither to "clean up" Skid Row nor to improve its denizens. The point was, instead, to maintain a state of *relative* safety and tranquility.[19] For instance, rather than curtailing excessive drinking and drug use, officers directed their energies to- ward mitigating the *consequences* of excessive consumption, whether in the form of a drunken brawl, a complaint from nearby merchants, or general annoyance to the city at large. As one Skid Row officer told Bittner, "In the last analysis, I really never solve any problems. The best I can hope for is to keep things from getting worse."[20]

Informed by broader conceptions of the area, officers in the twenti- eth century developed what Wiseman describes as an "almost mysti- cal" ability to "read" people and situations to determine their relative threat to rabble management.[21] Officers' "special sensitivity" carried an important spatial component as they assigned specific meanings to the different streets, buildings, and sections of the neighborhood to better anticipate future disruptions. For instance, officers might devote extra scrutiny to Skid Row residents who strayed too far from their SRO hotel rooms, often arresting them even if they had commit- ted no crime. Officers predicted that one of these residents *might* get too drunk, fail to make it back to his room, pass out in the roadway, and be struck by a motorist driving through Skid Row on the way to a more "decent" neighborhood.

Given finite time and resources, Skid Row officers recognized that they could not possibly intervene in every situation in which it might be warranted. In response, they developed what Bittner calls an "ideal economy of intervention" to effectively and efficiently deploy their enforcement powers.[22] In the rabble management era, officers primarily directed interventions toward those individuals and events that posed the most immediate threat to containment and preventive protection. In one commonly cited case, Bittner describes an officer's handling of two Skid Row residents named "Dakota" and "Big Jim."[23] When the officer noticed a growing romantic relationship between the two, he predicted that Dakota would likely rob Big Jim's SRO room. Adhering to the ideal economy of intervention, the officer decided to preemptively arrest and jail Big Jim, and not Dakota, to interrupt the likely chain of events. He did so despite the fact that Big Jim was the anticipated victim and had not committed any offense. Had he arrested Dakota, the officer theorized, Big Jim would have continued to strike up liaisons with other men who would be just as likely to rob him. The most economical approach was to simply remove Big Jim from the equation. While such interventions may occasionally have funneled residents into more rehabilitative settings, this result was peripheral at best. In fact, as anthropologist James Spradley shows in his study of Skid Row alcoholics, rabble management typically worsened material destitution and alienation.[24]

Patrolling the Recovery Zone: Rehabilitation and Reintegration in Today's Skid Row

Today, almost five decades after Bittner's observations, the once-prevailing view of Skid Row as a rabble zone has given way to a definition of Skid Row as a recovery zone.[25] This shift has had a profound impact on how officers conceive of neighborhood residents and their responsibilities toward them. Whereas officers in the twentieth century directed little effort toward reforming residents, who were seen to be beyond the possibility of help, contemporary officers are expressly oriented toward the task of *recovery management*, in which they attempt to reform even the most destitute and deviant. The new perspective was readily apparent from my earliest interactions with Central Division officers.

During one of the instances in which I myself was detained, questioned, and searched, the two officers instructed me to direct any further questions (or complaints) to senior lead officer (SLO) Andre Thomas. They informed me that SLO Thomas could often be found a couple blocks away, walking up and down the streets in front of the mega-shelters. When I pressed them for more information on how to locate the SLO, the officers chuckled, assuring me that the man was "pretty hard to miss."

Several weeks later, I learned what the officers meant. On the afternoon we first met, the SLO—known in the neighborhood simply as "Thomas"—was leaning assuredly against the trunk of his squad car, chewing on a toothpick. A sociable black man with a clean-shaven head, he carried a muscular, 260-pound frame that made him appear nearly as wide as he was tall. The sleeves of his uniform cut deep lines into his massive biceps. The front of his shirt pulled tight against his wide chest, putting serious strain on the buttons. Like Central Division's other SLOs, Thomas patrolled a dedicated subsection of Skid Row without a partner. While certainly empowered to issue citations and make arrests, his primary responsibility—as designed by the partnership between the LAPD and the mega-shelters—was to serve as a community liaison, directing individuals to social services, gathering intelligence on criminal activity, and generally responding to disruptions in and around the mega-shelters. Given Thomas's imposing physical presence, it is hard to imagine a more fitting personification of Central Division's new brand of coercive benevolence. With over a decade of experience on Skid Row's streets, the man carried the banner with tremendous pride.

Throughout my years of fieldwork I stopped and visited with

Thomas as much as I could. Despite our regular interactions, I waited a considerable time before informing him that our initial meeting had been a result of my own detainment. My admission clearly caught him off guard, and he immediately grew defensive. Quick on his feet and in keeping with his constant refrain that "the stuff you learn in school" was out of touch with "the stuff you learn on the street," he promptly reframed my run-in with the two officers in a positive light. According to Thomas, my detainment exemplified the consistent surveillance and "tough love" that those in Skid Row required to turn their lives around.

"Look around you," he instructed me. "What do you see?"

I took a moment to survey the street. "Uh, what do you mean?" I replied, unsure of exactly what he was asking me to notice.

Thomas pressed on. "Let me ask you this. What *don't* you see?" Recognizing my continued hesitation, he answered for me. "Look at this block right here. No dealers. No addicts. Nobody's robbing anybody. No women are getting raped. You see a bunch of people who aren't scared to start doing what they need to do to get *out* of Skid Row. This was *my* idea right here." He continued to level questions at me. "What's the best way to protect people? What's the best way to make sure they get the help they need? How do you keep somebody on the straight and narrow?" He paused to let the difficulty of the questions sink in. "A visible police presence," he answered. "That's how! Plain and simple. If it were up to me, I'd have one of me on every corner. Talking to you, talking to everybody. Really finding out what's going on."

Thinking back to my own feelings of helplessness while I watched an officer rifle through my belongings, I had difficulty masking my skepticism. "You'd put a cop on every corner, to talk to everyone who walks by?" I asked. "Is that even realistic? Don't you think everyone will have a problem with that?"

He replied immediately. "Who's gonna have a problem? The gangbangers? The guys smoking crack? The man planning to assault some old lady? I'm glad they have a problem with it. Maybe it'll finally get them to change what they're doing. Were *you* up to no good when *you* were stopped?"

I once again found myself unsure of how to respond.

"No," he answered for me again, "exactly. So you had nothing to worry about, right?" Thomas's message was straightforward. From his perspective, my detainment was but a minor inconvenience, carried out for the greater good of the neighborhood. It was an argument that has gained significant popularity as metal detectors, pat-downs, and drug-sniffing dogs have become routine sights in airports, schools, and areas like Skid Row.

"Let me ask you this," he continued. "All this violence and killing and whatnot that we have down here. You know what it's over? It's over something as simple as a crack pipe. 'You took my crack pipe and now I'm going to stab you.' Again, look around you. You can see with your own eyes. When I'm out here, that stuff doesn't even get started in the first place. They know better than to start up. I've been down here for a long time. Trust me. Me being here, right here, this is what gets people to sober up. You can ask anybody that I've dealt with out here. They come up to me all the time, even people that I've arrested. They say, 'Thomas, you saved my life. I was addicted and now I got my life together. I got myself a real job.' I've got career criminals coming up and thanking me for saving their life. I'm out here trying to set an example. They don't have to go down that road."

Like those patrolling in Bittner's time, today's officers recognize the need to safeguard residents from themselves and from one another.[26] Thomas's comments indicate, however, that today's Skid Row officers engage in preventive protection primarily on behalf of those living *within*, rather than *outside of*, Skid Row. Instead of merely containing problematic behaviors within the neighborhood's boundaries, officers see their mission as preventing these behaviors from developing in the first place, in large part by reforming residents' deviant lifestyles. In a further distancing of contemporary perceptions from the past, Thomas conveyed the belief that no one in Skid Row—whether an addict or a "career criminal"—was beyond saving.

Observing officers' interactions with Skid Row residents, I discovered that the new role that they envisioned for themselves grew out of the revised vision of the neighborhood authored in large part by the mega-shelters. This new ideal was nowhere more explicit than in the monthly newsletters Thomas wrote and circulated up and down Skid Row's streets. Running up to ten pages, the documents typically contain a personal message to residents, an original poem, a prayer, a crime report, the language of a select municipal ordinance, upcoming events hosted by the various mega-shelters, a "thank you" page listing organizations and individuals who were particularly helpful over the previous month, and instructions for providing anonymous information about criminal activity. Other patrol officers kept stacks of the documents on hand to distribute to those they encountered during their shifts.

The overriding purpose of the newsletters was to inform residents about the ongoing effort by Central Division, the mega-shelters, and the city attorney's office to rebrand Skid Row. One illustrative edition contained a four-page, personal message from Thomas, titled "Skid Row: We Have Faith in You. It's Time You Have Faith in Us," intended to educate residents on the neighborhood's new identity, function, and corresponding behavioral norms:

Hello again Central City East (Skid Row). . . .

I along with my fellow officers have proven our desire to make your community a safe haven for many to rehabilitate and thrive. . . . In my walks through skid row over twelve years, I have discovered the rehabilitative aspects of . . . what has been dubbed a recovery zone. . . .

The Los Angeles Police Department Central Division has recognized that the majority of the community desires to make Skid Row a true community for individuals struggling with the disease of addiction, homelessness, and mental illness. . . . Our goal is to make the influence of the service provider community stronger than that of the drug dealers and gang members who prey on the community. . . .

Think on this for a second. When your favorite celebrity is struggling with addiction and needs to "get clean" do they go to the night
clubs to do so? Absolutely not. . . . In Skid Row many individuals
cannot afford to go to Malibu or the mountains for a secluded safe
environment to change. But with your support, the police department along with the City Attorney's Office can begin to make Central City East a place where people can have a better chance at taking their lives back from the grips of addiction.

God bless you all,

From your Senior Lead Officer Andre Thomas

The newsletter emphasizes the reconceptualization of Skid Row, from
an area where residents were permitted to freely consume alcohol
and drugs if they remained out of the public eye, to an area where
these individuals must learn to *desist* from problematic behaviors.
As a space now associated with treatment and healing, Skid Row
has thus become what health geographers refer to as a "therapeutic
landscape."[27] To drive home the point, the newsletter draws parallels
between Skid Row and another, more established therapeutic landscape: Malibu, California. For many residents of southern California,
the nearby beach town of Malibu has become synonymous with detox
clinics catering to celebrity clients.[28] Officers referred to Skid Row as
a "poor man's Malibu," operating much like a rehabilitation facility or
halfway house expanded to the neighborhood scale.

In my initial months observing officers, I had difficulty reconcil-
ing the officers' purported goals of facilitating treatment and healing
with the unprecedented rates of citation, arrest, and incarceration in
the neighborhood. I questioned whether officers' claims of rehabilitation and support might have simply been post hoc justifications
that masked an underlying, more exclusionary intention. As I came
to know a number of officers on a personal level, however, I saw that
this was not the case. Officers smoothed the seeming discord between
punishment and compassion, and saw the two as mutually dependent. They reformulated coercion *as* care.

This perspective was frequently rooted in officers' unexpected critique of the local public welfare system. According to officers, negligence on the part of state, county, and city governments had left them with the responsibility to address broader social issues (unemployment, homelessness, drug addiction, and mental illness) despite being equipped only with coercive legal tools (handcuffs, batons, and handguns). Given that police officers often self-select into divisions and units whose daily responsibilities and demands resonate with their own sensibilities, ideological commitments, and style of work, the de facto social work role turned out to be one of the principal attractions of working in Skid Row.[29] As had SLO Thomas, many officers specifically requested assignment to Skid Row and repeatedly declined opportunities to move to other divisions.

A case in point: Officer Manuel Rodriguez, or "Manny," as I came to know him. Although Central Division was one of Manny's first assignments after graduating from the police academy, he planned to remain in the area as long as the department would allow. His attraction to Skid Row and his eagerness to fulfill the social work role stemmed primarily from his previous military service and his commitment to assisting other veterans. This background was also the source of our immediate friendship. When Manny heard that my kid brother had recently enlisted in the Marines, he immediately peppered me with questions about my brother's unit, rank, and deployment. Later, when I informed him about my brother's growing desire to leave the military, Manny suggested that we meet for a beer once he went off duty. He offered to provide advice I could pass along to my brother for navigating the bureaucracy of the VA, finding a job in law enforcement, and dealing with other issues commonly faced by former service members.

In what would become the first of our near-weekly happy hours, Manny and I sat in the dark bar of a Mexican restaurant in the Echo Park neighborhood, three miles north of Skid Row. As usual, Manny dominated the conversation. He seemed as eager to unload pent-up frustration as I was to lend an ear and take notes. For nearly twenty minutes, Manny railed against the VA for failing to adequately dispense veterans' benefits.

"Instead of taking care of them," he complained, "they're sending them all down there to fend for themselves. Telling them, 'We can't do anything for you.' It's bullshit. These are the guys that need the most help. They fought for this country. They've got PTSD, they're all messed up. They need serious counseling. Jobs too. And the VA just turns their back." He squeezed a lime wedge into his bottle of Corona as he spoke. "Every day I drive down there I see this one dude limping on a cane because of some IED in Fallujah, and I'm like, 'That could have been me.' I'm so lucky. You got other guys that can't sleep because they have nightmares. They don't trust themselves around their families. They end up down there self-medicating." He held up his beer as he said these words, toasting himself, indicating that perhaps he too had struggled with readjustment to civilian life.

"So what's the solution?" I asked, as Manny took a long swig.

He let out a loud sigh and put the bottle back down on the bar. "The better question is who *else* is helping these guys? We get a lot of flak, but the truth is, we're the only ones doing anything about it." His tone grew agitated. "Everybody wants to talk about 'Support Our Troops,' and all that, but I don't see them down there dealing with what I see every day. *We* are the ones pulling them out of the gutter and getting them help. *We* are the ones making sure they don't get stuck down there. If it was up to some people, we would just leave these guys alone and let them drink themselves to death. They say we shouldn't arrest them when they're stumbling out in the street getting hit by cars. It shows how out of touch with reality some people are. That's my brother out there. Not my real brother, like yours, but when you go in, you become brothers, you know? I can't *not* help him out. I swore an oath." He took another thoughtful sip. "It's like this. I'm not a therapist. I don't work for the department of housing. I'm not DPSS [Department of Public Social Services]. I'm a cop. I'm just doing what I can. At least when I arrest a guy I can get him into the system. At this point, that's a victory. Once he's there he's gonna sober up. He's gonna get a chance to clear his head. He's gonna have a roof and a bed. He can hit the reset button. And from there he can get into a program at one of the missions. Now, is it perfect? No. Of course not. But that's what we're gonna have to do until those suits in Washington decide to take care of the men and women that gave their lives for this country."

For Central Division officers like Manny, arresting those in need of help, while certainly not an ideal response, nonetheless represented the most effective means to "get people into the system." While I was not able to pinpoint the origin of this idea—it was in place well before I began my research—the historical account of Skid Row policing suggests that it most likely appeared in 2003 with the creation of the Streets or Services and Homeless Alternatives to Living on the Street programs.[30] By transforming arrests and citations into an official form of social service intake, these programs provided the institutional basis by which officers recast aggressive enforcement as a benevolent intervention.

Officers quickly (and easily) reframed even the harshest patrol practices and punishments as inherently therapeutic interventions. Consider Central Division's intensified drug enforcement. With the launch of the Safer Cities Initiative, the division assigned twenty-five additional plainclothes narcotic officers to carry out "buy/bust" sting operations. During buy/busts, officers approach suspected addicts and ask them for assistance in obtaining narcotics. Officers increase the attractiveness of these deals by promising in-kind or monetary compensation up to double the street value of the narcotics in question. When individuals follow through with the deal, officers arrest them for distribution or for possession with intent to sell, which results in significantly longer prison sentences than a simple possession charge. Strikingly, almost half (47 percent) of all narcotics arrests in the first year of SCI were for distribution or possession with intent to sell. Nationally, drug sales accounted for less than 18 percent of all narcotics arrests in that same year.[31] What is more, a new set of sentencing reforms enacted in conjunction with SCI disqualify Skid Row arrestees charged with drug sales from plea bargaining to lesser offenses. The enforcement strategy also disqualifies arrestees from California's Proposition 36, a ballot initiative passed in 2000 that allows those convicted of nonviolent drug possession charges to receive probation and drug counseling in lieu of incarceration. In one of the more egregious cases, a homeless, crack-addicted man was sentenced to three years in state prison for serving as a middleman in the sale of 0.0067 ounces of cocaine.[32]

Looking at these developments, most observers would not hesitate to describe the policing policies as punitive. Skid Row officers, however, consistently lauded the *rehabilitative* quality of their intensified enforcement, insisting that harsher penalties were the surest path to altering residents' lifestyle choices. One afternoon I stood with a plainclothes narcotics officer as his partner loaded an arrestee into the back of a squad car. As he debriefed the day's most recent sting operation, he grumbled about the fact that so many resources—a four-man narcotics team, four uniformed patrol officers, and a total of six police vehicles—had been devoted to a single buy/bust arrest.

"We wouldn't have to do this if it wasn't for this Prop 36 crap," he complained. "It's 'cause these deferred entry judgments are barely a slap on the wrist. They get a soft judge and he just lets them walk. They don't even check to see if the guy even showed up at their program." In the face of what officers saw as lax enforcement by local courts, the buy/bust stings provided the necessary means for increasing accountability and encouraging change. "Now they're finally starting to see what happens to them if they keep fucking around. They see that if they keep shooting up and smoking, we're gonna get them eventually. They stay cleaner for longer when they know we're on top of 'em."

At other times, officers reframed buy/bust stings as a form of therapy in and of themselves. In a monthly meeting with local social service providers, the Central Division captain insisted that the stings caused residents who witnessed or heard about the arrests to reconsider their present and future lifestyle choices. "It's like going through one of these drug programs we have here," he told those in attendance. "It's kind of like AA [Alcoholics Anonymous] or NA [Narcotics Anonymous]. One of the important things they teach you in those programs is that you have to get away from your old party friends because they're a big part of the bad influence holding you down." Several representatives from the mega-shelters nodded in agreement as the captain spoke. "That's *really* what we're doing," he continued. "When you see your buddies all over the place getting popped over and over again, what are you going to do? Eventually you're going to get the message that it's in your interest to get as far away from these guys as possible, right? You're going to find new friends that aren't such losers."

The revised meaning of punitive measures had a profound effect on the professional identities of, and interactions between, Central Division officers. As sociologist and police ethnographer Peter Moskos observes, within the culture of the police station, an officer's citation and arrest statistics often serve as indices of his or her competence and compassion.[33] While a department's top brass may reward officers for producing higher "numbers," and occasionally even demand that they do so, fellow patrol officers tend to see colleagues with elevated statistics as inexperienced, overly aggressive, lacking street-smarts, and devoid of compassion for the citizenry. Moskos finds that being "gung-ho" is frequently interpreted as a sign of sloppy policing.[34] This sentiment was particularly strong among Skid Row officers during the rabble management era. According to Bittner, "To arrest someone *merely* because he committed some minor offense [was] perceived as containing elements of injustice."[35]

For officers engaged in therapeutic policing, however, the opposite was frequently true. The coupling of legal sanctions with social services had the effect of reversing, or at least tempering, officers' previously negative judgments of colleagues who were quick to ticket or arrest. Rather than reflecting a penchant toward injustice, an officer's elevated numbers could be taken as a sign of his or her commitment to social justice more broadly. For an officer like Manny, for instance, arresting a needy vet exhibited his deeply felt concern for fellow service members' well-being. Arrests represented quantifiable proof that he remained a faithful brother-in-arms. Like others in the division, Manny kept a rough running count of how many of his arrests produced an SOS "diversion"—that is, when residents opted into rehabilitation programs rather than continue on to jail. Officers not only proudly recited their tallies in conversations with me, but also called their diversions to each other's attention.

The lighthearted banter immediately following arrests provided a prime opportunity for officers to communicate and "prove" their competence as recovery managers. At first, I was largely oblivious to the significance of officers' subtle practices of self-promotion, as they crassly teased one another while loading arrestees into the back of their squad cars. Their wisecracks seemed nothing more than an attempt to cut the tension that often hung in the air after officers finished subduing an unruly or difficult suspect. For example, after arresting a particularly intoxicated and flirtatious woman, an officer teased his partner by pointing to the woman in the back of the squad car and informing his partner that his "girlfriend wants to make out." As one might expect, the partner retorted by insisting that the woman was "saving herself" for the instigating officer. In other instances, officers ribbed each other by joking that male arrestees were another officer's "sweetheart," "homie," or "father." I initially wrote these jibes off as yet another example of the ritualized "masculinity tests" found in male-dominated settings.[36] As I reexamined my notes, however, I saw that these playful back-and-forths also provided opportunities for officers to confirm their social worker identity.

One subtle yet illuminating exchange took place early one morning on a street adjacent to the Central Division station. At approximately 6:20 a.m., the officers were arresting individuals who had violated the municipal sidewalk ordinance, which prohibits sitting, lying, or sleeping on the sidewalk between the hours of 6:00 a.m. and 9:00 p.m. They did this every week; soon an SOS caseworker would arrive at the station to escort any new program participants to one of the partner facilities. Out on the street, four patrol cars sat idling along the curb. Six officers huddled, snapped on black latex gloves, and began using their batons to rattle cardboard lean-tos and camping tents to wake their occupants. Officer Martin loaded two would-be sleepers into the back of his squad car and waited for his fellow officers to clear the remaining bodies off the sidewalk so the group of officers could move on to the next block. I stood with Officer Martin as he watched Officer Connor pull a Latino man off a make-shift cardboard bed, search him, handcuff him, and put him into the back seat of his car.

As Officer Connor closed the door, he walked in our direction. He had a playful smirk on his face. Teasing Officer Martin, he pointed back to his squad car and asked, "Isn't that your little Mexican buddy that you brought in last week?"

"What?" Officer Martin asked through a yawn. He squinted, trying to look through the back window of the car parked some thirty feet away. "Aw man. I think it is."

"Don't worry," Officer Connor replied in a mocking tone and through a widening smile. "I'll let you take care of him next week."

Officer Martin replied sharply. "If *you're* bringing him in, sure. Get this: A week ago I pulled in three for 41.18(d) [the sidewalk or-dinance]. They were hanging out behind a dumpster. Smelled like shit. Stunk up the whole back seat. I told them I didn't want to see them back there ever again, and what would happen if I did. And you know what? If you go over to the Union right now, you'll see all three of them front and center. New clothes, showered, haircuts. Spic and span. I'm making *your* job easier out here."

"Making *my* job easier?" Officer Connor asked skeptically. "I'm making *your* job easier. I just brought in a couple dudes that were drinking out in front of the Russ [an SRO hotel]. I damn near had to bring in the hotel manager, too, he was so busy screaming at them for pissing on the wall. Damn near got ugly. I saw one of them the other day. He went straight from booking over to a job program. He's doing culinary work, he said. Like a food safety kind of thing. I'm sure he's got the certification by now." Appearing pleased with himself, Officer

Connor offered Officer Martin a final jab. "Looks like I'm the one do-ing all the work around here, eh?"

Officer Martin gave off an air of indifference, striding to the far side of his squad car without a word. As he rounded his trunk, he turned back to Officer Connor and held up three fingers. He silently mouthed the word "three," referring to his recent diversions. In the same motion he pointed to two arrestees seated groggily in the back of his cruiser. "Take a good look," he instructed Connor. "Go on over there [to the Union Rescue Mission] tomorrow and give these two a big sloppy kiss for me."

As it turned out, neither of these officers visited the URM to check up on the men and resolve their friendly competition. Even if they had, it is unlikely they would have found them. As noted in the pre-vious chapter, nearly a third of SOS participants abscond from the program within the first twenty-four hours. The median length of stay is a mere three days.[37] And yet officers hold firm to the belief that they are catalyzing a meaningful and relatively smooth rehabil-itation process. How can this be? Much of the answer lies in the fact that Central Division officers evaluate their diversionary efforts ac-cording to a particular set of statistics. Rather than record how many individuals successfully complete rehabilitation programs, Central Division tracks only how many are admitted—roughly 2,225 in the first forty months of SCI.[38] Throughout my fieldwork, I asked offi-cers to reflect on the success of their diversions. If they were able to produce a statistic, it was always their total number of admissions.

Regardless of ultimate effectiveness, such bouts of paternalistic one-upmanship were unheard of during the rabble management era, when officers expressly forswore social work tasks.[39] While today's patrols remain concerned with maintaining tranquility and protect-ing the interests of nonresidents, like the irate hotel manager in Offi-cer Connor's account, these immediate aims have been eclipsed, or at minimum joined, by concern for Skid Row denizens' long-term con-ditions and future life chances. Propelled by a new normative geog-raphy, shifting organizational norms, and pressure from peers, contemporary officers strategically oriented their time on patrol toward bringing about the maximum number of diversions. Yet, converting residents into clients of social services was no simple task. Successfully diverting residents hinged on two additional processes. First, it required that officers appropriately "diagnose" individuals and their problems. Second, it required that they apply the most appropriate intervention.

Reading Recovery

In the current era of recovery management, Skid Row officers continue to rely heavily on their intuitive assessments of Skid Row residents. However, in reconceiving the neighborhood as a recovery zone, officers' perceptual schemas revolved primarily around determinations of whether a resident was actively engaged in rehabilitation; that is, whether an individual was "using" the recovery zone in the appropriate manner.

As in the rabble management era, space played an important role in officers' attempts to read social situations. Reenvisioning Skid Row as a halfway house expanded to the neighborhood level, officers' interpretations of residents' identities, propensities, and probable future actions were strikingly similar to those documented among staff working in rehabilitation facilities. In one of the best-known ethnographies of halfway houses, D. Lawrence Wieder finds that staff members view certain physical spaces—such as a secluded bathroom or basement—with additional scrutiny and suspicion because these spaces provide opportunities for relapsing into problematic behaviors.[40] Skid Row officers constructed similar cognitive maps but at the neighborhood scale. Officers assigned new meanings to Skid Row's public spaces based on the kinds of behaviors they believed those spaces to facilitate and promote, constructing what we can think of as an "ecology of recovery" that recategorizes neighborhood spaces according to their physical and metaphorical distance from the mega-shelters.

The ecology of recovery led officers to divide the neighborhood into three distinct sections. The first section, known informally as "the Bottom," corresponded to the eastern half of Skid Row, stretching five blocks from San Pedro Street to the neighborhood's eastern boundary at Central Avenue. The Bottom is made up primarily of light industry, seafood warehouses, and block-long storage yards with high brick walls and barbed-wire fences. The area includes a number of secluded alleyways, alcoves, and lots that allow an individual to escape the gaze of anyone, including officers, traveling along the nearby street or sidewalk. The second section, what officers referred to as the "institutional side" or "the Top," corresponded to the western half of the neighborhood, running from San Pedro Street to the western border of Main Street. As the nickname implies, this section houses the majority of social services and the Central Division police station. SRO hotels and low-rent apartments are distributed in both the Top and the Bottom. The final section in the ecology of recovery corresponds to the spaces *within* the walls of the mega-shelters.

Officers directly referenced this ecology in constructing the legitimate use of the neighborhood. Residents who used Skid Row "correctly" advanced along a specific trajectory through the hierarchy of its sections—from the Bottom to the Top, in the direction of and into one of the mega-shelters. Once there, the cognitive map took on a topographical quality that corresponded to the mega-shelters' continuum-of-care model of service delivery. As residents demonstrated a commitment to improving their lives through approved behavior, they increasingly moved off the ground floor, or "graduated," into one of the residential programs on the upper floors. The top floors represented the last stop in the optimum trajectory before an individual was deemed ready to leave Skid Row and rejoin mainstream society. When officers spoke about "falling to the Skid Row lifestyle," they often turned their bodies to point in the direction of the Bottom. While sharing their impressions of the neighborhood population, officers sometimes reported "near" success stories, in which individuals had, in the words of one veteran patrol officer, "made it all the way up to the third floor of the mission" before being "sucked down to the Bottom again."

This hierarchy of neighborhood spaces served as an officer's most immediate resource when encountering situations in which an individual's commitment to rehabilitation required additional evaluation. An illustrative incident transpired one afternoon outside of Gladys Park, located in the Bottom. I was sitting against the park's tall green iron fence, engaged in a conversation with a group of residents, when a squad car slammed to a halt. Two officers immediately approached and handcuffed a man standing thirty feet away. A moment later, a second squad car pulled to the curb, driven by two officers whom I knew. We exchanged greetings as they approached. They stood next to me, twenty feet away from the ongoing interrogation, to keep the gathering crowd from coming too close to the incident. While they clearly had no information about the other officers' reasons for the detainment, they used their current spatial location and their previous encounters with the suspect to piece together the plot.

"Oh, is that Shorty?" one of the officers said to his partner and me. "I've known this guy for a while. They call him Shorty. He used to be up at the program at the Midnight [Mission]. Sometimes we would get calls in there and I'd see him all the time. He seemed like he had his stuff together, engaged in the program, you know? He seemed like he was really close to getting out of this crap. But I guess he jumped ship and came back down here. Fell off the wagon, I guess. It's a shame."

With his realization, the officer walked over and spoke to the initiating officers. After the officer familiar with Shorty filled them in, the initiating officers promptly arrested Shorty and loaded him into the back of their squad car. When the officer returned, he reported that he had suggested that Shorty be arrested rather than released.

"We'll see if this gets him back on track and his head on straight," the officer said to me. "He didn't have anything on him, but it looked like he was looking to score."

The two support officers were quick to construct an authoritative narrative without any information about why the initiating officers had detained the man in the first place. Apparently Shorty's presence in the Bottom rendered further investigation unnecessary. Gladys Park, it should be noted, sits only four blocks east of the Midnight Mission—a telling demonstration of just how large of a moral gulf the officers perceived between these two Skid Row spaces.

Given that officers viewed the Bottom and the mega-shelter facilities as antipodal within the ecology of recovery, they interpreted presence in either space as a rather straightforward indicator of an individual's intended use of the recovery zone. Officers tended to view residents' presence in the intermediary space of the Top, outside of the shelters, with far less certainty. The five or so blocks adjacent to the missions contained individuals located at very different stages of self-transformation. According to officers, some in this section were "on their way up," having recently made the decision to move away from the Bottom, while others were "on their way down," having lost their way after being enrolled in social service programming. As a result, officers exercised more caution in interpreting the propensities of those found in the Top.

One particular patrol practice exemplifies the sensitivity with which officers attempted to make this distinction. In a practice Skid Row residents refer to as "prowling," officers routinely drove slowly through the Top, using their cruiser's public address speaker to issue orders to nearby pedestrians. On one occasion, an officer drove five miles per hour down San Julian Street in front of the Union Rescue Mission. The driver spoke loudly through the crackling speaker. "Attention ladies and gentlemen," he began. "There are people trying to get help here in the mission. If you want to get help you're welcome to be here. If not, if you want to poison yourselves and engage in criminal activity, you're going to have to leave the block. I will not let you interfere with their positive change. If you decide you want to get better, you can come back." The car traveled to the end of the block, made a U-turn, and the driver repeated the message as he pulled down the street once more. Several groups vacated the block altogether, while others stepped out of sight into the courtyard of the mega-shelter.

After the officer made three passes, only five people remained on the entire block.

When I spoke with officers about this practice, they described it as a crucial, and relatively easy, technique for discerning individuals' "real intentions" without even having to exit their squad cars. The tactic's utility was rooted in the officers' notion that, just as they were "sizing up" residents, residents were closely watching them. This view is not unique to Skid Row. According to sociologist Patricia Paperman, patrol officers frequently manipulate their own presence and visibility to provoke manifestations of suspects' affiliations with deviance, affiliations that are typically revealed through suspects' attempts to mask their fear, tension, or surprise.[41] While patrolling the Top, Skid Row officers accentuated their visibility to differentiate those "on their way up" from those "on their way down," and to prevent the latter from corrupting the former.

In addition to interpretations based on residents' spatial location and their reactions to visible police presence, officers relied on more direct means of discerning the threat individuals presented to Skid Row's new normative geography. By prohibiting a range of mundane activities, the city's reinvigorated quality-of-life ordinances greatly increased officers' legal authority to make contact with residents. Officers used impromptu detainments and interrogations as a diagnostic tool that enabled them to better determine residents' intended use of the recovery zone. As with their more indirect means of investigation, officers' face-to-face inquiries mirrored methods more commonly associated with staff members in rehabilitation facilities and therapeutic communities. In halfway houses, for instance, many staff members use a technique Barry Sugarman has called "motivational testing" to determine individuals' openness to rehabilitation, their lingering commitments to problematic and addictive behaviors, and their compatibility with program structure and requirements.[42] Skid Row officers similarly "tested" those they detained along the streets and sidewalks of Skid Row. Like halfway house staff, officers' interrogations revolved around a central question: "Why are you

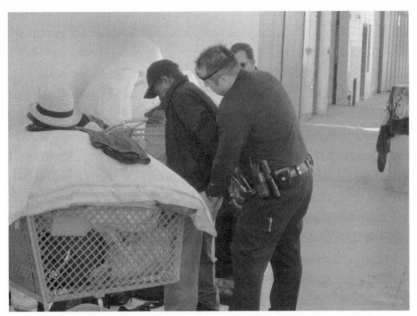

A routine stop-and-frisk.

here?" Indeed, it was a rare occasion when officers *did not* initiate detainments by asking an individual's purpose for being present in the neighborhood.

Central Division leadership specifically ordered its officers to take up this line of interrogation. I learned this when I questioned the lieutenant in charge of the daily administration of SCI whether the practice reflected larger protocols. "Oh yes," the lieutenant replied instantly. "We actively ask the reason why they are down here. Sometimes people will admit that they are here to drink in public and smoke dope. They really say this to us. The other ones, well, they'll say something like they're here 'visiting friends.'" The lieutenant made quotation marks in the air and laughed softly. "Right, of course, because this is just such a great place to hang out, right? As if there weren't better parks and places to do that in other parts of the city? You just really start to read between the lines about what they're really up to. We can pretty much tell the people that are living here because they are genuinely trying, because of the concentration of the service providers, or maybe because they are righteously homeless. That is versus the individuals who want the lifestyle or are predators from outside of the area."

One of the officers who oversaw preshift "roll call" meetings told me that he feared he had begun to "sound like a broken record" on this issue. "I know they're so sick of me saying this by now," the officer said with a sarcastic smile. "But a big part of patrolling this area is debriefing the vast majority of individuals that they come in contact with. After a while you start to learn people's responses. You start to be able to recognize the people who have no good business being down here."

These comments draw attention to the fact that Central Division officers attached more meaning to a person's physical presence in Skid Row than they might in a "normal" neighborhood. Whereas a response like "visiting friends" or "hanging out at the park" might be seen as an appropriate justification for one's presence in other areas of Los Angeles, it became the basis for increased suspicion and further investigation when uttered in Skid Row. Officers treated those in the area not necessarily as "residents" of Skid Row, but rather as "users" of Skid Row.

With instrumental use of the neighborhood serving as a dominant criterion of classification, officers sorted Skid Row's various inhabitants along an explicit moral continuum. At one end of the spectrum were those deemed to be "illegitimate users"—those officers believed to be "committed to the lifestyle" and thus content to make Skid Row their permanent homes. On the opposite end were those perceived as "legitimate users," who possessed a sincere and demonstrable intention of improving themselves and eventually leaving. One of the most immediate ways in which residents could demonstrate that they belonged on the latter end of this spectrum was to present officers with tangible proof of their desire for rehabilitation in the form of mega-shelter identification badges. Issued to program participants, these ID badges include the name of the facility, the name of the program, and a client photo. While intended to regulate access in and out of the mega-shelters, the IDs also allowed residents to essentially "carry" approved rehabilitative spaces with them when they ventured beyond the walls of the facilities into other spaces within the ecology of recovery.

One afternoon I stood on the corner of Sixth and San Pedro Streets with Officer Garcia, a middle-aged, seasoned officer, and his partner, a diminutive woman who had recently arrived from the academy. Under Officer Garcia's direction, the two spent the better part of an hour detaining, interrogating, and ticketing pedestrians who attempted to cross the street after the traffic signal's "countdown" had appeared and the red hand had begun flashing.[43] I looked on as Officer Garcia—one of several officers known throughout the neighborhood as "Mr. Ticket" on account of their tendency to write frivolous citations—narrowed his focus on three men who had entered the crosswalk during the countdown. When the men reached our position, he pulled them aside and asked for identification. Two of the men produced driver's licenses while the third handed Officer Garcia an ID badge from the Union Rescue Mission. Officer Garcia leveled a number of questions at the men, beginning with "What are you all doing down here?" The men answered that they were on their way to a small market on the next block. The two men with licenses reported that they were currently living in an SRO building three blocks to the west. The man with the badge replied that he was staying in one of the dormitories at the mega-shelter while enrolled in a recovery program. Officer Garcia asked the two without badges if they were in programs as well. Upon hearing their negative reply, he wrote up two crosswalk violation citations. The men began to complain, but Officer Garcia quickly silenced them, threatening to arrest them if they did not "move along."

"How come you let that guy off the hook?" I asked quietly as the men began walking away.

Officer Garcia remained silent for a moment as he watched them leave. "We've got to cut them some slack every once in a while," he responded assertively. He appeared to stand up even straighter with the prospect of providing a teaching moment for both me and his less experienced partner. "Right there you saw one who is at least trying, while the rest are just full of excuses. You heard them. They were pulling out all the stops, trying to say anything to make me rip up those citations." He turned slightly, directing his next words more toward his partner. "If you let them," he instructed her, "they'll lay the whole sob story on you: 'My car broke down. My old lady is sick. My dog died.' They'll talk about how they're broke and can't pay the ticket. You heard me. I told them to start saving up their money! It's not that hard." He pointed in the direction of the mega-shelters. "It's all right *there*. They can get their GED. Get an eye exam. Get some new glasses and some work clothes. They can even get their teeth fixed, for God's sake. If they're depressed they can see a counselor or talk to a pastor. And it's all *free!* So there's really no excuse anymore. It just goes to show how service-resistant these people are."

For officers like Garcia, possession of a mega-shelter ID conveyed a wealth of information about a resident's willingness to take responsibility for his or her own rehabilitation. Lack of a badge carried an opposite, equally powerful significance. As Officer Garcia's explanation illustrates, the badges derive their symbolic significance from the increasing range of comprehensive social services and programs now offered by the area's rehabilitation facilities. As he put it, "There's really no excuse anymore." The crosswalk interaction also captures how officers extended the label of illegitimate users from those involved in serious crime to anyone living in Skid Row who refrained from actively using the area's rehabilitative resources.

Officer Garcia's description of the two SRO residents as "service-resistant" demonstrates the extent of this categorization. The notion of service resistance has become increasingly popular among municipal leaders and law enforcement professionals who wish to blame prolonged poverty and chronic homelessness primarily on individuals' active refusal of services. As poverty scholars have shown, this discourse obfuscates and marginalizes the role of structural causes, such as the dearth of affordable housing or insufficient public aid, and instead castigates the poor for lacking the desire to properly govern their own conduct.[44]

Officers' new perceptions of the mega-shelters as a cure-all for a plethora of personal problems—ranging from unemployment and inadequate education to health problems, depression, and poverty more generally—led them to describe both unhoused *and* housed residents as equally service-resistant, equally unwilling to take advantage of available resources to move up and out of Skid Row. This diagnosis gave rise to a set of coercive measures designed to instill new attitudes and behaviors.

Solving Problems: The New Economy of Intervention

Whereas officers in the rabble management era favored interventions that ensured the most tranquility and quarantine for the least amount of effort, contemporary officers privileged a set of interventions they perceived as most effective in propelling residents along a trajectory of recovery that would ultimately take them out of Skid Row altogether. While SOS diversion was the most direct such measure, converting arrestees immediately into mega-shelter clients, that style of intervention was only available when SOS caseworkers were on duty at the station. The rest of the time, officers had to search for alternative means of producing a similar result.

Officers consistently complained (to me and to each other) that their collective effort to funnel residents toward rehabilitative settings was constrained by practical and legal concerns. While officers conceived of the mega-shelters as the best solution to Skid Row's various problems, the facilities' guidelines made enrollment and program participation strictly voluntary. Officers openly bemoaned their lack of legal authority to simply load problematic individuals into their squad cars and physically (even forcibly) deliver them to the mega-shelters. Compounding this difficulty, Central Division had come under intense scrutiny following a nationally publicized scandal in 2005, in which local law enforcement agencies were caught "dumping" various populations—parolees, addicts, mentally disabled people, and unhoused individuals—on the doorsteps of the mega-shelters.[45]

Yet, however constrained these officers felt, the zero-tolerance approach had given them a powerful resource. The newly minted municipal ordinances provided an *indirect* means of compelling residents to initiate and remain committed to their own reform. By selectively enforcing municipal bans on minor infractions and commonplace activities, officers sought to manipulate a neighborhood social ecology and incentive structure that they believed to propel service resistance and poor decisions. As the SCI lieutenant explained, "Ultimately it's our job to set the standard. There is really nobody else who is doing it. When you look out on the streets, most people have pretty much communicated to us that they aren't willing to make good choices in their lives. So our job is to help them to make the *right* choice. If they don't want to make the *right* choices to get better, to move up and out of here, then we have to step in."

The effort to compel individuals to "make the right choice" manifested in four principal interventions: (1) punishing long-term residence; (2) enforcing perpetual movement; (3) constricting the availability of alternative resources; and (4) protecting vulnerable future clients. Through these four patrol practices, officers attempted to instill levels of introspection, self-discipline, and future-orientation that would lead residents to begin taking steps toward rehabilitation. By initiating the process of self-improvement *outside* of the mega-shelters' walls, officers also attempted to condition residents to be more receptive to future program demands, thereby ensuring an elevated level of commitment and a higher probability of completion. While recovery management provided the organizational lens through which Central Division officers understood Skid Row, its population, and officers' responsibilities on patrol, there was notable heterogeneity among officers regarding their preferred patrol practices. I observed almost every officer deploying each of the four practices at one time or another. However, individual officers typically exhibited a preference for one or two of these techniques, based largely on their own background, patrol schedule, and personal conception of what recovery management meant in action.

Punishing Long-Term Residence

Given officers' construction of Skid Row as an instrumental and transitional space, extended residence in the neighborhood was taken as a clear sign that an individual was unwilling to engage in serious rehabilitation. Legitimate use of Skid Row thus took on an important temporal quality, rooted squarely in the recent influx of mega-shelter facilities. As one officer instructed me, "With the concentration of services for people down here, we've come to learn that the people who really want to get better do so quite quickly. They take full advantage of the services and they're up and out. This means that the vast majority of people who remain here are here because they choose to be here." Officers advanced the view that the longer individuals were allowed to remain in the area, particularly in the Bottom, the more attached they became to its "lifestyle." This posed a serious problem, because entrenched residents undermined the others' attempts at rehabilitation.

To counteract this effect, some officers selectively enforced quality-of-life laws to create graduated penalties that corresponded to an individual's length of residence in the area. This practice was most common among officers who were relatively more committed to the ideals of community engagement. These officers tended to take greater pride in learning the names and backgrounds of residents. They passed out business cards more frequently, and often encouraged residents to call on them when necessary. With this deeper level of contact, they were able to more quickly distinguish newcomers from long-term residents. Armed with this knowledge, they used (the threat of) enforcement to prevent the former from becoming the latter.

Officers Marshall and Diaz were two such officers. During a patrol, they spotted two black men sipping beer from tall aluminum cans wrapped in brown paper bags. As he approached the men, Officer Marshall called out to the older of the two by name. "Damn, Charlie," he said, shaking his head. "Again? You know the drill. Pour out those beers." The two men snickered but immediately began draining the contents of their cans into the gutter. Officer Marshall continued, addressing Charlie but pointing to his younger companion. "I see you've got yourself a new drinking buddy over here. You planning on bringing this guy down with you?"

"Aw man," Charlie replied, with a large, intoxicated smile. "This is my homeboy."

Officer Marshall looked toward the other man. "I haven't seen you before. Let's try to keep it that way, huh? Trust me, you don't want to become this guy's 'homeboy.'" The officer paused, looked westward on Sixth Street, and continued to address the younger man. "Why don't you take off and leave your homie with us?" Officer Marshall pointed toward the bright white façade of the Midnight Mission two blocks away. The younger man appeared surprised that he was being excused without further punishment but promptly crossed the intersection in the direction of the mega-shelter. Officer Marshall called after him. "Don't let me see you again, you hear?" The officer turned back toward Charlie. He put him in handcuffs, patted him down, and began to lecture. "We do this way too often, man. You ever going to learn?" The officers spent the next few minutes communicating with dispatch to check if Charlie had any outstanding warrants. Among other pieces of biographical information they demanded, Charlie provided his address—a residential hotel on Main Street. When the warrant check came up negative, Officer Marshall wrote Charlie a citation for possession of an open alcoholic beverage (LAMC 41.27(d)). As he turned to leave, Officer Marshall turned back toward Charlie and concluded his lecture, "You know, it's going to be like this until you get your shit together. It's your call."

Officer Marshall's intervention represents a contemporary analogue to Bittner's example of Big Jim and Dakota.[46] As in Bittner's case, the economy of intervention dictated that the officers only mobilize the formal law against one of the two individuals.[47] Rather than employ selective enforcement to prevent a crime, however, the officers in the contemporary case mobilized the available law as part of a conscious strategy to teach both men the benefits of "using" Skid Row in the correct manner, to direct both men toward the desired trajectory of rehabilitation. Officers Marshall and Diaz later explained their selective enforcement by insisting that, as they made permanent settlement more costly for Charlie, he would eventually come to view rehabilitation and exit from the neighborhood in a more favorable light.

Enforcing Perpetual Movement

While some officers employed graduated penalties to discourage long-term residence, others mobilized quality-of-life ordinances to impede settlement in a more immediate sense. This practice stemmed from the idea, commonly articulated throughout Central Division, that individuals engage in problematic behavior—particularly drug and alcohol consumption or sales—when they are allowed to remain idle in a single location. In response, officers turned again to the municipal ordinance that bans sitting, lying, or sleeping on the sidewalk to maintain constant movement through neighborhood space. Officers routinely parked their squad cars at one end of a street and walked the length of a block, issuing citations or instructing individuals they encountered to "move along." In a conversation following one such occasion, one officer told me, "It's pretty hard to spark your crack pipe while you're busy walking." Officers candidly offered this rationale for their discretionary enforcement to anyone who inquired, and even to those who did not.

SLO Thomas championed this practice. Thomas even devoted an entire edition of his newsletter to informing Skid Row residents that one of the ultimate reasons for issuing citations and making arrests was to keep residents on the move:

> When I began enforcing the sidewalk ordinance in my area it had less to do with sitting or sleeping on the sidewalk. . . . In Skid Row, people are not sitting or sleeping for "life sustaining" reasons. During the day, many are sitting so they can use narcotics. When they are sleeping, it is more likely due to crashing from a four-day cocaine binge or bad heroin overdose. While they sit, the drug deal-

ers we can't keep in jail, see the sidewalks as prime real estate for their trade. . . . There are excellent programs on Skid Row. . . . But when drug dealers are waiting right outside their doors, it's difficult . . . to succeed.

Thomas's newsletter clearly articulates how officers attempt to use selective, discretionary enforcement of quality-of-life laws to discourage, if only for a short time, the drug-related behaviors they perceive as detracting from the gravitational pull of the mega-shelters. Officers further insisted that, by denying residents comfortable spaces in which to recuperate from side effects and withdrawal symptoms, they could force individuals to reconsider their inappropriate choices. Officers thus reframed what some might see as police harassment as repeated lessons on the consequences of poor decision-making. As one senior officer explained, "Just imagine that you were getting woken up every single time you decided to drink too much. Come tomorrow, you might rethink climbing back into that bottle. In time, you're going to seek out somewhere warm and safe, somewhere like the Midnight, where you're not going to have an officer breathing down your back."

Constricting the Availability of Alternative Resources

A third discretionary intervention officers used to manipulate behavioral incentives and to promote an eventual exit from Skid Row entailed mobilizing municipal ordinances to constrict residents' access to vital resources that existed *outside* the confines and control of the rehabilitation facilities and programs. Echoing the logic of the proposed "feeding ordinance"—the ban on charitable food giveaways detailed in the previous chapter—many in Central Division explained residents' supposed resistance to services as rooted in an aversion to the strict rules imposed on them by the mega-shelters. The logic goes something like this: In order to receive the mega-shelters' resources of food, clothing, beds, or job training, clients must demonstrate an ongoing commitment to behavioral change, including complete abstinence from drug and alcohol consumption, willingness to perform

"Idle" pedestrians at the corner of Fifth and San Pedro Streets.

daily manual tasks, and attendance at various classes. Residents prefer to acquire vital resources without engaging in this quid pro quo, and those who can have little incentive to submit to the demands of self-improvement programs. Some officers, therefore, wanting residents to enroll in the programs, sought to curtail the availability of resources provided without these coercive rehabilitative mandates.

This practice was most frequent among officers who envisioned strong commonalities between themselves and residents. In Manny's case, for instance, it was his shared veteran status. Other Latino officers drew a parallel between the struggles faced by their immigrant parents and the dilemmas confronting recent immigrants in Skid Row. Similarly, some black officers recognized that their own upbringing, in South Central and without a father figure in the home, was common among those they now patrolled. Like Manny, these officers envisioned themselves as guardians of this population, with a duty to steer residents toward a better future. This practice also had a temporal dimension. Every Sunday, independent philanthropic orga-

A morning line for oatmeal provided by the Catholic Worker organization.

nizations and religious congregations descend on the neighborhood to deliver various forms of charity. In the early afternoon, congregations from across southern California travel en masse to distribute assistance in the form of food, clothing, and coffee.

With the launch of the Safer Cities Initiative, some patrol officers attempted to thwart charitable efforts and thereby limit residents' ability to physically sustain themselves without enrolling in rehabilitative programs. On one such afternoon, I watched as Manny and his partner disrupted a church group's attempt to provide free food. Dressed in their Sunday best, three women and two men stood behind a small collapsible table handing out sandwiches on a usually deserted street in the Bottom. Given that over 60 percent of both housed and unhoused residents of Skid Row report these giveaways as a regular source of food, the group drew a significant crowd.[48] On the far side of the table, roughly twenty men and women massed in an orderly line waiting to be served. The church group passed out their sandwiches with a smile and a quick "God bless you." Once individuals received their food, they took a seat on the curb or leaned against the nearby concrete wall to eat.

I followed close behind Manny and his partner as they walked briskly toward the table. Several of those who had been eating promptly stood and walked in the opposite direction. As we approached, one of the women addressed the officers with a smile. "Good afternoon, officers. Can I interest you in a turkey sandwich?"

Manny returned the politeness as he stood in front of the table, blocking the next man in line from receiving his sandwich. "No, no sandwiches for us today, thank you."

"How about some water?" one of the men asked, holding up a small bottle of Arrowhead Spring Water.

"No, no water either, thank you," Manny's partner responded. After several minutes inquiring about the group's church, an AME temple located in South Central LA, he informed them of his ultimate reason for interrupting their activity. "So, unfortunately, I'm going to have to ask you to pack up today. I know that you all came down here to help out. A lot of churches do. But what they don't realize is that just giving people food out here in the streets is really just making matters worse."

"Making matters worse?" another one of the women defensively asked. "How exactly is feeding hungry people making matters worse?"

"Well, there's a number of reasons," Manny continued calmly. "Right now it's hard for you to see, but we're the ones who have to deal with all this after you all leave and go back home."

The woman was clearly growing agitated. "Deal with what?"

"For starters, all the trash. See these?" Manny picked up a Styrofoam plate off the table. "These are going to be all over the gutters. That brings the rats and the roaches and diseases. We have a population with compromised immune systems down here. You don't want to get them sick, do you?"

"We're going to clean everything up before we leave," the man said. "We promise."

Manny grew more assertive. "It's not just the trash and the rats.

People down here need help. They don't need food. They can get food at any one of the missions. They serve three meals a day. But do you know why they're not eating at the missions? Because they can't be in there drunk or high or starting fights. They have to follow the rules. And the fact of the matter is that a lot of the people don't want to do that. They want to stay out here and keep doing the same stuff that landed them down here in the first place. So a lot of people think they're helping, but they're actually hurting. If you really want to help, there are plenty of places that would be happy to let you volunteer your time instead of rewarding them for not getting their lives together."

Despite this firm explanation, the group showed little intention of backing down. The man continued. "I understand, but all we're doing is giving these people a little nourishment and a prayer. We're not breaking any laws, sir."

Technically, the man was right. As the LA City Council has yet to approve the proposed ban on street giveaways, no city statutes prohibited the group's activity. Still, the officers had a number of legal resources at their disposal. The city's vague quality-of-life laws, particularly the ban on "unreasonably interfering with the free passage of pedestrians," provided officers with alternative means for achieving the same result.

"Look," Manny replied, clearly agitated. He gestured to the small group of people that had remained throughout the dispute. "If you want, I can give you a ticket right now for blocking the sidewalk." He motioned behind him to the group's SUV parked several yards away. "And for parking in a red zone."

"No, no, that won't be necessary," the other man immediately responded, silencing his fellow congregants. "I'll move my car. A ticket isn't necessary. Can we have a minute to pack up?"

"That's fine," Manny responded. "Just don't make me repeat myself when we come back by here."

"No, no, you won't," the same man assured.

Appearing satisfied, Manny's partner offered a few parting words of advice. "Like he said, if you're *really* serious about helping people, you can call down to the station and get a list of good places to volunteer. There are much better ways to do this. Trust me." In 2009, Skid Row officers formalized this referral process and began distributing fliers with the names, addresses, and phone numbers of approved social service facilities to philanthropic groups distributing food.[49]

As we walked away from the group, Manny turned to me to debrief the interaction. This had become our standard routine. He explained his handling of the "do-gooders"—officers' blanket term for those providing street charity. "This shouldn't be a vacation down here for people," he instructed me. "To an extent you could say a part of our job is to make this place as uncomfortable as possible so that people finally hit rock bottom and get themselves into a mission." Eliminating food giveaways was thus designed to literally starve Skid Row residents into rehabilitative settings.[50]

Protecting Vulnerable Future Clients

To make their interventions as economical as possible—to "police smarter," as a senior officer put it—some officers engaged in the peculiar practice of aggressively targeting individuals they suspected would be *most* receptive to rehabilitative programs. A subset of Central Division officers took a particularly interventionist stance toward women, viewing them as more amenable to social services and the accompanying demands of behavioral change. These officers were more likely to spend time on patrol distributing homemade toiletry kits containing feminine hygiene products, moisturizer, and razors. These officers were also more likely to participate in events like "Ladies Night"—a gathering created by one of the division's senior officers to provide women residents with self-defense lessons and instructions for reporting domestic violence and sexual assault. One such officer explained the importance of focusing on women. "Women are much easier," the officer explained. "They aren't steeped in that tough-guy, macho, gangbanger mentality. They don't want to fight everybody. So once they start getting help, it sticks a lot faster."

Officers felt a need to move fast, however, because women were also easy targets for crime and victimization. "The longer these women are down here," one patrol officer explained, "the more they get abused, the more they start to lose trust in people because everyone takes advantage of them."

To head off this growing distrust, these officers were quicker to detain women, using interrogations to inquire about their safety and issuing citations as a form of service referral. Officer Wallace, who patrolled the western side of Skid Row, was among those most devoted to this practice. Once, while standing with him on the corner of Fifth and Los Angeles Streets, I noticed Officer Wallace closely watching four middle-aged pedestrians—a woman and three men—make their way across the intersection in our direction. The woman and one of the men were arguing, yelling at each other as the other two men added their own occasional comments in support of the man. Halfway across the street, the woman suddenly shoved the man in his ribs. He responded by getting in her face and yelling even more loudly. This caused the woman to speed up, as though attempting to walk away. By the time the group reached our location, however, the man had caught up with the woman and was speaking sternly, though more quietly, in her ear. Officer Wallace stopped the group as they began to walk past us. He asked each for identification and inquired as to their destinations. They all produced IDs and said they were heading to a market on the next block. Without further questions, Officer Wallace excused the men but not the woman.

"Friends of yours?" he asked after the three men had walked away.

The woman was only beginning to cool down. "Who, them? Yeah."

Officer Wallace continued to probe. "You sure? It didn't look like that from over here."

"He's just an asshole," she replied tersely. She stood with her hand on her hip, clearly annoyed. "Can I go?"

Officer Wallace frowned. "Not yet. You're sure you're OK? You're not in any danger that I need to know about, are you?"

"I told you," the woman said. "He's just being stupid. I need to go, OK? Can I go?" Her frustration peaked when she noticed Officer Wallace begin writing in his citation book. "You're about to give me a ticket, now?"

"You crossed against the light," he responded without looking up from his writing.

"That's some bullshit!"

"Listen," Officer Wallace ordered, pointing at the woman with his pen. She stared upward in defiance, tapping her foot. She bit down hard on her lip, as though holding back another outburst. "Listen," Officer Wallace repeated more loudly. The woman finally looked him in the eye. He continued. "I'm giving you this ticket. *But*"—he paused—"you're not going to have to pay this fine." He paused again as she looked upward in defiance. "Are you listening to me? Listen to me," he ordered. "They have a ticket clinic over at the Midnight Mission. If you take this over there, they'll take care of it for you. All you got to do is link up with someone to talk to. There's counselors and caseworkers in there. That's all you have to do, OK? And then they'll tear this ticket right up. Can you do that?"

The woman protested, leading Officer Wallace to repeat his instructions once more. They argued for another couple of minutes until the woman appeared convinced that Officer Wallace would not take back the citation. Once he dismissed her, she stuffed the citation in her front jeans pocket and stormed off in the direction of her companions.

I looked for the woman throughout the remainder of my fieldwork, but neither I nor Officer Wallace ever saw her again. Neither one of us knew whether she ever took her citation to the clinic. This did not seem to bother Officer Wallace, however. "She'll likely go running right back to that abusive relationship," he lamented later. "But at least now she knows that she has better options down here. It might take a while, but someday she'll reach a point where she's ready to do better for herself." Like his fellow officers, Wallace anticipated that each successive police interaction would bring these "better options" into clearer relief. For now, he had done his part.

||||||||||||||||

Officer Wallace's routine attempts to pull women away from abusive partners and push them toward social services marks a noticeable departure from the explicitly nonrehabilitative model of rabble management popular during the mid- and late twentieth century. If the rabble management school of policing primarily emphasized quarantine and social exclusion, the recovery model sees Skid Row as an instrumental and rehabilitative space.[51] Instead of isolating the poor out of sight, today's officers hope to improve them to the point that they might reenter conventional society. To this end, officers read and give meaning to the people, places, and situations they encounter through a revised perceptual framework. Rather than evaluate scenarios in terms of the potential threat they pose to Skid Row's containment, officers now make assessments based on perceived threats to rehabilitation. Contemporary officers also operate under an explicitly therapeutic economy of intervention. Given their revised conceptualization of Skid Row and their own responsibilities toward the neighborhood, contemporary officers weigh their various interventions against their efficiency in funneling residents toward more approved trajectories of self-improvement. They mobilize the discretionary authority granted by the zero-tolerance approach to convince Skid Row residents to govern themselves through healthier, more responsible choices.

While this perspective dominates Central Division, it is not monolithic. Officer heterogeneity extends beyond the concrete practices of recovery management. During my fieldwork, I encountered a small number of officers who appeared less committed to the ideals and mandates of therapeutic policing. Among these officers, Officer Hill appeared the least convinced that the Skid Row population could ever be redeemed. Whether speaking to me, his partners, or residents, the man never once indicated that he carried out his actions for residents' own good. He seemed concerned only with the fact that a law had been broken. In fact, Officer Hill seemed utterly disgusted with the population. He quickly snapped on his black latex gloves any time he interacted with residents. Afterward, he lathered his hands and forearms in sanitizer. He constantly grumbled about how "dirty" residents were. Of all the officers I observed, Hill was one of the quickest to confiscate property. He routinely took crates, blankets, and backpacks out of the hands of homeless people and locked these items in the trunk of his car. He repeatedly called the nearby BID office to seize shopping carts, luggage, and tents that were too large to fit in his squad car. When Officer Hill intervened, homeless residents were likely to be left confused and propertyless, clutching a citation in their hands.

Interestingly, although Officer Hill and Manny Rodriguez seemed to be driven by nearly opposite conceptions of their responsibility to Skid Row residents, there was a striking similarity in the objective results of their interventions. While Manny's interactions often included a sympathetic lecture or a handshake, he was just as likely to confiscate homeless people's property as Officer Hill, especially if they were veterans. He was just as likely to exacerbate residents' material hardships. This means that one of the *least* therapeutic officers and one of the *most* therapeutic officers often engaged in equally punitive patrol practices. Both were equally capable of making life untenable for Skid Row residents.

Officer Hill represents a dwindling minority in a division that is increasingly oriented toward recovery management. As officers like Thomas, Garcia, and Rodriguez gain in seniority, enlist fellow patrol officers to distribute newsletters about the neighborhood's new identity, school rookies on how to use citations to incentivize self-improvements, and lightheartedly assess fellow officers' skills at diverting residents from the streets to the mega-shelters, they actively institutionalize recovery management and its constituent practices as part of the division's organizational culture. The process of self-selection in and out of divisional assignments has additionally contributed to a critical mass of officers who understand their daily patrols as a form of outreach social work. Even Sergeant Morgan, who bemoaned what he saw as a loss of autonomy in the zero-tolerance approach, supported the disciplinary practice of prohibiting panhandlers from continuing to shirk "real jobs" in the formal labor market.

On a more theoretical level, this emerging vision of Skid Row residents and their associated deviance and crime represents a movement away from a "criminology of the other" and toward a "criminology of the self."[52] A criminology of the other essentializes difference. The social deviant is seen as, at her core, fundamentally different from "us." While a select few can be remade and reintegrated into society, those deemed beyond help are quickly quarantined, often in neighborhoods of exile like Skid Row. In contrast, a criminology of the self holds that the deviant is, at the most base level, a normal, rational consumer, someone "just like us." Reintegration, then, becomes a matter of reawakening (or recovering) the ability to, in the words of the lieutenant, "make the *right* choice." As a result, those who remain poor and destitute are seen as *willfully* poor and destitute. As they continue to make the "wrong" choices, they deserve to be punished harshly.

This view, and the resulting interventions, raises some obvious questions. Do these patrol practices work? Do they in fact engender self-discipline and promote better decision-making on the part of Skid Row residents? Spending time alongside those on the receiving end of such sanctions, I discovered that the constant threat of police discipline did in fact propel residents to alter their lives. In fact, Skid Row residents went to extreme lengths to mitigate the weight of policing that pressed down on their routine activities. The changes they enacted, however, were hardly the kind desired by officers. Rather, residents found new, subversive ways to deflect, manipulate, and obstruct law enforcement and its paternalistic demands. I detail these efforts in part II, showing how ubiquitous and intrusive policing gives rise to a contradictory culture of everyday resistance. On the one hand, residents' diverse forms of resistance provide avenues for them to assert autonomy and ensure freedom from unwanted police contact. On the other hand, residents' tactics carry the potential to fracture the community and amplify residents' social, economic, and moral marginalization.

Part II

Becoming Copwise

CHAPTER THREE

Training for Survival

On a sweltering August afternoon I stood on San Julian Street, just outside of the Midnight Mission. The sun radiated off the asphalt, awakening the smell of urine that accumulated in thin puddles along the gutter. As usual, the street was littered with debris and bustled with activity. Seemingly oblivious to the surrounding commotion, a mountain of a man known simply as "Steel" clutched a heavy barbell in his hands. At his feet sat an assortment of dumbbells, PVC pipes, and other pieces of homemade weight-lifting equipment. Steel grunted as he repeatedly curled the barbell to his chin. Thick rivulets of sweat ran from the spaces between his cornrow braids down his face, disappearing into his long-sleeved denim Fubu shirt. Even through the XXL shirt he wore, the outlines of the fifty-three-year-old's hulking back and biceps were clearly visible. Steel let out a final exhale and passed the barbell to the next man in the tight semicircle, who repeated the process.

This group of about thirteen men cleared debris from the sidewalk to perform physical exercises together three or four days a week. Through their workout routines, they carved out a small but cohesive community amid the turbulence of Skid Row. Between groans of physical exertion, the men caught up with each another, told dirty jokes, and debated current events. On this day, hot topics included the outlook for the Los Angeles Lakers in the upcoming basketball season and the diminishing beauty of supermodel Tyra Banks. After ten minutes of playful bickering, however, the group fell silent as they caught a glimpse of an LAPD squad car creeping slowly up the block. The men stood frozen, eyes cast to the sky. After the cruiser turned the corner and disappeared from sight, someone muttered "fucking pigs" as the men re-formed a semicircle around the weight-lifting equipment.

Tony, a toned and muscular man, spoke first, providing news about another group member. "Ya'll hear that Sammy got popped yesterday?"

"That idiot?" Steel responded as he bent over and picked up a pair of dumbbells. "I ain't surprised. That fool deserved to get popped, running the streets 'til two in the morning, hanging with those shady females. What else does he think is gonna happen?"

A squat man, ironically nicknamed Big Ron, agreed. "That's what I been telling him, but he don't wanna listen. I told him he needs to get more serious about these workouts. Stop hitting that bottle and start hitting these weights. A man can't get his mind right 'til he gets his body right."

"He better get serious about it real quick," Steel added decisively, "or else he better get used to wearing them peels [prison jumpsuits] for a while."

For the next hour, the group exchanged news about recent police activity in the neighborhood—a topic that often dominated their conversations. They reported who else "got popped," cataloged recent citations they had received, and poured over the details of other run-ins they had heard about, observed, or experienced firsthand. As the workout came to a close and the men began departing in separate directions, Big Ron noticed two mounted police officers guiding their horses through a nearby intersection. The officers stared down at one of the men, a fair-skinned black named Dice, who was walking in their direction. Seeing this, Big Ron called out with a notable urgency in his voice. "Hey young buck!" Dice turned to listen. "I better see you back here next week. Five-oh [the police] is out rolling hard today." Big Ron pointed at the officers. "So just be smart, aight? Mess around and you'll end up sitting in a cell right next to Sammy's dumb black ass." Dice nodded and continued up the street.

It turned out, however, that Dice was not yet "smart" enough. Despite Big Ron's warning, he was arrested two days later for loitering outside of his SRO hotel. He rejoined the group the following week, having spent a night in jail. After a brief chiding, Big Ron and the others offered detailed instructions on how Dice might avoid future arrests. Between push-ups and other exercises, they engaged in a very different kind of training.

|||||||||||||||

Therapeutic policing, with its omnipresent surveillance and regulation, has dramatically impacted the cultural context of Skid Row. Beginning in this chapter, I show how this street-level model of poverty governance reverberates through the neighborhood even (and perhaps especially) long after officers have left the scene. Facing the constant threat of police contact, punishment, and discipline, residents developed a range of circumspect tactics to evade, deflect, and subvert officers' coercive interventions. These "everyday forms of resistance" provided Skid Row residents with a distinct schema for evaluating conduct and making sense of their experiences, thereby playing "an active part in the generative process through which shared meaning, value, and—ultimately—culture are produced and reproduced."[1] Residents' maneuvers became tightly woven into the "social fabric of everyday life"—that "vivid and pressing milieu" in which local residents come to understand themselves, others, and the larger community.[2]

This chapter focuses on the daily lives of Steel and his crew to illustrate the extent to which residents reorganize their routine activities, peer associations, and even the minute management of their physical bodies to cope with ubiquitous law enforcement. Steel and the others developed and refined sophisticated techniques for minimizing unwanted police contact in an attempt to reduce the likelihood of arrest and incarceration. Whereas the preceding chapters elaborated how the police leverage the law to rehabilitate Skid Row residents, this chapter considers how residents' attempts to resist policing contribute to their efforts to develop indigenous forms of self-improvement and recovery that stand in stark opposition to therapeutic policing. This chapter also explores the contradictory nature of residents' tactics of resistance, showing how these techniques can become a further engine of atomization.

Welcome to Purgatory

Looking back, it seems only fitting that Steel's first words to me came in the form of unsolicited advice. "You really wanna get jacked?" he asked over his shoulder, suspended from a recently erected pull-up bar in the small courtyard of Skid Row's Gladys Park. We had been working out near each other when Steel struck up the conversation. "If you wanna take it to the next level then you gotta grab the bar wider, like this." He executed five quick pull-ups, showing off his impressive wingspan. Dropping down, he introduced himself and invited me to give it a try. I humbly accepted his suggestion, and for the next half hour Steel showed me multiple ways of utilizing a single pull-up bar to exercise almost every major muscle of my body. "For a long time this is all I had to work with," he proudly stated, pointing to the thin steel bar. "This was my whole gym right here. Around here, you gotta make the best of whatever you can get your hands on." I took this opportunity to explain my interest in learning about everyday life in the neighborhood. Steel nodded his head in approval as I spoke.

On my first mention of policing, however, he quickly cut me off. "You been rolling around with one-time [police]?" he asked in a cynical tone, hardly giving me a chance to answer. The advice continued. "Listen to me on this one. Don't believe the hype, you hear? No matter what they say, not everybody down here is doing dirt. There's a handful of niggas like me that's trying hard as hell to stay out of trouble and do right with our lives. It ain't easy in a place like this." In what I now recognize as an eager attempt to prove his point, Steel invited me to rendezvous with his "crew" two days later for one of their regular gatherings. As I participated in the group's daily workout sessions over the following months, I learned that their effort to set themselves apart from the "typical" Skid Row resident was at the heart of their struggle to survive in the neighborhood.

As unofficial leader and mentor of the group, Steel blended workout tips with life lessons. Born and raised in the Pueblo del Rio housing project in South Central LA, Steel had recently completed a seven-year prison sentence for multiple counts of robbery. Beginning with an arrest at age twenty-one, he had accumulated a total of seventeen years in prison on charges stemming from a lifetime of involvement with crack cocaine and the Pueblo Bishop Bloods gang. Having been convicted of two felonies, Steel knew a third conviction would send him to prison for twenty-five years to life under California's "three strikes" law. Steel vowed to never again return to the Pueblos in hopes of avoiding this future. Upon his release, he traveled instead to Skid Row—a halfway point (both geographically and symbolically) between LA's massive jail system and South Central.

Steel was certainly not the first inmate to make this journey, nor would he be the last. The launch of the Safer Cities Initiative, with its unprecedented levels of citations and arrests, has increased the number of individuals traveling along the circuit that runs between Skid Row, the Twin Towers Correctional Facility, the LA Central Jail, and the patchwork of correctional facilities up and down the state. As a result, Skid Row has become the most common point of prisoner reentry in the southern California region, with an estimated one-third of the city's active parolees residing in its fifty square blocks.[3] The major service providers now operate shuttles to and from nearby detention facilities. On the suggestions of fellow inmates and prison staff, Steel secured a shelter bed at the Los Angeles Mission.

Yet despite the concentration of reentry services, conditions in Skid Row can undermine former prisoners' attempts to remain sober and avoid further involvement with the criminal justice system. Steel devised a plan to "stay out of trouble," however, using rehabilitative techniques he acquired in prison. During his most recent incarceration, he had devoted a majority of his time to the "weight pile"—the collection of iron weights that can be found in many prison exercise yards.[4] Steel sometimes credited the prison weight pile with saving his life. "It gave me a way to escape all the bullshit," he told me one morning as we sat on a park bench recording his life story. "When I started hanging with the O.G.'s at the pile,[5] I stopped kicking it with all the knuckleheads I knew from the block. I started working on my addiction. I realized it don't matter how much weight you can lift if you're just gonna keep pumping drugs and booze into your muscles. You gotta take care of your body if you want it to get bigger and stronger." By the time of his release, Steel had put on twenty-five pounds of muscle.

Steel said his decision to maintain his workout routine on the outside was a "no-brainer." Every morning when the shelters emptied their cots, he walked to Gladys Park, where he devoted two hours or more to intense exercise. As a testament to Skid Row's concentration of ex-offenders, Steel serendipitously reunited with one of his former cellmates, Big Ron, who permitted Steel to crash on the floor of his apartment. As roommates, the two amplified their commitment to the prison-inspired workout regimen. Scavenging weight-lifting supplies, they assembled what they referred to as the "Skid Row weight pile" along the sidewalks of San Julian Street and in Gladys Park, transporting their equipment to and from Big Ron's apartment in a battered and rattling red shopping cart. Over the ensuing months, the two attracted other men from the neighborhood, several of whom were ex-offenders similarly hoping to kick lingering addictions and avoid returning to prison.

A common pattern emerged when I spoke with the men regarding their arrival in Skid Row and their attraction to the group. While Skid Row had been a logical destination given their lack of resources and alternative options, they nonetheless felt reluctant, even ashamed, to take up residence in the infamous area. These sentiments are far from unique. In their influential study of precariously housed individuals across the LA region, geographers Jennifer Wolch and Michael Dear find that Skid Row is the one place their respondents overwhelmingly attempted to avoid.[6] "For them," Wolch and Dear report, "Skid Row is a kind of purgatory."[7] This revulsion arises not only from the

Pull-ups in Gladys Park.

neighborhood's material destitution, but also from Skid Row's *symbolic* denigration, its "territorial stigma." Sociologist Loïc Wacquant argues that as economic and social marginality become concentrated in isolated and bounded territories, these "neighborhoods of exile" come to be perceived as a kind of social dumpster, where only the refuse of society would choose to dwell.[8] To reside in Skid Row is to subject oneself to a "taint of place" that intersects with other stigmas associated with extreme poverty, race, or a criminal record. As a result, residents experience a tension between internal self-perceptions and spatially imposed identities.

This tension preoccupied the men who found their way to Steel's crew, particularly those who had grown up in nearby South Central and had preconceived opinions about Skid Row. They were now resigned to living alongside some of the same individuals they had belittled and even exploited in their former lives. When I asked Big Ron if he "hung out" in Skid Row prior to his incarceration, he responded with a look that indicated the absurdity of my question. "Hell naw," he protested. "We only used to come near here if we really needed to offload a package in a hurry. Me and my boys would just roll up and all the crackheads would bum-rush us, like a stampede." He used his fingers to mimic the scurrying of small insects. "Now I gotta deal with these motherfuckers every time I walk out of my place. I'm surrounded by them. Plus, they wanna come talk to me like I'm their best friend or something, asking if I'm holding." His tone grew agitated. "When they come at me I'm like, 'Do I *look* like I belong in this hellhole?'" This question seemed directed as much to me as to his imagined interlocutor. He raised his eyebrows and held his arms out to his sides, inviting a closer examination.

Big Ron's statement captures one of the main effects of territorial stigma: the elaboration of "infra-differences" and the stimulation of secondary marginalization. Wacquant notes that, in their efforts to salvage an ideal sense of self, residents of denigrated neighborhoods turn against their neighbors, engaging in mutual distancing and emphasizing micro-hierarchies detectable only at ground level.[9] Residents join the public chorus in castigating such familiar scapegoats as "hoodlums," "welfare cheats," and, in Big Ron's case, swarms of "crackheads."[10] Many of the men at the Skid Row weight pile explained their attraction and dedication to the group in precisely these terms. Consider Tyrell, a soft-spoken, burly man. Upon his 2006 release from the California Men's Colony Prison, some two hundred miles to the north, Tyrell used his "gate money" to purchase a bus ticket to Los Angeles. He followed the suggestion of his cellmate and walked the two blocks from the Greyhound station to Skid Row. "As soon as I got down here I was like, 'Oh shit. This is my life now.' Right when I saw the boys, I didn't feel alone anymore." He snapped his finger. "I knew they weren't gonna just sit around and keep poisoning themselves like everyone else. God showed me some other niggas out here that's just like me."

But territorial stigma also carries important material consequences. It reshapes interactions with state agencies, particularly the
police, who are likely to modify their conduct and procedures within
a stigmatized area in line with a "reflex suspicion of deviance if not
outright guilt."[11] Skid Row residents quickly become aware of the
blanket police suspicion and undiscerning application of stop-and-
frisks within the neighborhood's boundaries. For one of the men in
Steel's crew, a dreadlocked man named Tex, it was only a matter of
minutes after his arrival in the neighborhood before he found himself in handcuffs. Upon his release from the Men's Central Jail, Tex
wheeled his battered green suitcase the mile and a half to Skid Row.[12]
Tired from the trek, he set down his bag to buy a single cigarette—
known locally as a "loosie"—from another pedestrian. Before he
could pull the quarter from his pocket, however, two officers on bicycles detained, handcuffed, and searched him for narcotics against
a nearby wall. Not finding any contraband, the officers issued him
a citation nonetheless, stating that the placement of his bag had violated Los Angeles Municipal Code (LAMC) 41.18(a)—an ordinance
that prohibits obstructing the sidewalk. Unable to pay the nearly $200
fine with his monthly General Relief income of $221, Tex ignored the
ticket. What he did not realize was that, over the next eight months,
which he spent sleeping in SROs and the streets, the fine had increased to over $500, and a warrant had been issued for his arrest. He
found out when he was rustled from his tent at 6:15 one morning for
violating LAMC 41.18(d)—a different ordinance that prohibits sitting,
lying, or sleeping on the sidewalk between 6:00 a.m. and 9:00 p.m.
The officers arrested him on the basis of his current offense, the outstanding warrant, and his unpaid fines. After three days in jail, a judge
issued Tex a twelve-month suspended sentence and an additional $195
fine, warning him that any future citations or arrests would result in
harsher sentencing.

Interactions such as these teach residents a fundamental lesson
about life in Skid Row: "staying out of trouble" or refraining from
drug activity and criminal behavior is not enough to avert repeated

detainments, citations, arrests, and spiraling legal entanglements. In response to this dilemma, the men of the Skid Row weight pile not only worked on their rehabilitation but developed proactive measures to avoid unwanted police contact. They invested considerable energy in their performances of infra-differences, in hopes of escaping officers' default assumptions of criminality. Specifically, they minimized the scrutiny and suspicion they might otherwise draw from officers by amplifying the symbolic and physical distance that separated them from those they viewed as "belonging" in Skid Row. While these efforts did provide some reprieve from police contact, and even reinforced the therapeutic capacity of the weight pile, they did so at the expense of validating and exacerbating the same territorial stigma pressing down on them.

Becoming "Copwise"

The evasive actions of the Skid Row weight-lifting group emerged in response to the conditions of ubiquitous policing. Nevertheless, they bear close resemblance to the tactics documented among residents in neighborhoods characterized by *inadequate* policing. Sociologist Elijah Anderson, drawing on four decades of analyzing urban street life, demonstrates that when police protection is lacking, inner-city residents develop techniques to take personal safety into their own hands.[13] They cultivate what he terms "street wisdom"—a cognitive framework that "allows one to 'see through' public situations, to anticipate what is about to happen based on cues and signals from those one encounters."[14] By generating a "system for categorizing the denizens of the streets and other public spaces," individuals refocus their attention on "a host of signs, emblems, and symbols that others display in everyday life."[15] Given the rationalization that street criminals select victims based on outward signs of vulnerability and unfamiliarity, "streetwise" residents learn to display "safety signals"—dressing in certain attire or monitoring eye contact, for example—which ward off danger and reduce unwanted interactions.

Cultivating street wisdom is no simple task, however, and requires significant "offstage" preparation and reflection.

As police officers now saturate Skid Row in record numbers, residents respond by developing "cop wisdom"—a cognitive framework designed to reduce unwanted police interactions. Among the men at the weight pile, Dante, an outspoken man well known for his black nationalist commitments, offered a concise notion of what it meant to become copwise. We paused our workout one afternoon to watch a nearby arrest. Dante snickered as the arresting officer slapped handcuffs on a disheveled black man and pulled a clear plastic vial from one of the man's pockets. Employing the image of a predatory animal stalking its prey, he reflected on the practices of Skid Row police officers: "Living down here is like living way back in Africa, you feel me? You got a lion out there in that tall grass just waiting to jump out on your ass. If you don't wanna be lunch then you gotta be ready. It's simple though. The lion, he's lazy, so he's looking for that easy kill. He's looking for the weakest in the herd. Remember, you don't gotta outrun that lion. Shit, nobody can do that. All you really gotta do is outrun the slowest nigga on the safari. It's the same with these motherfucking po-po. It's all about figuring out their psychology and making sure yours is better. They can't jack up everybody."

Thus, despite being up against "lions," the men of the weight pile saw themselves as capable of maintaining at least some control over their fate in the streets. As Dante points out, Skid Row officers do not behave randomly. Rather, they are guided by a set of subjective and practical constraints. While police saturate the neighborhood, their time and resources on patrol are finite. They cannot possibly intervene in every instance of (suspected) criminality, and they must privilege certain individuals and behaviors as most in need of their immediate attention. I was impressed by how closely the men's theories about police behavior mirrored those proposed by the classic police ethnographies discussed in the last chapter. But instead of basing their findings on officer interviews and systematic observations of patrols, the men drew on their own experiences. Armed with this "data," they used their time together to formulate what we might think of as a folk ethnography of policing, in which they attempted to model police "psychology"—the general tendencies and considerations motivating officer behavior. By sharing these experiences, they built a collective repository of knowledge about precisely which characteristics make some individuals more likely than others to attract police scrutiny. Throughout these exchanges, the men tended to explain police intervention as determined primarily by a potential suspect's outward appearances and associations.

Consider the men's analysis of Tex's earlier citation for blocking the sidewalk. One morning, after Tex had uncharacteristically missed seven consecutive workouts, Big Ron approached him and asked him about his recent whereabouts. "We missed you last week, buddy. Where you been at?"

Tex reminded Big Ron of his suspended sentence and the judge's stern warning. "I been laying low, man," he said in a low, dejected tone. "I ain't trying to go back to court. Those bike cops were out all last week. They're the ones that popped me for that bullshit ticket that I'm still dealing with."[16]

Big Ron quickly dismissed Tex's fears. "Aw man, you ain't got to worry about them fools no more. Trust me. They ain't fucked with me in a minute. You know why? It's 'cause I stay on top of my shit. That's the key. Let me ask you this. What do you think those pigs were looking for when they rolled up on your ass?"

Tex sighed. "They were looking to give me a ticket for blocking the road. It's bullshit cause I was only stopping to buy a Newport. I was just . . ."

Big Ron cut him off. "Naw naw, man. I mean what is this pig *really* looking for? He don't give a shit about your bag. That's just a smoke-screen. What he's *really* looking for is to see if you're high or if you look like you're *about* to get high."

"But I wasn't high," Tex countered, "and these motherfuckers still fucked with me."

Big Ron was undeterred. "That's my point. You wasn't trying to get high, but that's not the way you *looked*." Big Ron stressed this last word. "Think about it. You just got out of jail so you're looking tired. You probably ain't had much to eat so you're all thinned out. Plus, you're talking to this cat you clearly don't know. You're digging in your pocket for some change. Yo, imagine that you're one of these pigs. Put all the facts together. What does that look like to them? It looks like you're a straight dopefiend, and it looks like you're buying some dope. Of course they rolled up on you! They wanted to get all up in your pockets."

Tex nodded his head. His mood appeared slightly elevated. "I see what you're saying. I kinda asked for it."

"Look," Big Ron said as he put a consoling hand on Tex's shoulder. "Now you're on top of your shit like the rest of us. You ain't the same man they fucked with before, right? You been putting on some good size. You been hitting the iron. You ain't got that same look in your eyes that you had when I met you. People can see that you're a man that respects himself." Big Ron gave Tex a playful shove, which was returned with a reluctant smile.

Big Ron's folk analysis exemplifies how the men collaborated to make seemingly unpredictable police interventions more legible and manipulable. The men put themselves in officers' shoes to reconsider the neighborhood and its inhabitants from a vital new perspective— they attempted to "see like a cop." Seeing like a cop entailed a double interpretation: to anticipate how an officer will behave, one must anticipate how officers anticipate addicts will behave. Engaging in this thought experiment—asking how officers might construe any given action—the men adjusted their own behaviors and appearances so as not to be "mistaken" for those they perceived to be officers' most sought-after targets.

Sobriety Signals

Just as streetwise residents learn to project safety signals, Steel's crew learned to exhibit "sobriety signals" designed to reduce their relative level of suspicion in the eyes of officers. Sobriety signals rested on a negation: to communicate that they were less deserving of police attention than others in the immediate vicinity, the men presented outward proof that they were *not* under the influence of drugs or alcohol. They mindfully refrained from engaging in what they termed "dopefiend shit." This was the men's term for the unconscious behaviors they believed to be the most visible symptoms of prolonged substance abuse.

According to Mike, a former auto mechanic who was addicted to crack cocaine for over ten years, "When you're high you do all kinds of stupid shit you don't even realize. Like you see dudes out here that always be scratching their arms. Or like some guys lick their lips a lot. It's because your body gets all hyper." He mimicked uncontrollable fidgeting as he said this. "When I got really high, I was always rubbing the top of my head. You know, like smoothing out my waves." He repeatedly stroked the top of his head to make his curls lay flatter. "It wasn't 'til I kicked my habit that I even realized I had damn near rubbed myself bald!" Mike tilted forward to show me the thin patch of hair on the crown of his head.

When the men reflected on their former lives, they overwhelmingly described addiction in terms of an alienated and antagonistic relationship between their body, driven primarily by the need to satisfy physical sensations, and their mind, which became increasingly overpowered. The men frequently spoke of being "trapped" in addiction, held hostage by their body as it oscillated between the ecstasy of the last hit and the misery of the ensuing withdrawal and "dopesickness."[17] Dice offered a compelling depiction of this internal battle during a particularly taxing workout. Big Ron and I watched as Dice completed a forceful set of shoulder presses, slammed the dumbbells at his feet, and loudly clapped his hands together in accomplishment. "There we go," he let out with a heavy exhale. We both complimented him and exchanged "dap"—a local handshake. "Thanks man, I'm trying," he responded. "Not too fucking bad for a nigga who used to be a all-star crackhead, huh?" Pausing to catch his breath enough to continue speaking, he pointed to a group of three men who were standing in a huddled circle on the opposite side of the street, passing what looked like a glass pipe. "I was bad there for a little bit, man. I wasn't living no life. . . . It was like I was on cruise control. Like a dream where you just float over yourself and can't do nothing. On autopilot, doing stupid shit, being on the hunt, sparking up the pipe. There was two of me, and the real me was just along for the ride."

For the men, this antagonism between mind and body produced more than just self-inflicted pain and suffering. Residing in Skid Row means spending one's daily life in front of an audience of officers who are fixated on even the most seemingly innocent of actions. As in Big Ron's analysis of Tex's detainment, the men anticipated that merely the *appearance* of the loss of bodily control can quickly result in unwanted police attention. Much like a poker player's "tell," the men saw addicts' inadvertent movements and habitual gestures as precisely what betrays their addiction to onlooking officers. "The crazy thing," Mike complained, "is that they're teaching them that kind of stuff in the academy. They got all kinds of videos and shit, so these guys know you're high from just looking at you. They can see that shit from halfway up the damn block! They see you before you even see them."

During my first few months working out with the group, several of the men took it upon themselves to show me how to identify those nearby who had lost control of their bodies, who were "flying on autopilot" and thus likely to draw the notice of any nearby officers. At times, the behaviors they pointed out were readily apparent. One morning, for instance, they taught me about "runners." As I took my turns straining through pull-ups in Gladys Park, I heard a loud yell erupt from the nearby corner. I spun around just in time to see a man push his way out of a small group assembled on the sidewalk and break into a full sprint in the middle of Sixth Street. I watched in confusion as the man ran west on Sixth at top speed, dodging pedestrians and oncoming cars. One of the men behind me excitedly shouted, "We've got ourselves a runner!"

Steel provided me with clarification. "That's what happens when some people hit that pipe, you know what I'm saying? Everybody responds to that shit a little different. For some niggas, they just gotta run. It gets in their body and their legs just start going. He can't stop his legs even if he wants to. That fool will keep going 'til his legs damn near fall off."

"Or 'til the cops roll him up," Rashaan interjected in disgust. "Now you know why ya'll won't never catch my ass jogging. Not 'til I'm clear on the other side of Spring [a major street separating Skid Row from the financial district of downtown]. I walk. Nice and easy." He gave these words an exaggerated slowness. "Around here, cats pay a hefty price for pressin'." He raised his hand to his mouth as though he were holding a walkie-talkie. He made the sound of radio static before pretending to speak with police dispatch: "Ten-four. We got another crackhead running down the street. Requesting back-up. All units respond." He put his imaginary radio down and continued, "Go jogging around here and I might as well draw a damn bull's-eye on my ass."

More often, however, the men cast their spotlight on more subtle behaviors that, while liable to escape an untrained eye, might pique the interest of passing patrols. "Look at this nigga right here," Steel might say, directing my attention to someone walking up the street. "It's like he's *begging* these fools to jam him up." On one such occasion, Steel pointed out a young Latina pacing back and forth just outside the green metal gate of the park. She furiously chewed on the drawstring of her dark red sweatshirt. Every so often she timidly spoke to passersby, who generally paid her little mind. "Check it," Steel said in a near whisper, as if not to alert her that we were watching. "See how she keeps tugging at her hair. She's in bad shape, man. She know she better cop soon or she's about to be in a world of hurt. That right there's a dead giveaway. Watch. Money says when five-oh hits the corner, they're about to jam her up."

Tony suddenly appeared over my shoulder, pointing to a man sitting on a nearby curb. "Naw dog. If it's *my* money, it's on this one over here: Squeaky Clean." I quickly understood the impromptu nickname. I watched as the man incessantly wiped his face and picked at his clothing, perhaps removing small pieces of imaginary lint or dirt.

"Yup," Tony added with confidence, "Squeaky is going to jail today." As it turned out, passing patrols singled out neither the young woman nor "Squeaky." When officers instead detained and arrested an intoxicated man as he stumbled past the park, Steel and Tony grumbled in lighthearted disappointment, joking that they had both "lost."

This game served as more than simple entertainment to pass the time between exercises. The exchanges held an important instructional quality. As Steel and Tony debated the fates of those around them, they cataloged and continually reinforced the dos and don'ts for staying off the police radar: never move faster than a walk, refrain from sudden or nervous movements, keep hands out of pockets, and most important, avoid self-grooming at all cost.

"That's why you don't see me messing with my waves out here no more," Mike offered, as he reflected on his former tendencies. "Shit, if I got an itch, you better believe I'm waiting to scratch that shit 'til I get off the block!" Chuckling, he shot his right hand to his cheek to scratch an imaginary itch and then jerked his arms back to his sides. With a joking smile he darted his eyes back and forth as if to determine if he was being watched. "I just keep my hands like this." Standing rigidly, he took three stiff steps in a small circle, evoking images of Frankenstein's monster. He then relaxed his body with a high-pitched laugh.

While Mike was clearly being dramatic, his pantomime captures how resistance and recovery became wedded at the weight pile. Efforts to display sobriety signals hinged on the men's ability to wrestle command of unruly bodies from the grip of drugs and alcohol. The men saw their participation in this collective activity as the most effective way to protect against future relapse while communicating difference to onlooking officers. Within the context of Skid Row policing, however, the men's new mode of sober living stood in stark opposition to the lifestyle changes demanded by officers. As they became increasingly devoted to the weight pile, the men became less willing to enroll in formal recovery programs housed in the mega-shelters located just steps away.

"Working the Pile" versus "Working a Program"

While the men of the weight pile regarded the mega-shelters as a necessary and often unavoidable aspect of life in Skid Row, they tended to keep their excursions into these formal spaces of recovery brief. They might use the emergency services, but in general they refrained from enrolling in formal programs.[18] The men railed against what they saw as the mega-shelters' infantilizing and disparaging qualities. The experiences of James, one of the longtime homeless members of the group, illustrate their dogged refusal to participate in the mega-shelters' programs. James had been sitting on a milk crate one evening when he was suddenly surrounded by several LAPD squad cars, arrested for violating one of the sidewalk ordinances, and ferried to the Central Division station. As part of the SOS program (detailed in chapter 1), James was given the option to either spend several days in jail or enter a residential rehabilitation program in one of the mega-shelters. James chose the latter. Yet, around noon on his tenth day there, James walked out of the facility, determined not to return. He headed directly to the workout already underway in Gladys Park, where he boasted of his "escape." As the session continued, I talked with James about why he left the program.

"It wasn't for me," he told me dismissively, jumping up to the pull-up bar. "In those places, all they wanna do is talk to you like you're some kind of retard, like you're a little kid. 'Go there, do this, check in at this time, lights out at that time, wake up at this time.' Then they wanna tell you what you're thinking, as if you don't know what's going on in your own head, right?" He paused to complete his thought, his chin hovering above the bar. "It's a waste of my damn time, I shoulda just said 'fuck it' and taken the jail time. At least I woulda been out after like a day or two."

Other men joined James in the sentiment that the mega-shelters resembled, and in some cases were even worse than, jail or prison. The men especially complained about the facilities' highly regimented structure—8:00 p.m. bedtimes, 5:00 a.m. wake-ups, "work detail," lice inspections, and physical (and sometimes sexual) abuse on the part of prison guard–like staff.[19] Big Ron tellingly referred to the Midnight Mission as "Sixth Street Lockdown."

The men also recoiled from mega-shelter programs because they reduced the physical and symbolic distance between themselves and other Skid Row residents. Marcus, another group member experiencing prolonged homelessness, had exhausted the time limits that the mega-shelters place on emergency shelter beds. Yet, rather than enter into a recovery program and gain the benefit of a guaranteed nightly bed, he continued to sleep under a cardboard lean-to on Winston Street, only a few feet from the LA Mission and the Union Rescue Mission. "Those motherfuckers in there have given up," he told me one evening as I helped him gather boxes from a storefront on Fourth Street to make his bed for the evening. "I'm not like them. I'm not trying to be friends with those fools, so why the hell am I gonna bunk up with them, listen to their complaining and excuses all night long? That's why I might crash for the night, but that's all I can handle."

Consider the men's contentions in light of the discourse of "service resistance" examined in the previous two chapters. Steel's crew did in fact "resist" the mega-shelter services. Their avoidance, however, was not grounded in an unwillingness to alter their former lifestyles, or in complacency in the face of the squalor of the street (as officers contended). Rather, the men believed that shelter-based programs have deleterious effects on the ability to maintain self-worth. It is worth noting that James and Marcus, arguably the most destitute of the group, were among those who were most averse to the mega-shelters. Of all the men, they possessed the fewest material and symbolic resources to combat the mega-shelters' constant assaults on their idealized visions of themselves.

Embodying Sobriety, Accentuating Difference

Research on racial and class domination shows that subordinate groups often develop distinct interactional styles, spaces, and "hidden transcripts" by which they can more effectively transmit and refine their resistant practices.[20] A well-known example is the practice of the "dozens," or "dirty dozens," in which young black males trade rhymed insults about one another's mothers and sisters. Victory is achieved by not losing one's temper, and by devising ever more clever insults.[21] As Scott has argued, these exchanges provide valuable training in self-control and anger management necessary for young black men to survive in America's climate of racial hostility. Practices such as these enable vulnerable groups to better prepare for future interactions with members of the dominant group, in which the stakes are much higher.[22]

Amid their exercise routines, Steel and his crew created a similar interactional space in which they honed the skills and resources they believed to be necessary to deflect officer scrutiny. Emphasizing the communicative capacities of the body, the men practiced drawing attention to their muscular and healthy physiques as a way of proving their "true" identities to onlooking officers. Through an aggressive, though playful, style of exchange—what the men referred to as "shit-talk"—they continually cast doubt on one another's muscularity and strength in a manner that simulated potential threats to their claims of difference.

Consider the following scene. During a routine session on San Julian Street, Dante stood in the middle of the circle that had been formed along the sidewalk. As he labored through a final repetition of arm curls and set the dumbbells at his feet, Rashaan called out from his place along the perimeter. "What happened Dante? You're looking like you're having a rough time. You falling off or what?"

"Oh shit," Tyrell chimed in from the side with a wide smile of anticipation, recognizing that a bout of shit-talk was underway.

"I'm saying," Rashaan continued, taking a few steps toward Dante, "I ain't never seen you straining like that, making that face like you're sucking on that glass dick [crack pipe]!"

Still standing in the same location on the sidewalk, Dante kept a half smile on his face, slowly nodding his head as if calmly waiting for Rashaan to finish his comment. "Oh, you're over here saying that

I fell off, huh?" With the same calmness, Dante pulled the sleeve of his shirt up to his shoulder and raised his arm to flex his bicep. He stared into Rashaan's eyes. "Take a look at this. Does this look like a nigga that's been out on the chase? Does this look like *falling off* to you? You see niggas around here looking like this? You wish you had a pump like me. Let's see what *your* ass is hiding." He pointed at Rashaan's left arm. Taking this cue, Rashaan similarly lifted his sleeve and flexed his bicep, which was noticeably smaller than Dante's. The two stood mirroring each other, mouths tight and eyes locked, as the rest of us added an assortment of comments.

"He's got you!" Tyrell shouted at Rashaan.

"That's how you do it," added Marcus.

After several seconds, Dante snickered at Rashaan, "You need to look at your own damn arms before you start talking all that shit. If anybody's falling off, it's you. You're gonna have to work harder if you ever want a pump on like this." He flexed his bicep even harder with a grimace.

"OK, OK. You all right. You all right. Keep getting that work in, boy." Rashaan walked forward and the two men embraced in a handshake and a hug. Amid laughter from the rest of the group, Dante picked up the weights and began his next set of bicep curls. Rashaan smiled as he shrugged his shoulders and returned to his place along the wall.

Shit-talk proceeded in a rather predictable manner. One man would cast direct, though easily deflected, doubt upon another man's continued abstinence. For several minutes the men would take turns, pointing to their arms, chests, shoulders, or backs to one-up each other. In doing so, they attempted to disprove any lingering insinuations about substance abuse and relapse by providing embodied evidence to the contrary. These responses drew out explicit comparisons between a group member's own physical attributes—a "pumped-up" bicep or prominent veins, for example—and those outward characteristics the group associated with addicts—severe emaciation, collapsed veins, and abscessed flesh. I was particularly struck by the timing of shit-talk. These exchanges seldom commenced until at least twenty minutes into a session. The men seemed to be allowing each other time to "warm up" their somatic defenses for any attacks that might arise. Possessing few other ways of emphasizing their difference, they accentuated their physiques to create what Erving Goffman terms a "disidentifier," which is "a sign that tends—in fact or hope—to break up an otherwise coherent picture . . . in a positive direction desired by the author."[23] Getting "jacked" at the weight pile thus constituted a means to better escape getting "jacked up" by police.

"If You Ain't Smoking, then You Must Be Slanging"

Given the number of hours I spent closely documenting how men like Rashaan and Dante arduously prepared themselves to step back out onto Skid Row streets and back under the gaze of officers, I found myself asking the obvious question: How effective were these impression-management techniques? To what extent did these displays of sobriety actually deflect officers' attention? I certainly recorded a fair share of "success stories." Most often these boiled down to instances in which someone claimed that he *should* have been detained but was not. Some men reported officers simply driving past them without notice. Others reported officers choosing to target someone else instead of them. The best answer to my questions, however, arose when several in the group relayed that officers were suddenly interrogating them at an *increased* rate. Listening to these accounts, it appeared that the uptick in detainments had resulted not because the men's outward signs of sobriety were unbelievable or ineffective, but because their displays had become *too* convincing.

One afternoon, our workout came to an abrupt halt as Reggie stormed into Gladys Park. He violently kicked the tall metal gate as he entered. The park maintenance worker, who had been napping nearby, nearly fell out of his chair at the sudden sound. Paying little attention to the maintenance worker's drowsy curses, Reggie made his way over to the group under the pull-up bars. He was clearly upset. He also looked like hell. The white T-shirt he wore, one of several that he meticulously washed and ironed on an almost daily basis, was wrinkled and streaked with Skid Row's familiar grime. His collar, stretched well beyond its normal shape, hung low and exposed the top of his chest. A bruise, dotted with small specks of blood, was beginning to form on his forehead.

As he approached, he began ranting. "These fucking pigs . . . I swear . . . next time I'm gonna . . . I swear . . ."

Confused, several in the group pleaded with Reggie to calm down long enough to explain. He responded with only more ranting. Suddenly Steel's voice cut through. "Calm the fuck down," he ordered in a rare show of frustration. "Stop bitching and speak on it."

Taking a deep breath, Reggie massaged a faint red welt that wrapped around his wrist. We formed a tight circle around him as he recounted his run-in with officers with his usual flair. He had been walking on San Pedro Street near a prominent social service organization and was unexpectedly detained as he attempted to sidestep a group of men who were openly smoking crack. The officer slammed Reggie's face into a nearby concrete wall before cuffing him. While the interrogation and search did not turn up any contraband on Reggie, the officers found lighters, pipes, screens, and multiple vials of crack cocaine on the other men. Twenty minutes later, the officers released Reggie.

Before leaving the scene, Reggie told us, he had turned the interrogation back on one of the officers. "I say to this asshole, 'Look at these idiots over here. Do I strike you as the kind of man that's out here getting high with these jokers?'" Reenacting the conversation, Reggie held both arms straight out in front of his chest. He turned his wrists over and flexed his forearms, which were toned and powerful. "And you know what this fucking pig said to me? He looked me dead in the eye and said, 'No sir, I don't. But that's not why we stopped you.' Do you know why he said he jammed me up? Get this, he said, 'We didn't stop you because we thought you were out here *buying*. We stopped you because it looked to us like you were *distributing* to these guys.'"

With this, the rest of the group let out a collective groan. Big Ron seemed especially frustrated.

Reggie continued matter-of-factly. "Can you believe that? A nigga can't win down here. They think there's only two kinds of people in Skid Row. If you ain't smoking or slamming, well damn, then you must be slanging."

Reggie's frustrations were understandable. He had proudly extended the discipline of the exercise regimen to his day-to-day affairs. This included twice-weekly visits to the neighborhood's lone public laundromat and a weekly haircut by one of the "sidewalk barbers." Given the instability and lack of resources that characterize Skid Row, these habits did not come easily. In retelling the details of his detainment, it appeared that Reggie had in fact been successful in communicating his diligence and sobriety to officers. In doing so, however, he unwittingly aligned himself with an alternate, and no less suspect, category—that of drug dealer. Reggie now looked more like those individuals officers believe travel into the neighborhood to sell narcotics or enlist desperate addicts as lookouts, middlemen, and "hooks."

Negotiating Safe Passage

When the men were less successful at presenting physical displays of difference, they considered additional variables to account for officers' misrecognition and the resulting police contact. Their analyses turned from questions about problematic appearances and behaviors to questions about problematic locations and times. Even the best sobriety signals could be rendered mute if deployed in contexts that gave rise to elevated police scrutiny.

Back in Gladys Park, Reggie continued recounting details of his interrogation. Demetrius interrupted him midsentence to dive into an unsolicited analysis of the incident. "You said you was over on San Pedro?" he asked, piecing together the facts. "Over by the Weingart [a prominent social service provider]?"

"Yeah, right there on the corner," Reggie answered eagerly, "by the bike rack. Wassup?"

Nodding his head assuredly, Demetrius paused in thought before giving his opinion. "Well, that's the new dope spot."

"Oh word?" Reggie responded with defeat.

"Yeah, you didn't know?" Demetrius provided an update. "Get this. A few weeks back I noticed that a bunch of young bloods set up shop right there. They looked like they was running a solid business for a minute. They were making that good cheddar 'til five-oh caught a whiff. Now the undercover squad has been crashing and bashing on their asses on the regular."

"Straight up," Steel agreed. "Just about every time I'm heading down here for a workout or over to the store I see they've got *somebody* in cuffs."

"See," Demetrius emphasized, "that's why I been walking clear around that mess lately. I been sticking to Crocker [a parallel street one block to the west]. I'm not about to get scooped up in one of those surprise sweeps like you did. You gotta stay one step ahead, you know what I'm saying? Crocker's good 'cause it's hardly got anybody on it. There's not enough easy customers for it to be a good dope spot, so they don't really pay it no mind. Nobody's really standing around. The foot traffic keeps moving. San Pedro, though, it's got a grip of people standing in their little cliques all up and down that block. Even the rookie cops can see that's gotta be one of the most lucrative serving spots around. I'm telling you, that whole street is bad news."

Efforts to see like a cop thus not only encouraged the men to renegotiate their relationships with their bodies; it also spurred them to reflect on and revise their relationships with neighborhood surroundings. Demetrius's advice to Reggie captures how the men's evasive maneuvers had the potential to reshape their "daily round," the term urban sociologists use for the day-to-day routines that individuals devise to satisfy their various needs.[24] Research on the daily round of the urban poor has focused almost exclusively on disruptions caused by the violence and crime that erupt in the absence of police protection.[25] For example, in his description of a neighborhood overrun by gangs in the 1990s, Sudhir Venkatesh observes, "The manner by which [residents] can move about in [the neighborhood] and surrounding spaces—both *where* they can visit and *how* they get there—is effectively altered once they are forced to acknowledge and incorporate street gang inscriptions."[26] By anticipating the behaviors of those who might do them harm, streetwise residents identify and avoid "hot spaces," "no man's lands," and other places in which they will likely be victimized.[27] Doing so, however, often constricts residents' opportunities for meeting new acquaintances, interacting with peers, building community, and developing social capital, factors that have been shown to mitigate the negative effects of poverty, unemployment, and lack of adequate housing.[28]

When policing is hypervigilant, residents reinterpret their physical and social environment not only in terms of associated risks of crime, but also in light of their perceived likelihood of unwanted police contact. Recent research confirms that this tactic is by no means limited to Skid Row. In one of the few studies to consider the lived experience of ubiquitous criminalization, Alice Goffman describes the behaviors of "wanted men" in a Philadelphia ghetto.[29] Goffman reports that, due to outstanding warrants or parole and probation violations, these individuals withdraw from many of the vital institutions on which they previously relied (including hospitals, courts, schools, and workplaces), having deduced that these settings carry an elevated risk of apprehension. Victor Rios similarly finds that criminalized youth become "socially incapacitated," unable to take full advantage of community institutions, once these institutions have been coupled with the criminal justice system.[30] My fieldwork suggests that as policing becomes embedded ever more deeply in the minutiae of day-to-day reality, even individuals not currently "on the run" take up techniques of evasion that reorganize space and time.

Reexamining their daily rounds through the lens of policing, Steel's crew carefully reviewed the specific streets on which they traveled, whom they associated with in public view, and at what particular times of day they did so. I first became aware of this mental schema when I began to spend more time with the men beyond the confines of our workouts. Much to my frustration, our exchanges elsewhere in the neighborhood could be surprisingly impersonal and abridged, even as we seemed to be building more intimate connections at the weight pile. While Tyrell, for example, had assumed the role of my "tutor" in both weight lifting and Skid Row life, he sometimes rushed through our conversations when we serendipitously ran into each another out on the streets. On two occasions, we concluded our brief greetings some twenty feet apart, Tyrell walking backward and not slowing his brisk pace up the sidewalk. Writing up my field notes, I described Tyrell as "a fast moving target." As I would soon learn, this was precisely his intention.

When Tyrell breezed through a subsequent chance meeting, I risked an unwanted intrusion and caught up with him as he continued up the street. "Sorry man, I'm just making sure I catch the 9:28 bus," he said as I jogged to his side. "I gotta get to the grocery store." As we walked together, Tyrell shared that he had timed the walk from his building to the bus stop, which took him exactly four and a half minutes. Much to my own surprise as a native of Los Angeles—a city in which traffic congestion makes bus "schedules" comically irrelevant—we arrived at the stop just as the bus pulled to the curb. Figuring that I had already come this far, I asked Tyrell if he would mind if I tagged along. A bit surprised, but clearly pleased, he motioned for me to follow him onboard.

Once we settled into our seats, his abruptness gave way to his typically relaxed demeanor. "The way I see it," he began, "there ain't no sense in just wasting my time standing out here on the corner. If I really wanted to spend my damn time standing around shooting the shit with everybody, I'd catch the bus over on San Pedro." I realized that Tyrell had walked to a bus stop farther from his building than the San Pedro stop. The bus was now traveling the route we had walked, heading back toward the intersection that Tyrell was determined to avoid as a pedestrian. Minutes later, Tyrell gave a simple nod, a wordless signal for me look out the window. I saw a chaotic scene at the San Pedro stop. A collection of disheveled bodies lay on pieces of cardboard while others assembled in small groups, chatting, smoking cigarettes, or waiting to use the large green public toilet that stood on the corner. "It's like this all day and night over here," Tyrell complained. He pointed back in the direction from which we had just come. "Right now, at this time of the mornings, up the street is still nice and quiet. I try to get all my errands done before noon." We had not traveled a block before Tyrell signaled for me to look out the window again, where two officers questioned an irate woman in handcuffs. "Five-oh still got the skeleton crew out here right now. They won't really start hitting the block hard for a couple more hours. They know that a lot of people are still passed out from partying last night. When they wake up, the cops will roll out. That's when you get caught up."

Steel's crew avoided getting "caught up" by moving with a sense of purpose, either swiftly cutting through or altogether avoiding the congestion that characterizes many of Skid Row's sidewalks. Others in the group sometimes referred to this as "putting your blinders on" or "keeping your head down." "You know that old saying 'two's a crowd?'" Tyrell quizzed me. "Well down here, it's more like 'two's a dope deal.' These cops see a couple people chilling and they think, 'Shit, they *must* be up to no good.' It don't matter if that's your homeboy or your minister or the damn president of the United States. They're gonna jam you up, pocket-check you, and try to see if you're hiding something."

As the bus traveled its route, Tyrell shared the other walking paths that he had similarly "stop-watched," including the trip from his apartment to our workouts on San Julian Street, to Gladys Park, and to a half dozen other locations in Skid Row. "Most days I just stick in my little triangle." He traced the shape in the air as though drawing on an imaginary map. Interestingly, Tyrell's daily path through the neighborhood kept him nearly entirely in the Bottom, in the part of Skid Row that officers associated with those least committed to recovery and least willing to enter the mega-shelters.

"I wake up, get my errands done, then I head up to get my pump on. Then I usually gotta go to work." Tyrell had recently found sporadic, under-the-table employment sweeping the floors of several warehouses in the Garment District, located four blocks south of Skid Row. "After that you'll see me heading straight home. It's simple. I just stay on my little path. . . . You stand around too long bullshitting with the wrong people, and trouble is gonna come find your ass, whether you want it or not. I done paid the price for trouble already." Tyrell laughed deeply, exposing the large gap that formerly held his four bottom teeth.

It took us fifteen minutes to reach our destination, a discount warehouse grocery store in MacArthur Park, a Latino neighborhood west of downtown. Tyrell used his EBT card to purchase cans of tuna fish and several packages of skirt steak. "Gotta feed your muscles," he instructed as we approached the cashier. I helped Tyrell carry the groceries back onto the bus. As we returned to the front of his building, he exchanged greetings with several men standing outside. While he met the bunch with a smile, his gait did not flag, as he concluded the interaction calling, "Peace out, fellas," over his shoulder. I felt relieved that I was not the only one he brushed off in the streets.

I asked if the other men lived in the building. "Yeah, of course," he replied instantly. "We're all neighbors in these two buildings." He paused for a moment as he fished for his keys in his pockets. "I don't really see them all that much anymore though. I mean, I'll stop and kick it for a bit. But it's the same thing every day, just sitting around talking bullshit. I know how it goes with those guys. Somebody is gonna pull out a pipe, or a bottle of whiskey or something." It was nearly noon. Tyrell emphasized that as the patrols intensified, spending time with his neighbors increased the probability of a police stop or, in the event that any of them possessed contraband, the possibility of arrest. Eager to get off the street, he told me goodbye and ducked inside his building for the rest of the day.

In this manner, the men synchronized the rhythm of their daily lives with the rhythm of policing. They spent significant time piecing together detailed records of patrol schedules and logistics to determine precisely where and when their distancing techniques would be the most convincing. They limited their uses of the street to periods when they anticipated officers would interpret their outward displays in the desired fashion. They consistently weighed the importance or benefit of any given excursion into the neighborhood against the chances of its resulting in detainment.

As a result, the men tended to spend the greater part of their days and nights alone in SRO and apartment rooms above the street. Steel and Reggie were notorious "nappers," heading directly home after workouts for their daily "siesta." The two sometimes bragged about who slept the longest. Tyrell and Dante preferred visual entertainment, regularly swapping stacks of pirated DVDs they had purchased from the area's sidewalk vendors (a group discussed in the next chapter). With the two of them viewing as many as four or five "flicks" per day on portable players purchased at the discount electronic stores lining Skid Row's southern boundary, it was not uncommon to hear the grunts of a taxing workout mixed with heated amateur film analysis. The men promoted their various retreats to private space not merely as a means to escape the gaze of the police, but also as a therapeutic practice that was a vital component of their collective project of recovery. The time spent napping or watching DVDs was by no means idle or unproductive. Rather, the men defended these behaviors as "active" pursuits. Developing solidarity with their bodies required adequate time to recuperate from strenuous workouts. The rules and regulations in Skid Row housing units, where visitors must often pay a guest fee (usually $5 per visit) or else risk forcible removal, further reinforces this isolation.

Beyond diminishing the men's engagement in community life, patterns of self-sequestration inhibited their full separation from prison life. Following our workouts on a string of chilly January days, Tyrell and I headed to his SRO hotel to, in his words, "let our muscles mellow out." After passing through the security door and climbing the narrow stairs to his bare fifteen-by-fifteen-foot room, we spent the afternoons watching his collection of classic gangster movies. As we sat on the floor, propped up against his twin-size bed, eating canned tuna by the spoonful, Tyrell recounted his three-year "bid" in Chuck-awalla. As *The Godfather II* played quietly in the background, he recalled the intense solitude he felt behind bars, a solitude he continued to feel now "on the outside." In this moment it struck me that Tyrell and the others had carried far more with them from prison than an exercise routine. Their approach to surviving Skid Row involved actively reconstructing the defining conditions of incarceration, locking themselves away in their SRO "cells" save for a few hours in which they ventured outside to engage in recreation at the weight pile. With increased participation in the exercise routine, even those few in the group with little history of imprisonment resorted to self-imposed confinement. This behavior captures a concrete mechanism by which hyperpolicing amplifies what scholars of urban poverty theorize as an increasing "fusion of ghetto and prison culture."[31] Paradoxically, in their efforts to avoid police contact and possible reincarceration, the men kept one figurative foot squarely inside the prison.

But even as the men curtailed the spatial and temporal windows in which they accomplished their daily round, they could not entirely escape the police. Even the most calculating and reclusive members of the group reported at least the occasional police stop. On those occasions when the men were unable to avoid such contact, they resorted to a form of "tactical conformity" designed to mitigate its negative effects.[32] Earlier we saw that most of the men in the group disdained the mega-shelters. Yet, through collective analyses of their interactions with officers, a number of the men concluded that an affiliation with the mega-shelters, or more accurately the *appearance* of such an affiliation, constituted a valuable currency that could be exchanged for continued freedom. The men at the weight pile exploited officers' tendency to grant leniency to individuals enrolled in the mega-shelters' formal rehabilitative programs for their own purposes. This tactic proved particularly attractive for men like James, who had little recourse to private space.

James recounted a story in which he was detained as he sat near a group of fellow homeless men. James panicked when the officers asked each of the detainees for identification, then remembered that he had held onto the identification badge from the mega-shelter when he absconded from the SOS program. He dug for it at the bottom of his duffle bag. Much to his surprise, when he produced it for the officers, they ended his interrogation and simply ordered him to "move along." Once he was a safe distance away, James turned around and saw that the remaining men—none of whom had a similar form of identification—were quickly handcuffed and arrested. Beginning that afternoon, James began wearing the badge prominently on the outside of his shirt at all times. "This guy right here," he boasted, pointing proudly to the laminated piece of paper hanging on a lanyard around his neck, "this is my ticket. This is my get-out-of-jail-free card."

In a later conversation, James conveyed clear recognition that the only way he could continue his self-directed, informal mode of recovery among his weight-pile peers was by feigning commitment to the formal, police-enforced model of recovery. "They think everybody down here is a criminal or a dopefiend," James complained. "They think there's no way in hell I could be on the straight and narrow without being in a program. But that's not reality. So I say, OK, it's all good. I can play the game. I can tell them what they wanna hear. Oh, they want some proof?" He held the badge out in front of him. "Bam! I got their *proof* right here." To my knowledge, none of the other group members made overt attempts to acquire their own get-out-of-jail-free cards. Independently, however, Steel, Rashaan, and Demetrius each reported that they routinely told officers they were "in a program" or en route to a meeting with a caseworker. While these claims did not prevent them from being handcuffed and searched, each believed that his pretensions shortened the length of the interrogations and reduced officers' proclivity to run his name through the parole, probation, and warrant databases. Rashaan figured that this technique had saved him from receiving a jaywalking ticket on at least two occasions.[33]

As successful as the men's maneuvers may have been while individually traversing Skid Row's streets, the tactics were largely in-effective during their daily assembly at the weight pile. With their weight-lifting equipment scattered across the sidewalk, they could hardly claim to be in transit. Nor did they appear to be enrolled in formal programming. Officers eventually came to regard the group, routinely convening at the same location for hours at a time, as prob-lematic, as bad as, if not worse than, the others they saw "stagnating" along the sidewalks. In time, the group attracted the full attention of Central Division.

The End of the Skid Row Weight Pile

Ironically, it was precisely the men's regularity and dedication that led to the weight pile's eventual dissolution at the hands of the police. On what began for the group as a typical afternoon, four uniformed officers—the Central Division captain, a sergeant, and two patrol officers—arrived on San Julian roughly thirty minutes into a work-out session. According to the men, the officers stood quietly watching them from the opposite side of the street for several minutes. Once the officers made their way to the group, the captain relayed that he had heard about their gathering, and that he had come to personally disband them. Despite Steel's pleas, the captain stated that he would no longer allow the men to "turn the sidewalk into a prison yard." He would not allow them to continue "distracting people" who were try-ing to access services. He warned that if any of his officers saw them assembling in the future, he would arrest them.

I recapped the incident with the group. They were angry, confused, and quieter than usual.

"Aw fuck them," Dante exclaimed, breaking one of the longer moments of silence. He began making an argument that the group should simply ignore the captain's threats. He reminded them of one of the justifications Steel had offered to the captain—the men were not harming anyone.

Steel rebuffed him in his usual calm tone. "Naw, but you heard the man. He said, 'It's starting to look like the prison yard out here.' I knew right when he said that that they're really not trying to fuck around. I'm not trying to test them, either. My P.O. [parole officer] is a straight asshole, and I know he's just looking for anything he can to get me. I ain't going out like that, G."

"But if we ain't breaking the law, then they can't do shit," Dante argued.

Demetrius chimed in. "Yo, it don't even matter. I swear, maybe if I was on just regular old probation I wouldn't even sweat it. I'd be like, let these pigs try to arrest me. I think all my old P.O. woulda done is just laughed at that shit. But since I caught that paperwork for my pistol, I been on summary probation. It's all different. I don't know what the fuck the judge would do if I showed back up in court, even if it was on some stupid made-up shit like this."[34]

"We'll see," Steel said in an assertive tone, ending the discussion without announcing a future course of action.

It turned out that this would be the last time that the men would convene on San Julian Street. Given the men's constant attempts to instill commitment and prevent attrition, I assumed that the group would convene again two days later, on the regular schedule. When I arrived at the usual location, however, it became apparent that the group would never rematerialize in its previous form. Four of the men showed, but there was no sign of Steel. Tyrell stood with me for fifteen minutes before hastily returning to his building. Over the next hour, Reggie, James, and Dante also came by, though none stayed longer than five minutes. After an hour and a half, I too made my way off San Julian Street. The same process unfolded at Gladys Park, though over a longer period of time. I had expected that with their exile from San Julian Street, the men would make the park their primary meeting place.[35] This was not the case. After two weeks, the number of participants began to dwindle. If the men worked out in the park at all, they did so individually and at sporadic times.

Without stable housing arrangements, mailing addresses, telephone numbers, and the regular sociality provided by the weight pile, the men fell out of contact with one another. I too had a hard time tracking them down. I devoted additional time to walking the neighborhood in the hopes of a chance meeting. One early morning, some seven months after the initial interaction with the captain, I nearly tripped over James as he napped on the sidewalk. After another arrest and another short stay in a mega-shelter, James was now sleeping in a tent on Towne and Sixth Streets. James was a large man, standing six-foot-four with a wide frame. Yet, in his tank top, he appeared noticeably thinner than he had the last time I saw him in the park. I sat with him and we caught up. Within weeks after the weight pile folded, he said, he returned to spending time with his former homeless encampment group. And he began using heroin again.

"That was really rough on me," he said with a cast-off look. "I dunno, I guess I just kinda figured, 'Hell with it.' It's messed up that the cops can just come by and order people around like that. We weren't hurting nobody. Shit, you'd think they would want us to keep doing what we were doing. We were the only ones out there actually really trying to do right. What they need to do is take care of the *real* problems around here."

I asked for news about the other men. James informed me that Tony had been arrested by undercover narcotics officers and that Rashaan had been picked up on a parole violation. I gained additional information when I ran into Tyrell, who was (quite uncharacteristically) standing in the courtyard of one of the social service organizations I had once heard him criticize. He had been sleeping at the facility since a fight with the manager of his hotel led to his eviction. He had been one of Steel's closer friends, but the two had lost touch when Steel moved back to the Pueblos, back to the environment to which Steel attributed his former patterns of offending.

I called Officer Manuel Rodriguez shortly after my conversation with James. After a few minutes catching up, I told him about Steel's group, the time I spent with them, and their recent disbanding by the captain. I tried to withhold my own personal disappointment about the splintering of a group with whose members I had become close friends. Manny shared no such displeasure. Quite the opposite. Based on my description of the incident, he wholeheartedly agreed with the captain's course of action.

"Before you know it," he told me once I finished the story, "guys like that would have infected the whole neighborhood."

"But they weren't really doing anything wrong," I replied in defense.

"Sure they are," Manny said immediately.

"How so?"

"First of all," he began, "they're setting a bad example for everyone else. What if your little brother came home from the Corps and for some reason ended up down there. Would you want him hanging out with those guys? Would you want him spending his time around a bunch of big boys straight out of lock-up?"

I had difficulty containing my skepticism. "I wouldn't care," I answered. "It's not like they're out there beating people up. They're just exercising. Working out. Getting healthy. It can't be *that* bad."

Manny kept his even tone, as if to emphasize the cool rationality of his position. "You can't listen to that stuff they're telling you. These guys think they're out there helping the community, helping out the young guys. But the truth is that they're actually hurting the community. Trust me, Forrest, I see it every day. It's called being in denial. If they were really serious about getting healthy, why are they still down there? It's because they *want* to be down there, so they can live by their own rules. It's why they got locked up in the first place. All they're doing is making excuses and teaching everyone else how to make excuses. It might seem innocent at first, but it's only a matter of time before more and more people join in. It turns into a party. The dealers show up. And then all the work we've done has been for nothing."

We debated the matter for another ten minutes. Throughout, Manny refused to admit any benefits that Steel's crew and their daily exercise routine might have carried. Instead, he saw them as deserving of even more intensive police supervision. It was essential, he insisted, for Central Division officers to keep even closer tabs on the men to ensure that they did not attempt to reconvene.

||||||||||||||||

The group's dissolution punctuates the role of therapeutic policing in shaping residents' everyday lives. The Skid Row weight pile largely grew out of its participants' shared desires to avoid arrest and (re)incarceration, to begin a new, positive chapter in their lives. Refashioning limited resources and shared biographies of marginalization, the men leveraged their workouts as an indigenous and self-directed model of recovery. Their daily meeting at the weight pile constituted a genuine attempt to rein in lingering drug addictions and provide some insulation against the neighborhood's manifold threats to sobriety. One might see this effort as evidence of the success of Central Division's recovery management approach. Constant threats of punishment did, in fact, propel these residents to alter their former behaviors and make new lifestyle choices. But their informal program of self-reclamation, developed on the streets among peers, was not the kind of rehabilitation the LAPD had in mind. As long as Steel and his crew refused to formal programs at approved facilities, they remained subject to persistent detainments by Skid Row police.

Clearly overmatched in this struggle, group members attempted to use their collective cop wisdom to resist policing. By engaging in a folk ethnography of policing and learning to see like cops, the men attempted to avoid provoking suspicion and to minimize adverse interactions with officers. These techniques of evasion reorganized the men's waking hours, infiltrating peer group dynamics, their interactions with other residents, and even their conceptions of space and time as they negotiated their daily round.[36] The group's sudden fracture underscores the fragility of their indigenous recovery program. The men understood the subtext of the captain's orders. "They ain't messing around no more," Mike lamented one afternoon in Gladys Park after it became clear that we would be alone in our workout for the fifth straight day. "The captain's on the case now, so that means that they all got their orders. If they see us, that's all she wrote. There's no getting out of that one. It don't matter if it's over there or over here. They put the BOLO [police dispatch code for "be on the lookout"] on every single one of our asses." The men felt marked, not only when they convened as a group but even when they traveled the neighborhood on their own. In the course of a single interaction, the captain had dismantled the foundation on which the men's evasive tactics rested. Now squarely on the police radar, they anticipated that their former distancing techniques would prove obsolete; they had been pulled back under the blanket of suspicion applied to all neighborhood residents.

The Skid Row weight pile provides an opportunity to reflect on the relation between hyperpolicing, territorial stigma, and resistance. For Wacquant, territorial stigma is a central factor in propelling the kind of aggressive and ubiquitous law enforcement deployed in Skid Row.[37] In examining policing from the perspective of its targets, it becomes clear that hyperpolicing also helps to propel and reproduce a neighborhood's denigrated status. My time alongside Steel's crew demonstrated that residents' attempts to cope with omnipresent policing exacerbates territorial stigma by amplifying the importance of micro-hierarchies. In their efforts to minimize their contact with the police, the men displaced officers' attention onto those they believed to be more deserving of it, those who truly "belonged" in a place like Skid Row. In no way were these tactics concerned with reducing the absolute number of detainments, citations, or arrests. Instead, Steel's crew saw themselves locked in a zero-sum game, in which their continued freedom and unmolested travel through the neighborhood could come only at the expense of fellow residents. It was a game they eventually lost.

Of course, some residents learned to play this game by a different set of rules. They learned that their ability to remain in public space while avoiding unwanted police contact required them to more actively monitor and regulate the individuals and behaviors in their immediate vicinity. In the next chapter, I detail the subversive tactics taken up by a long-standing group of Skid Row street vendors, who mobilized their cop wisdom to maintain rigorous control over an entire intersection. Rather than avoid addicts and dealers, the vendors took it upon themselves to police illegal behaviors. Here too, however, their application of cop wisdom came at a larger price to fellow residents and the community at large.

CHAPTER FOUR

Cooling Off the Block

Jackson moved with his typical nervous energy as he set up his "sidewalk shop" on the corner of Fifth and San Pedro Streets. The late afternoon light gave a sense of urgency to his motions as he unloaded his wares from his battered shopping cart onto the worn blue tarp he spread across the sidewalk. Six dented cans of chili, a bundle of women's cosmetics, a stack of college textbooks. The scavenged inventory looked remarkably similar to those of the three other street vendors who had set up only feet away. With a nod of satisfaction, Jackson grabbed a splintered broom that hung from the chain-link fence behind him and began to sweep cigarette butts, soiled paper napkins, and other small debris into tight piles. He squatted low to better grip the broom's broken stub of a handle, muttering in annoyance as passing pedestrians disrupted his meticulous tidying.

Jackson's complaints suddenly grew audible as he glanced up from his task and noticed that a group of four visibly drunk men had assembled on the corner, pulling tall cans of Old English malt liquor out of brown paper bags. Jackson jogged in their direction, veering slightly from his path to tug on the shirt of another vendor, a clean-shaven, bald man named Larry, who followed without question.

"Hey y'all," Jackson said forcefully as he pushed his way through the perimeter of the group. "You gotta get your drink on somewhere else, you hear? Y'all can't be partying over here."

While startled, the men appeared undeterred. Jackson was hardly an intimidating figure; his high-pitched voice matched his five-foot-five-inch frame. One of the men swallowed a mouthful of malt liquor, teetered slightly, and leaned in to offer a slurred response. Just as the words formed on his lips, however, Larry's deep voice suddenly boomed from above. Standing almost a foot taller than Jackson and outweighing him by at least a hundred pounds, Larry stared down at the group through his dark sunglasses.

"Time to leave, fellas, and I'm only gonna tell you once. I'm really not playing, so don't test your luck."

Silence.

The four men exchanged defeated looks with bloodshot eyes. Putting up no further fight, they rewrapped their cans in brown paper bags and vacated the corner.

Hands on his hips, Jackson watched with satisfaction as the four staggered their way up San Pedro Street.

IIIIIIIIIIIIII

I spent roughly two and a half years alongside Jackson, Larry, and fourteen other street vendors as they conducted business along Fifth Street, one of Skid Row's main thoroughfares. As the above scene captures, they devoted their time on the block to far more than simply hawking their wares. Tidying the sidewalk, quelling arguments, and, most notably, intercepting alcohol and drug consumption, the men maintained a vigilant system of informal social control. The vendors' active prohibition of illicit activities stood in stark contrast to the ambivalence shown by Steel's weight-lifting crew, described in the previous chapter, whose members made no attempt to correct the behaviors of anyone outside of their own group. In fact, Steel's crew often exploited others' visible signs of addiction as evidence of their own moral superiority, and even as a callous form of entertainment. Despite their divergent stances, however, both groups' responses to surrounding behavior were rooted in a preoccupation with policing. The vendors' informal regulation of Skid Row's sidewalks was an alternative tactic for coping with the omnipresent threat of unwanted police contact. By focusing on the vendors' daily regulation of Skid Row's sidewalks, this chapter explores additional ways that Skid Row residents mobilize the cop wisdom they develop through the course of repeated police interactions. In doing so, it sheds further light on the capacity of the police to shape the cultural context of the neighborhood.

The experiences of the sidewalk vendors also provide insight into the process of "third-party policing," which is one of the most significant developments in the field of criminal justice over the last three decades. Responsibility for controlling crime no longer rests solely with the police but has been diffused throughout social space.[1] In conjunction with zero-tolerance policing policies and quality-of-life ordinances, cities are increasingly pressuring citizens to step outside of their routine activities to regulate the actions of their fellow citizens.[2] Cities now penalize landlords for their tenants' nuisance behaviors, prosecute pawnshop owners for their customers' gun violence, and fine parents for their children's truancy.[3] The vendors' voluntary mode of regulation reveals that therapeutic policing policies like the Safer Cities Initiative have the power to diffuse social control even further into the hands of citizens. Skid Row policing has extended third party policing "all the way down," so to speak, forcing even onlookers and pedestrians to become accountable for the behaviors of nearby residents with whom they may have no direct link. This chapter shows how this process unfolds and presents a number of the unforeseen, and often contradictory, consequences of this development. While therapeutic policing compelled the vendors to create and maintain a drug-free zone on adjacent sidewalks, these benefits came at a significant price. The constant threat of police interference forced the vendors to adopt the gaze of the police and to act as surrogate officers, thus engendering a perverse mode of privatized enforcement that undermined the commonly theorized benefits of informal control, undercut possibilities for rehabilitation, and worsened the social and economic marginalization of Skid Row residents.

The Fifth Street Vendors

Like many of America's most impoverished neighborhoods, Skid Row is home to an active informal, street economy.[4] The off-the-books exchange of vital goods and services—from food to haircuts to cash loans—rests at the heart of area inhabitants' myriad efforts to make ends meet. In an early effort to sketch the contours of underground commerce and make connections with its participants, I took up one of the more common enterprises I had observed: I began selling individual cigarettes. Each morning I bought several packs of Marlboro Reds at a liquor store on my way into Skid Row. I paced up and down Fifth Street advertising my wares, which I sold at the standard neighborhood price of twenty-five cents per cigarette. On most days, I was lucky to break even after three to four hours of work. I later learned that the cigarettes I saw others sell were cheap imitations smuggled from Mexico. Instead of a profit, however, I earned entrance into the social world of Skid Row's street vendors.

I met Jackson first. Prior to moving into Skid Row, Jackson had spent much of his adult life employed as a machinist in LA's once-booming aerospace sector. Jackson's story conveys the human impacts of southern California's decades-long process of deindustrialization, which dislocated many of the region's semiskilled black workers. Facing a string of downsizings, layoffs, and evictions, Jackson and his wife, a small woman named Leticia, reluctantly moved into a dilapidated SRO hotel room on Skid Row's western border. There, the situation turned from bad to worse.

"That's when we got into crack," Jackson recounted matter-of-factly one afternoon as we shared a basket of fries in a noisy downtown diner. While the couple had frequented bars after work and occasionally smoked marijuana on the weekends, they did not experiment with harder drugs until they moved into Skid Row. "At that place, you got people knocking at your door at all times of the day. It's easy to fall into it." For the next two years, the couple spiraled further into addiction. To pay for their mounting habit, Jackson began peddling "knickknacks" he scavenged from downtown alleyways.

Jackson was at the height of his addiction, smoking crack at least once a day, when he and I first met. He pulled me into his familiar sales pitch as I sold cigarettes nearby. Complimenting my "smart looks," he pointed to a small stack of books he had "checked out" from the library at the nearby University of Southern California. As a graduate student at crosstown rival UCLA at the time, I chuckled when I spotted the USC insignia stamped on the first page of a copy of Herman Melville's *Moby Dick*. I eventually gave in and purchased the novel, using the opportunity to explain my research. Jackson's receptiveness surprised me; in fact, he invited me to set up shop next to his tarp and volunteered to "show me the ropes." He insisted that it would be mutually beneficial: when pedestrians stopped to buy my cigarettes they might be enticed to buy one of his products, and vice versa. And so our partnership began. At sunset I helped Jackson load his remaining wares into a rickety baby stroller, and he invited me to join him the following day. I agreed, and over the course of the next weeks, Jackson introduced me to more than a dozen other vendors.

Maintaining a Drug-Free Zone

Throughout my time on the corner, I marveled at the rigorous public order the vendors maintained along the sidewalk. Of all the nearby activities they stepped in to regulate, none received more concerted reproach than drug-related behavior. One of my first glimpses into their antidrug efforts occurred on only my second day alongside Jackson. In fact, one such intervention solidified my position as Jackson's unofficial assistant. Early that afternoon, Jackson was sifting through a mound of wrinkled clothes in his baby stroller. I noticed that a small glass crack pipe had slid out of the pocket of a jacket that had been resting atop the other items. Keith, a round man whom I had only met minutes earlier, saw me staring at the pipe and called Jackson over in a quiet voice. Despite Keith's attempt to shield their con-

Sidewalk shop selling small electronics.

versation from me by turning his back, I could make out enough of his stern instructions to understand what was transpiring.

"You know you can't have that out here," Keith reprimanded Jackson in a hushed tone, gesturing behind him toward the pipe. "Ain't no room for that out here." For the past year, Keith had been trying to help Jackson get clean. He occasionally held onto Jackson's cash while they worked and he constantly forbade him from "mixing business with pleasure."

As Keith lectured, Jackson turned and suddenly noticed the pipe sitting in clear view. "Aw, shit," he said, looking clearly ashamed. He tried to reassure Keith. "I know, I know, I know, It's just . . . yeah . . . OK . . . I'll take care of it right now. Don't you worry. I got this."

Jackson quickly walked back to the stroller, where he put on the jacket, shoved the pipe back in the pocket, and turned to me. "I gotta run home real quick," he said. "Watch my stuff." Before I had a chance to respond, Jackson started walking in the direction of his SRO. He returned a half hour later without his jacket and, I assumed, without the pipe. Thus began a regular pattern in which Jackson would pull me aside four or so hours into the workday and tell me that he had to "run home," "talk to Leticia," or "check on something," leaving me to tend his shop. He was, quite obviously, running off to get high. In the lead-up to excusing himself, Jackson tended to grow irritable toward me, the fellow vendors, and customers. He always returned noticeably energized, talkative, and eager to fill my notebook with tales from his past.

In those first days I wrestled with the thought that I might be passively facilitating Jackson's drug habit. By watching over his shop, I gave him the freedom to take off in search of a hit while continuing to make profits. Three months later, however, Jackson began to curb his addiction. After a string of long days in which he never once excused himself, I realized that I had played at least some part in his turnaround. While I may have been enabling him to leave and get high, my presence also enabled him to *return*. Returning to the corner meant that Jackson had to leave his stash and pipe back home. It meant that he was able to separate himself, if only for the duration of the day, from the dealers and addicts he complained were fixtures at his SRO building. It meant surrounding himself with fellow vendors who not only demanded abstinence while on the job, but who stepped in at the first glimpse of drug paraphernalia.

Sociological research on the informal economy of poor communities tends to support this latter reading of my role. By holding Jackson's place on the corner, I was helping to maintain his exposure to what Mitchell Duneier, in his ethnography of street vendors in New York's City's Greenwich Village, calls the "rehabilitative forces of the sidewalk."[5] According to Duneier, vending allows even the most impoverished, addicted, and otherwise defeatist individuals the opportunity to "become innovators—earning a living, striving for self-respect, establishing good relations with fellow citizens, providing support for each other."[6] Street vending's distinct blend of entrepreneurialism and mutual accountability thus creates "a way for a person to devise new goals and exercise control in a limited domain, which through a process of generalization can affect other aspects of his life."[7]

While I continually observed the kind of intense peer regulation that Duneier had documented along sidewalks three thousand miles away, I turned up an important difference between vending in Skid Row and in Greenwich Village.[8] In Skid Row, the vendors appeared to be far more active in extending the rehabilitative forces of the sidewalk beyond their immediate group of peers. Indeed, the Fifth Street vendors strictly prohibited any and all drug activity, whether by vendors or by unknown passersby. My field notes are filled with scenes in which, upon noticing a nearby pedestrian attempting to roll a marijuana blunt or load a crack pipe, one of the vendors would take several steps toward the culprit, issue a reprimand, and shoo him or her away.

As I got to know the neighborhood better, I realized that the frequency of the vendors' interventions could largely be attributed to their geographic location in the area's drug ecology. While setting up shop on this block of Fifth Street promised the highest level of foot traffic, it also placed the vendors directly between San Julian Park and a collection of warehouses on Crocker Street—two locations that the local media and the LAPD have called the busiest "open-air drug bazaars" in the city.[9] Those who "score" at either location walk quickly from the completed transaction up Fifth Street before inconspicuously loading their pipe or needle. While the vendors' reprimands frequently startled users, they usually obeyed the commands. A shout from Keith or Larry sent them hurrying across the intersection and down the street with confused looks on their faces. In the event that individuals were so engrossed with their paraphernalia that they did not realize they were being addressed, additional vendors lent assistance by stepping toward the culprit and unleashing a chorus of reprimands.

The vendors came to each other's aid particularly quickly when dealers, rather than users, brought their activity into the vicinity. Some dealers conducted hand-to-hand transactions on the move, walking alongside their customers to better conceal the sale from anyone who might be watching. While they typically traversed the space before any of the vendors had a chance to address them, occasionally a dealer would pause directly in front of the vendors to complete the handoff.

Once, a young black man in crisp clothing and bright red sneakers approached with two disheveled addicts in tow. He stopped to dig into his pockets, pulling out a small clear baggie that he handed to one of them.

Keith, who was closely watching the men, called out immediately. "Hey man," he complained. "Yeah, you! I can't have you pushing that poison over here. That shit ain't cool."

"Eh pops, mind your shit," the young man responded.

"Listen sucker, this *is* my shit," Keith replied as he moved forward, visibly pushing out his chest.

I stood nearby with Craig, a wide and imposing man in his forties, as he made change for a customer who had purchased two *Star Trek* VHS tapes. While I remained silent (my usual response), Craig immediately added his own voice. "It's mine too," he boomed as he forcefully pushed past his customer and approached the dealer.

Slick, the oldest of the vendors, joined in, stroking his long graying beard as he walked toward the developing scene. "You heard the man. Push on!"

Larry joined the chorus last, in defense of Slick. "I'd listen to pops if I were you," he called out from his own shop, positioned the furthest from the commotion.

The young dealer's previous defiance evaporated. "Come on," he ordered his eager customers. "Fuck these assholes." He turned and led the two men in the direction of San Julian Park. Without another word, the vendors turned back to their regular activities.

Collective support proved particularly critical when verbal clashes turned physical. On one such occasion, a dealer stopped to conduct a transaction directly in front of Craig's shop. Craig immediately sprang into action, walking to the front of his tarp and ordering the man to "push on up the block." Rather than retreat, however, the dealer moved closer, bringing his face within inches of Craig's. They stood silent, eyes locked. Without warning, the dealer shot his arms forward and shoved Craig in his shoulder, forcing him to take several steps back.

"Hell naw," Craig shouted as he steadied himself, sprinting forward to deliver a shove of his own. Reinforced by his running start, Craig sent the dealer stumbling in the direction of another vendor named Chico, who shoved him toward the street. Knocked off balance, the man tripped and fell. His cell phone flew from his hands and broke into two pieces as it hit the pavement. Chico, Larry, and two other vendors immediately formed a wall between Craig and the dealer, who cursed the group as he collected the parts of his phone.

"You're lucky you got your boys here to protect your ass," the man yelled.

"You're lucky they're here to protect *your* ass," Craig returned.

"Is that right? You're a real bad ass, huh? Let's see if you're still talking when I got my piece." He lifted up his shirt to show his waistline, signaling that he was unarmed—for now. "Wait here, motherfuckers," he continued. "Y'all about to be some dead motherfuckers." He stared at Craig. "And you. I'll see you real soon." He smiled devilishly and walked away with an intentional slowness, keeping his eyes fixed on all of us until he crossed the intersection and started into a jog. While the dealer's threat of retaliation weighed heavily on my mind, it did not seem to faze the vendors. They nonchalantly returned to their positions and remained just as dedicated to this potentially dangerous system of sidewalk regulation.

The Eyes on Fifth Street

By continually interfering with the local drug economy, the vendors acted as what urban theorist Jane Jacobs famously refers to as "eyes on the street."[10] In *The Death and Life of Great American Cities*, Jacobs writes that eyes on the street are the key to ensuring community safety, order, and stability, particularly in disadvantaged neighborhoods with little recourse to police assistance:

The first thing to understand is that the public peace—the sidewalk and street peace—of cities is not kept primarily by the police, necessary as police are. It is kept by an intricate, almost unconscious network of voluntary controls and standards among people themselves, and enforced by people themselves.[11]

Often, Jacobs writes, the public peace is maintained by seemingly unlikely individuals. In fact, she argues that street vendors, like those along Skid Row's Fifth Street, are "great street watchers and sidewalk guardians if present in sufficient numbers"—quintessential examples of eyes on the street.[12]

Jacobs's reverence for informal regulation reflects a dominant current running throughout the intellectual history of urban sociology. Beginning with sociologists of the first Chicago School, researchers have consistently found that impoverished urban neighborhoods are beset by high levels of "social disorganization," defined as "the inability of a community structure to realize the common values of its residents and maintain effective social controls."[13] Given the long-standing association between social disorganization and crime, sociologists, criminologists, and public officials alike continue to search for ways to increase the presence and vigilance of capable eyes on the street.

Jacobs's writings have provided a counterintuitive platform from which criminal justice scholars and professionals have advocated for zero-tolerance policing policies like those currently deployed in Skid Row.[14] The best-known appropriation of Jacobs's ideas is undoubtedly Wilson and Kelling's broken windows thesis.[15] In their formulation, a more aggressive police stance toward problematic behaviors will reduce residents' fears of crime and criminals, and embolden them to become more active eyes on the street. The resulting elevated levels of voluntary regulation and guardianship will, in turn, reduce crime while increasing neighborhood stability.[16]

At first glance, the vendors' behaviors may appear to confirm Wilson and Kelling's propositions.[17] Their system of sidewalk regulation had in fact developed in response to intensified enforcement, particu-

An afternoon chess break. Photo: Nathan Stuart.

larly Central Division's crackdown on narcotics activity. Under closer examination, however, I discovered that the vendors' strict prohibitions developed through a very different mechanism than the one proposed by Wilson and Kelling. The vendors' ban on drug activity derived, not from a reduction of the men's fears of nearby addicts, dealers, or other criminals, but from their increasing fears of police, a growing desire to avoid police contact, and the need to protect against the cascading impacts of criminal justice entanglements.

The underlying impetus for the vendors' interventions became most apparent at moments when their informal controls broke down, when they were *unsuccessful* in disrupting drug activity. On one such occasion, I met Keith outside of his SRO building to walk to Fifth Street. We began setting up for the day. We were earlier than usual, so I was surprised to see that Stevie, a thin vendor with a shiny gold front tooth, had already arrived. Before we reached Stevie's location, however, Keith stopped to talk with a small group of friends leaning against a nearby wall. As I stood quietly at Keith's side, I watched

Stevie advertise his products to passing pedestrians, eventually convincing one of them to buy two packages of his homemade incense. As Stevie stuffed a crumpled wad of cash into his front jeans pocket, something suddenly caught his attention. He raised his nose to the air. A second later I picked up the faint odor of marijuana.

"Come on, y'all," I heard Stevie call out a second later in his slight southern accent. He walked determinedly toward a group of four young black men who stood in a thin cloud of smoke in front of a takeout restaurant on the corner. I moved a few steps closer but maintained my distance.

If the group had heard Stevie, they certainly did not show it. In one quick motion, one of the men, wearing a silk do-rag, passed folded bills to another man in a Los Angeles Dodgers baseball cap.

Stevie began with a tone of disgust. "Smoking? Serving? Y'all know you can't be doing that shit out here."

He clearly had their attention now. The man in the Dodgers cap turned and looked Stevie up and down with defiance. "Look G," he said sharply, "just do your thing. Don't worry about this, aight?" He thrust his shoulders forward as he said this last word. Stevie flinched slightly but stood firm. I looked back toward Keith and realized that he had not noticed what was occurring only yards away. Stevie would not be receiving any assistance in the dispute.

In the midst of their quarrel, the man in the Dodgers cap suddenly broke from the group and walked hurriedly into the nearby restaurant. A second later, an LAPD squad car slammed to a halt in front of the remaining three.

"See this now?" Stevie called out in a vindicated tone as he turned back toward his tarp.

Two officers promptly exited the car and ordered the three men up against the wall. The blunt had mysteriously disappeared and, after fifteen minutes, the officers merely sent the men on their way. Before returning to their car, however, the officers turned their attention to Stevie. Keith walked to my side and we watched the interaction from a safe distance.

The officer took a forceful tone toward Stevie. "You know you can't be out here selling this stuff, right? We have to keep these sidewalks flowing and you're blocking people who are trying to get by."

Stevie pleaded his case. "No, see. That's why I set all this stuff up against the wall, so that it's not in the way. I don't want to block the sidewalk."

The officers appeared unmoved. Despite Stevie's pleading, the officers issued him a citation for blocking the sidewalk and instructed him to pack his belongings and vacate the area. They watched him pack his items back into his duffle bag before they drove up the street.

Within moments, the man in the Dodgers cap emerged from the to-go restaurant.

"See!" Stevie called out, walking toward him and flailing his arms in anger. "This is what I'm talking about. I told y'all not to be doing that shit around here. Now y'all is messing with my livelihood." He slammed a stack of CDs into his bag. "You saw those cops. They stopped over here because of *your* asses, not mine. And look, I got caught up in the crossfire. They would have just drove right past, but y'all gave them a reason to stop. I would have been fine."

Dodgers cap just shook his head. "Whatever."

Keith and I approached as Stevie finished gathering up his wares, grumbling the entire time.

"Don't even bother today," he instructed us, seeing that we had not yet unpacked Keith's inventory. "The corner is too hot with these motherfuckers pushing weed out here."

"How long they been out," Keith asked, clearly trying to stay optimistic.

"Only a few minutes," Stevie answered, "but they already got cops rubbernecking. I was fine all morning, but as soon as they show up, the first car that passes by and 'wooop' here they come, telling me to pack up my shit." Stevie spent a few moments recounting how he tried to make them leave the corner. "It's some bullshit. Their heat rubs off on everybody else out here. They just cost me two hundred bucks!" He waved the ticket in the air in front of him. "*Plus* the money

I'm not going to be able to make today. I should send the bill to those little jackasses." With this, Stevie heaved his bag onto his shoulder and walked across San Pedro Street, complaining under his breath.

"Damn," Keith said, looking toward the corner. "The cops in that car are gonna be back around. They'll circle a couple times. And if they radioed in to the switchboard, we're gonna have every cop looking real hard, even if those guys do take off. There's too much heat right now. They'll give me a ticket for sure." He sighed. "We gotta let the block cool off before we come back out." Keith and I resigned to rendezvous later that evening, hoping that the dealer would be gone by then. The possibility of setting up shop, as well as the profits Stevie and Keith hoped to collect that morning, were quickly dashed.

Cooling Off the Block

Through repeated police encounters like these, Stevie, Keith, and their fellow vendors learned a valuable lesson. The visible or even *suspected* presence of criminal activity on the corner drew swift notice from passing patrol officers, which set off a detrimental chain of events. It prompted officers to exit their squad cars, get off their bikes, or dismount their horses to investigate. Once officers finished inquiring into the matters that initially caught their attention, they frequently took the opportunity to deal with other issues that they might otherwise have overlooked or bypassed. The vendors, with their relatively large presence, were frequent targets of these secondary interventions. The vendors thus discovered a pattern long recognized by policing scholars, that the "uniformed patrolman . . . finds it virtually impossible to leave the scene without becoming involved in some way or another."[18] In the best case, officers merely interrogated them or quickly scanned their wares for drugs and weapons. In the worst case, officers ordered them to pack up and leave, issued them citations for blocking the sidewalk, confiscated their inventories, or, as was the case in the later years of my research, arrested them for outstanding fines or unlicensed street vending.

This new threat to the men's livelihoods forced them to alter their long-standing relation with the conditions that surrounded their sidewalk shops, particularly those related to the local drug economy. While they had strictly prohibited Jackson and other fellow vendors from getting high on the corner, prior to the launch of the Safer Cities Initiative they had regarded the drug-related behavior of strangers and passersby with far more ambivalence. In fact, a number of the vendors described a prior tacit "understanding" with addicts and dealers. Larry, for example, openly acknowledged that the presence of drug sales increased his own profits, because the vendors and the dealers drew from the same customer base. "We didn't bother them, they didn't bother us," he told me. "It was live and let live. To be honest, there were days where I made *more* money when cats were out here selling that chronic [marijuana]. When people get high, they get the munchies. Or maybe they want some new music. I was right there to hook them up." He pointed to a stack of dry ramen noodles and two notebooks stuffed with pirated CDs.

This unspoken truce eroded, however, once the men began to experience the collateral effects of the LAPD's new law enforcement campaign. On an unexpectedly chilly evening I probed Larry, Keith, and a stocky, loud vendor named Jerome about the period before the launch of the Safer Cities Initiative—what the men frequently referred to as the "good ol' days." Nostalgia quickly turned to frustration as they traced their escalating police encounters over the subsequent months.

"There used to be a whole bunch of us out here," Keith complained from underneath his trademark leather baseball cap, pulled down almost to his eyes. The four of us stood in a tight circle, breathing into our cupped hands to keep warm. "We used to call this whole area the Skid Row Swap Meet. I'm talking guys on both sides of the street, all day every day. It was good money, too." He paused, shaking his head. "But then the cops started picking us off one by one."

"Why'd they start coming after you guys?" I asked.

"Because they're assholes," Larry replied tersely, "and that's what assholes do." He turned to the side and spat at his feet to punctuate his statement.

"I'm saying," Keith agreed, though he added some complexity to Larry's account. "But they weren't as big of assholes *before*. They fucked with us, sure, but not how they do now, remember?" Larry nodded silently, allowing Keith to continue. "One day they started rolling through like a bunch of storm troopers. At first they were just jacking up all the young bucks that were stupid enough to do their business right out there in the open. But once all *those* guys were gone, that's when they started jacking us up too. What happened is that they couldn't be lazy no more. They finally had to do some real police work if they wanted to get the smart ones that were doing their business on the down-low. They started running around the hood trying to be all Matlock and shit, jacking *everybody* up, getting up in *everybody's* pockets."

Larry chimed in. "That's when they started looking over here all hard after they hit that corner." He took several quick steps backward, toward the intersection from which patrols tended to arrive. "They're just over here sitting in the cut, trying to find a reason to jump out. They're over here all like, 'I think he's about to make a sale.' And what they're trying to see is whether *I'm* involved in it. You know, if I'm contributing to the operation. Like, giving them cover, or hiding the package, or making change for them, or some down-low shit like that."

"And that's when *we* get caught up," Jerome piped in with frustration. "We get hemmed up even though it's some other cat that's the one over here pushing."

Larry grumbled. "That's what I was saying. It's a real asshole that doesn't wanna see the difference between what *we're* doing out here and what *they're* doing out here. That's why I'm steady telling these young bucks to move on up the block with that mess. They wanna sell that weed? All right. But go up to the weed corner. They wanna sell something else? There's a corner for that too. All I know is that this ain't that corner no more."

"Word," agreed Jerome.

The vendors' routine conversations about the antecedents of unwanted police encounters closely mirrored the collective folk analyses offered by Steel and his weight-lifting crew. Despite little or no contact with one another, the two groups arrived at nearly identical explanations for their own criminalization: unwanted police contact resulted from being caught in the crossfire of the LAPD's local war on drugs and minor crime, a war waged by officers unable or unwilling to recognize the differences between behaviors—like vending and drug dealing—that residents understood as fundamentally different. While both groups accepted that they could not eliminate police encounters altogether (they had been subject to the occasional police detainment and citation even prior to the launch of SCI), they believed they had at least some control over the situation. They could swing the odds of police contact in their favor by proactively reducing officers' likelihood of misrecognition. Steel's crew relied on tactics of mobility and self-presentation to physically and symbolically distance themselves from officers' "real" targets: individuals, scenarios, and locations they anticipated officers would associate with criminality. The Fifth Street vendors had fewer options. The nature of their economic enterprise precluded the possibility of simply sidestepping people and places that were likely to draw heightened police attention and intervention. Turning a profit required that they remain stationary and visible for hours at a time, in a location that provided a steady flow of potential customers. It was no coincidence that they amassed on one of the exact corners that Steel's crew took pains to avoid.

Facing this constraint, the vendors attempted to forestall police contact by reducing the presence of individuals, behaviors, and activities they anticipated would attract heightened police attention, or "heat," as they called it. As Larry's explanation illustrates, the vendors' efforts to "cool off the block" required them to reinterpret the street scene and their relation to it *as if* they were onlooking officers. Like Steel's crew, the vendors devoted significant energy to "seeing like a cop." Unlike Steel's crew, however, the vendors used this inverse perspective to do more than simply revise their own appearances. They acted as surrogate officers and engaged in a kind of *prepolicing*, revising the appearance of the surrounding public space and its inhabitants. The men singled out and regulated likely police targets before the police had a chance to arrive. In so doing, they hoped to ward off the officers' more formal, punitive, and blunt measures, which threatened to enmesh anyone unlucky enough to be standing nearby. Again, the resulting system of informal control stood in stark contrast to the kind of voluntary regulation anticipated by proponents of the broken windows theory. While the intensification of law enforcement did increase the vigilance of the neighborhood's eyes on the street, their resulting regulatory actions were primarily intended to *diminish* the reach, impacts, and effectiveness of the police.

When the Eyes on the Street See Like a Cop

In a neighborhood like Skid Row it is tempting to see *any* increase in collective, voluntary regulation as a significant improvement, no matter its underlying motives.[19] And in fact, the vendors' actions did effectively eliminate (or at least displace) drug commerce and other illicit behaviors. This raises important pragmatic questions for police, city officials, and anyone concerned with improving conditions in impoverished and marginalized communities. Does it really matter that the men's informal controls emerged out of their preoccupation with police? Or that they ultimately intended their prohibitions to subvert policing?

An answer to these questions emerged as I continued cataloging the spectrum of people and activities that ran afoul of the vendors. I found that the origins and objectives of voluntary regulation mattered immensely. The "why" of informal social control ultimately determined both who and what the eyes on the street came to see as "problematic" and how they addressed these problems. This process was readily apparent in the vendors' vigorous enforcement of the city's various sidewalk ordinances, which prohibit obstructing or sitting on the sidewalk. Knowing that these violations attracted the attention of passing officers, the men cooled off the block by forcefully disbanding groups of pedestrians, preventing homeless residents from sitting down to rest, and running off anyone who threatened to clog the nearby walkways.

One afternoon, I watched as Keith herded three older, slowly moving black women past his shop. His intrusion into their friendly conversation clearly annoyed them, and they gave Keith a piece of their mind. After a quick back-and-forth, however, they relented and walked up the street.

"We can't let the sidewalks get all bottlenecked," Keith lectured me, still heated from the exchange.

I nodded my head in agreement. "So you don't get a ticket for blocking the sidewalk, right?"

"Well, that, yeah," he replied. "The narcs come flying by and if they see a pack of people on the sidewalk they always assume that at least one of 'em is slanging. They figure that somebody's gotta be a dealer, so they put everyone up against the wall to find out."

As one might expect, some residents were less willing or able to abide by the vendors' orders to move along. When these individuals failed to obey or offered resistance, the vendors responded with the same ferocity that they applied to dealers. For example, they sprang into action when a mentally disabled homeless man dared to take a seat on the curb in front of the sidewalk shops one morning. Jerome walked over to him and demanded that he find a new place to rest. When the man did not immediately reply, Jerome raised his voice and repeated his order. This caught the attention of two of the other vendors, who immediately began berating the man, deriding him as a "lazy bum" and a "degenerate asshole" as they walked to Jerome's side. Once there, they bent down, grabbed the man under his arms, and lifted him several feet into the air. The man kicked violently as the three carried him to the far side of the block, where they indifferently deposited him against the wall of a building.

The vendors' severe treatment of nearby pedestrians illustrates how, in their efforts to mitigate the negative effects of zero-tolerance policing on their own lives, they felt compelled to "pay it forward," so to speak, by harshly regulating mundane and otherwise innocuous public behaviors. It was a perverse mode of informal social control that neither Jacobs nor Wilson and Kelling had imagined.[20] In outlining the ideal of how eyes on the street should operate, Jacobs writes that "safety on the streets by surveillance and mutual policing sounds grim, but in real life is not grim." "The safety on the streets works best," she cautions, when it is accomplished "most casually, and with the least frequent taint of hostility."[21] Clearly this description does not apply to Fifth Street, where the vendors maintained a forceful grip over the sidewalk. They operated as a hostile and unified front to any and all who threatened to heat up the block. The vendors accompanied their diligent, and ostensibly beneficial, prohibitions on drug activity with indifference and even cruelty toward fellow, noncriminal residents in a way that privileged the vendors' own well-being over that of their neighbors.

Beyond its capacity to engender animosity and aggression along Skid Row's sidewalks, the vendors' rigorous system of regulation undermined individual and community stability in additional and far more troubling ways. When eyes on the street were forced to see like a cop, their resulting behaviors served to negate and even counteract the theorized benefits of informal social control. In fact, the vendors' attempts to forestall police contact had the unintended results of facilitating crime, obstructing rehabilitation and upward mobility, and further exacerbating the territorial stigma that presses down on Skid Row residents.

Word on the Street

According to Jacobs, the most effective informal social control operates "through a web of gossip, approval, disapproval and sanctions, all of which are powerful if people know each other and word travels."[22] Eyes on the street contribute to this process by serving as nodes and relays within what Jacobs calls the "street grapevine system."[23] By spreading "the word" through the street grapevine, the eyes on the street provide fellow residents with the information necessary to anticipate, avoid, and quell potential disruptions. In her own research on New York City's Lower East Side, Jacobs observed that residents relied on these aggregators of information to learn, for instance, about "the presence of dope pushers in the neighborhood," that "the Dragons [a local gang] [were] working up to something and need attention," and that "two girls [were] agitating the Sportsmen toward a rumble."[24] This kind of information, Jacobs warns, does not circulate through neighborhoods that lack diligent eyes on the street.[25]

As Skid Row's most active eyes on the street, the vendors anchored a similar network of informational relays, through which they disseminated timely warnings about future disturbances. Unlike the eyes on the street that Jacobs celebrated, however, the vendors performed a function that has received surprisingly scant attention in research on informal social control.[26] Because they designated the police as the most immediate and detrimental disturbance to neighborhood life, the vendors' warnings primarily circulated information about pending police presence and interference. In a subversive reworking of the street grapevine, the word that the vendors spread was, quite literally, "police."

To better cool off the block, the men developed a simple, yet effective warning system to audibly alert one another when police officers arrived in the area. When the vendors spotted an approaching officer, they casually (though loudly) yelled out "One-time"—a slang term for police. Repeated down the line of vendors, the warning often traveled well beyond them. Even after I had spent several years in the neighborhood, I stood in awe of the waves of "one-time" calls that rolled for blocks in either direction, several hundred feet in advance of approaching LAPD squad cars. From my first days selling cigarettes two blocks from the vendors, I had marveled at the call-and-response as it echoed up and down the street. I eventually learned that many of these calls originated with the vendors. The men had developed a largely unspoken norm whereby those who arrived early enough to set up their shops closest to the intersection, which provided a clear sight line in all four directions, initiated the warning calls each time they spotted an approaching officer. The alerts provided fellow vendors with the vital seconds necessary to address the behaviors around their shops most likely to flag police attention.

Two aspects of Fifth Street's street grapevine system are particularly noteworthy in light of the discussion so far. First, while intended to protect one another, the vendors' "one-time" calls provided a boon to anyone within earshot. This meant that despite their hostilities toward nearby dealers and addicts, the vendors served as de facto lookouts for their activities. The warning system provided these individuals with a short time to abort transactions, stash supplies, and flee the scene before officers noticed them. This certainly helped the vendors cool off the block. At the same time, however, it protected the drug economy and made its participants less susceptible to police detection. It undermined the effectiveness of the LAPD.

Second, the warning system illustrates how copwise residents' tactics for coping with aggressive law enforcement can become cemented in a neighborhood's shared social practices. I myself had begun participating in the warning system well before I joined the vendors and learned its point of origin. Looking back, it is difficult to explain exactly why I had joined in when the calls reached my position more than a block away. It simply felt "normal," like something that everyone did. I might be standing and conversing with my cigarette customers when, midsentence, they would tilt their heads back and yell "One-time" at the top of their lungs. For better or worse, the street grapevine system seemed to be transmitting an embryonic form of cop wisdom throughout the neighborhood streets, allowing an increasing number of residents—both criminals and noncriminals—to more effectively anticipate and shield themselves against unwanted police contact.

Some of the more savvy vendors went to greater lengths to acquire and disseminate information that might help them anticipate and manipulate future police behavior. One such individual was Warren, an attractive black man in his midthirties. Warren had moved to Skid Row from North Carolina in 2000. An aspiring actor with a bright smile, Warren disappeared for a week at a time to work as an extra in the commercials and television shows that regularly film throughout downtown. He used the cash he earned "on set" to purchase scented candles, body oils, and imitation cologne. Among other things, this meant that Warren had significantly higher inventory costs than most of the other vendors. With more to lose, he developed an innovative tactic to forestall police contact, or "tame the market," as he put it. One day, Warren decided to befriend the senior lead officer (SLO) who oversaw the area where the vendors operated. He waited on San Julian Street for two days until the SLO appeared. Warren immediately approached, introduced himself, and engaged in a long conversation about his burgeoning acting career.

"He was actually pretty cool when we were just standing around shooting the shit," Warren recalled.

"What did you two talk about?" I asked, incredulously.

"No, seriously," Warren defended, "I just talked to him about what I'm trying to do out here. He was really hip to it. I just told him why I moved out here, where I'm living, how I've been doing commercials and now I'm trying to get hooked up with an agent. He was asking about the TV shows I was in. You know, a lot of people around here hate the guy, but he's nice enough when he's not trying to put you in handcuffs."

After this initial interaction, Warren went out of his way to engage in regular conversations with the SLO. Much to the surprise of many of the other vendors, who remained skeptical about the tactic, the relationship yielded significant results. In one of their regular conversations, the SLO informed Warren that, for the remainder of the month, Central Division would be amplifying its enforcement of the sidewalk ordinance within the SLO's patrol jurisdiction. He discreetly warned Warren that if he did not move to the opposite corner, just outside of the targeted area, Warren would almost certainly receive a citation and likely be arrested. Days later Warren found an opportunity to exploit this piece of intelligence, using the information to discipline fellow vendors he considered too hot to remain on the corner.

For some time, the men had been growing aggravated with Jerome, whose interactions with officers had grown increasingly hostile following what Jerome thought was an especially frivolous arrest. Those who set up near him suffered the consequences. On one occasion, Keith and another vendor named Carter received citations and nearly had their items confiscated when Jerome hurled insults at two officers who were driving past with their windows open. As the two vendors told it, the officers immediately slammed on their brakes, put all three of them in handcuffs, and searched them before ordering them to pack and leave.

"Jerome's too hot for his own good," Keith complained.

"He's too hot for *all* our good," Carter added.

Despite their repeated demands that Jerome follow the lead of the other vendors and not outwardly express his resentment toward the police, Jerome continued his behavior. Several of the men decided to teach Jerome a lesson. Their retaliation unfolded subtly. Three weeks after the incident with the passing squad car, I sat on a milk crate with Jerome, Carter, and a tall, mustached vendor named Terrance in our usual location. Warren arrived soon after. However, he did not unload his pack as usual. Instead, he pulled Carter to the side and shared what he had learned from the SLO. They spoke in hushed tones for fifteen minutes, then Warren quickly walked across the street and leaned against a wall. Several minutes later, as Jerome fiddled with his cell phone, Carter quietly conferred with Terrance. The two calmly packed their shops and headed in Warren's direction. As he began to walk away, Terrance gave me a subtle head nod and a hand signal to join them. I took the cue and followed them across the street.

"I can't stand that jackass," Terrance complained once we were on the opposite corner.

Warren was equally dismissive. "The man's so hot he's melting the damn asphalt." His contention was borne out minutes later, when a squad car pulled onto Fifth Street, moving slowly past Jerome.

"Watch this," Terrance said in a low voice, as he walked to my side. "Warren said they're jacking up people up and down the block this week. They're just looking for an excuse."

As predicted, the officers pulled over to the curb, placed Jerome in handcuffs, threw his inventory in the trunk, and drove off in the direction of the Central Division station.

Warren nodded in satisfaction. "Maybe he could use a trip to the station. Maybe it'll wake him up."

Warren's words proved prescient when Jerome reappeared on the block a month later, sometime after his jail term. His verbal outbursts toward officers were a thing of the past.

"A few weeks inside got the man's head back on straight," Warren noted after several of us spent the afternoon set up next to Jerome's shop without a problem. "He ain't a liability no more, so he's all good in my book." As long as Jerome remained calm and assisted the others in cooling off the block, Warren willingly shared the information gained from the friendship he cultivated with the SLO. Conversely, any time he deemed another vendor "too hot," Warren brought him in line with thinly veiled threats. "You don't want to end up like Jerome," he repeatedly warned as he adjudicated disputes and generally imposed his will. He received little opposition.

Handling Strangers

Throughout the criminological literature, strangers and neighborhood outsiders appear as prime threats to neighborhood stability, safety, and solidarity. Wilson and Kelling, for example, attribute crime, danger, and fear chiefly to strangers who "invade" neighborhoods with the intent of victimizing "decent regulars."[27] Jacobs shares this logic, writing that one of the foremost responsibilities of the eyes on the street is to "handle strangers."[28] The eyes on the street, as Jacobs notes, "observe strangers. They observe everything going on. If they need to take action, whether to direct a stranger waiting in the wrong place or call the police, they do so."[29] The "natives," as she calls them, have a duty to keep a sharp lookout for individuals who lack a legitimate reason for their presence in an area.

While both Wilson and Kelling and Jacobs consider the regulation of strangers a central concern, neither provides much explanation of

how natives determine who is a stranger in the first place.[30] How do
the eyes on the street know an outsider when they see one? What, precisely, are they on the lookout for? My research alongside the vendors
revealed that, in a hyperpoliced neighborhood like Skid Row, where
the eyes on the street see like a cop, they overwhelmingly adopted
and emulated *officers'* criteria for distinguishing dangerous outsiders
from those who "belong" in the neighborhood. This process was most
readily visible in regard to an individual's race or gender. Mimicking the heightened scrutiny that officers directed toward whites and
women, the vendors forcibly ejected members of these demographics
from nearby public space. In so doing, they perpetuated a detrimental
racial and gender order that carried dire consequences for their peers.

In chapter 2, I noted Central Division officers' diligence in detaining and interrogating those they suspected of entering Skid Row to
engage in criminal activity or exploit vulnerable residents. In addition to "predators," who sought to prey on the vulnerable, and "do-
gooders," who enabled poor lifestyle choices, officers reported that an
additional group of outsiders had now "invaded" the neighborhood.
With the ongoing redevelopment and gentrification of the adjacent
downtown, well-to-do whites had apparently begun descending from
their lofts and condos into Skid Row to buy or sell drugs. Officers considered these individuals relatively "easy to spot." While whites made
up approximately 53 percent of the population in downtown, they
constituted less than 10 percent of the Skid Row population.[31] In the
words of one patrol officer, "They don't look anything like the people
with a legitimate reason for being down here."

As usual, Skid Row residents quickly picked up on officers' scrutiny of nonpoor whites. Consider the experiences of Sam, a white,
unhoused man. As Sam attempted to pull himself out of alcoholism
and off Skid Row's streets, he was subjected to increasing suspicion
by police and, as a result, by the eyes on the street. I befriended Sam
in my first days alongside the vendors. When we met, he had a long,
scruffy beard and a mound of curly black hair that had recently begun
to grey. He smelled strongly of beer and walked with a slight limp.

Sam had come to Skid Row a year earlier, after a traumatic car accident that had cracked several vertebrae and ribs, shattered his knee, and broke his femur. Suffering from debilitating back pain and unable to purchase effective pain medicine, he started drinking heavily. With medical bills mounting and few other options, Sam made his way to Skid Row and secured a bed at the Midnight Mission. On only his second night, however, he got in a drunken fistfight with one of the mission's security guards and was immediately banned from the property. That night he began sleeping on the streets and using a shopping cart to transport his possessions, which consisted of a small tent, a tarp, a backpack, and a handful of pants and shirts.

Sam visited the corner several times a week to sell the items he scavenged from nearby alleyways. The vendors did not seem much bothered by Sam's race. When the issue did come up, it was typically in the course of playful bonding. Jackson, for example, liked to throw his arm around Sam and proclaim that they were "brothers from another mother." The running joke characterized the majority of Sam's lighthearted and welcoming interactions with the vendors. Hesitant to leave their shops to "go on a run," the men relied upon Sam and the rest of Skid Row's dumpster divers to help them replenish their inventories during working hours. Sam typically received between fifty cents and two dollars per item, and I once saw Sam make thirty dollars after unloading a shopping cart full of small electronics, hip-hop CDs, and magazines.

Scavenging provided Sam with just enough money for meals and beer, but it exacted a physical toll. Despite medicating his back pain with frequent swigs from a forty-ounce bottle of malt liquor, the long hours on his feet, repeated climbs into dumpsters, and the weight of the shopping cart continually aggravated his injury. Eventually, Sam's limited mobility and pain forced him to stop scavenging. Strapped for cash and finally willing to jump through the requisite bureaucratic hoops, Sam applied for, and began receiving, Supplemental Security Income (SSI). With his monthly SSI payment of $938, he rented a room in a residential hotel on Seventh Street.

For roughly five months, I did not see Sam on Fifth Street (or any-where else in the neighborhood, for that matter). When I unexpect-edly ran into him, I would not have recognized him had I not noticed the slight hitch in the step of the man walking toward me. His face was freshly shaven, his hair trimmed and combed. He wore a clean pair of jeans and a light blue, short-sleeved, button-up shirt. He had replaced his white-turned-grey Fila tennis shoes with a new pair of black Nikes. We hugged, exchanged greetings, and walked to grab lunch at the nearby Subway. Over the next hour Sam filled me in on his SSI, his hotel room, and how he was finally "getting it together." Sam proudly reported that he had not touched a drop of alcohol for over a month.

A week after our reunion, Sam reappeared on Fifth Street, carry-ing a milk crate and a large black backpack that contained a carton of cigarettes and a spindle of bootleg DVDs. Sam had learned the lo-gistics of sidewalk sales during the time he spent supplying the men. Now possessed of the capital necessary to build his own inventory, Sam had decided to try his luck at vending. The other vendors greeted him warmly. I stood next to Slick and Bishop, an older vendor with grey dreadlocks, as they joked with Sam.

"Somebody's out here getting their hustle on," Bishop called out in a playful tone. Sam smiled back, nodding his head.

"The man's a businessman now," Slick added.

The affection, however, was short-lived. I only picked up bits and pieces at first, but the vendors began expressing discontent about Sam's reemergence. Late one afternoon, I sat with Slick watching a bootleg copy of *American Gangster* on his portable DVD player when Slick saw that Sam was packing up his items for the day.

Veering significantly from his initial reception, Slick let out a quiet groan. "Thank god this motherfucker's leaving."

Carter, a man in his midfifties with long, chemically processed straight hair, echoed the sentiment. "Couldn't be soon enough."

I waited until Sam was around the corner before asking the men about their disapproval. "You mad at Sam or something?" I asked.

"I mean, I'm just getting kinda tired of him being out here so much," Carter bluntly replied.

"Definitely," Slick added.

I was unsatisfied with the answer. When I heard Slick's earlier comment, I figured he resented the additional competition that Sam brought to the corner. I continued. "You guys end up having the same inventory, huh? Is he messing with your prices? You guys gotta compete now?"

Their responses dismissed my initial hypothesis. "Naw, man. That ain't it at all," Slick snickered. "There's plenty enough money around here for all of us. I ain't even sweating that. We're all cool. Shit, I like the guy, he's a good man. We even trade movies sometimes if he thinks he needs one of mine. He don't bring no knuckleheads around and he ain't pushing like a couple of the other fools that come around here. So he's all right in my book." Slick stopped at this.

Now even more confused, I probed deeper. "So what's the issue, then?"

Carter spoke as if to finally shut me up. "Ain't everything up to us," he said bluntly. "If everything was up to me, shit would look a whole lot different around here. It's fucking po-po. That's the issue. They come rolling by quick and just kinda look over here real fast after they hit that corner." He pointed up Fifth Street, in the direction from which officers typically appear. "A lot of the time they don't even trip, but there's certain things that we know make them stop and give us shit. Sam sticks out like a sore thumb! When you're talking about Skid Row, white is black, you feel me? You know the cops are in their cars like, 'Hmmm, who is this white guy kicking it with all these brothers? This can't be no good. Let's go check this out.' That's all it takes and boom, you're jacked up with these motherfuckers confiscating all your shit. It don't even matter if you've done something or not. They just need an excuse to come over here."

Slick punctuated Carter's point. "That's right. Sam makes it a little too hot around here. I think if he keeps coming out at the same time again I'm gonna start coming out later."

Carter and Slick cut to the heart of the issue. Seeing like a cop, they anticipated that Sam's racial difference was likely to attract detrimental police contact. I found it particularly interesting that Sam's race had never been an issue when he was drunk and destitute. Only after Sam secured forms of housing, income, and clothing nearly identical to what the others had did his whiteness become a problem. It was as if by bathing Sam had washed away the dirt that had masked his underlying race. He was no longer "black enough" to be allowed on the corner.

Sam's repeated run-ins with Skid Row officers following his transition out of homelessness confirmed the vendors' worries. During our reunion lunch, Sam complained that Skid Row officers had detained and handcuffed him six separate times in a two-week period. "Now that I cut my hair," he said through a mouthful of sandwich, "it's like I got a flashing sign that says, 'Please arrest me.'" He went on to detail his most recent detainment, in which he was handcuffed outside of his apartment building while conversing with one of his black neighbors. To his surprise, the officers allowed the other man to leave the scene. They kept Sam in cuffs and questioned him about his "true" reason for being in Skid Row. "I remember they just kept asking me, 'What are you doing down here?' And I kept saying, 'I live down here.' And they didn't believe me, so I was like, 'I live right there!'" He acted out the incident, hands behind his back, nodding his head toward his fourth-story apartment. "They kept asking me if I was looking for drugs. They didn't believe that I lived upstairs. They were like, 'Come on, we know you don't live down here, tell us where you *really* live.'" Sam shook his head in disbelief. "It's like an episode of *The Twilight Zone*. Where else do the cops let the black guy go and keep the white guy in handcuffs?"

I might have discounted Sam's allegations of racial profiling, but I too had been accused of "trespassing" in Skid Row, and for similar reasons. Given my mixed-race background and light brown skin tone, I appear somewhat ethnically ambiguous. As the arbiters of racial classification in Skid Row, however, Central Division officers quickly put this ambiguity to rest. It was nearly eleven o'clock at night on a weekday evening, shortly after I had begun working alongside the Fifth Street vendors. I stood next to Keith, Carter, and four customers who were perusing their DVD inventories. The night was quiet, save a few occasional pedestrians and an episode of *Gangland* on Keith's DVD player. A patrol cruiser, yellow auxiliary light flashing, pulled to the curb in front of us. Without warning, the officers exited their car and charged me.

"Hands on your head! Hands on your head! Up against the fence!"

Before I had time to react, the first officer was on top of me. He spun me around with a shove. Grabbing hold of my backpack, he pushed my face into the chain-link fence. In the same motion he pulled my backpack off and threw it to the ground, where his partner unzipped it and started rifling through the contents.

As the first officer proceeded to pat me down, I spouted the first thoughts that came to my mind. "Officer, I'm a UCLA researcher." I rattled off a series of buzzwords I hoped might de-escalate the situation: "Chief Bratton." "Homelessness." "Evaluation." I felt the officer release his grip on my wrists. He turned me around. The other officer placed my backpack down on the ground.

He addressed me again, but his tone had changed remarkably. "All right. Well, you need to know that the only reason we stopped you is because we got a call that somebody fitting your description was out distributing narcotics on this corner."

"Huh?" I responded skeptically. "Someone fitting *my* description? Are you sure?"

"A white male in a black sweatshirt and a black bookbag."

"See, that can't be me," I said, shaking my head, confidence returning. I held my hand out, palm down, motioning for them to look at the shade of my skin. For me, it was noticeably darker than that of the two white officers. "I'm not *white*," I argued.

The first officer did not hesitate. "Down *here* you are," he said flatly. He pointed to the others, who were watching eagerly. "Look at these guys. Compared to them, trust me, you're white."

Unsure exactly how to respond, I changed tack and asked for the officers' names and badge numbers.

"You know what happens down here, right?" The officer asked defensively as he handed me a business card on which he had written his badge number, the reason for the stop, and the contact information for the senior lead officer, should I have further questions. "We're out here making sure that you don't get hurt," he offered. "We're just trying to look out for you. Do us a favor and just head on home, will you?" Looking to end the interaction, I followed their orders.

I returned to the corner two days later, where I was greeted with surprising fanfare. Keith had shared the story widely, emphasizing how I had quickly reversed the course of the interaction with the officers. For the next few weeks, I was made to tell and retell the details of how I "showed the cops what's up." At the same time, however, Keith, Carter, and several others insisted that I would have to do something to reduce the heat I brought to the corner if I were to continue hanging with them. While the officers had left the scene that night without detaining or dispersing the others, Keith argued that the vendors might not be as lucky the next time officers decided that I "fit the description."

In response, the men undertook a concerted effort to "blacken me up," as they jokingly referred to it. They instructed me to leave my running shoes and "butt-hugger jeans" at home. Apparently, I also wore my shirts too tight. They ordered me to start wearing basketball shoes, baggy pants, and a backward hat. Somewhat to my surprise, Keith also ordered me to change the way I jotted down field notes. In an early effort to appear less conspicuous I had stopped carrying my small spiral-bound notebook. Instead, I had taken to scribbling notes on a newspaper folded to the crossword puzzle. For me to appear "blacker," Keith insisted that I ditch this strategy.

"Everybody knows that niggas don't do crosswords," he instructed with a smile. "Come on! That's a dead-bang giveaway that you ain't really from around here. How many people around here do you see doing crosswords?" From his understanding of how cops thought, he had a point: crosswords demand a high level of literacy, a level that someone who "belongs" in Skid Row would not possess.

I hesitantly followed the men's instructions and, in return, they cemented my place on the corner. Sam, however, was not as fortunate. As he stayed clean and sober, he slid toward the opposite end of their racial spectrum. The vendors' hostility toward him only intensified in the weeks following his reemergence. Their desire to push Sam off the block manifested in two noticeable tactics. First, the men forced Sam to set up his shop one or two hundred feet away, or even on the other side of Fifth Street, so as to insulate them from any police attention Sam might attract. Having created this buffer, the men initiated a second tactic whereby they attempted to actually *increase* Sam's heat. The vendors used their cop wisdom to set Sam up for arrest, enlisting the police to finish the task they had been unable to complete on their own. With Sam present, they manipulated the grapevine system by keeping their voices low, or by refraining from police warnings altogether.

On the last evening I saw Sam, he occupied his usual place of exile further up the sidewalk. I myself stood closer to the intersection, next to Stevie, Slick, and Carter. Suddenly, Carter reached over and tapped Slick's leg, nodding toward the intersection. A police cruiser sat idling at the light, preparing to turn in front of us onto Fifth Street. Rather than call out "One-time," the men looked in unison down the block toward Sam, who was busy lining up the twenty or thirty DVDs he had pulled from his bag. Within seconds, Stevie, Slick, and Carter had packed their wares, leaving Sam as the only active vendor on the block. When the light changed, the squad car's lights began pulsating as the officers pulled to the curb in front of Sam. After searching his bags, the officers arrested Sam.[32] They gave little attention to the other men, who looked on from half a block away. The remaining vendors expressed notable satisfaction at this outcome, despite the fact that the heat from Sam's arrest ended their sales for the evening. With Sam in jail, they anticipated that the corner would be significantly cooler in the days to come.

Being white in a criminalized black space. Photo: Nathan Stuart.

The vendors' system of informal control similarly shaped gender relations in Skid Row's public spaces. As discussed in chapter 2, officers stop and question women with a frequency disproportionate to their numbers in the neighborhood. Recognizing that the presence of women led to increased police contact, the vendors strictly forbade women from lingering on the corner. Just as they had observed how often officers detained and interrogated whites, who were assumed to be slumming in the neighborhood, they recognized that officers suspect men to be either johns or pimps if they spend too much time flirting or even standing too close to women.

One of the only instances I witnessed physical violence erupting *between* vendors resulted from the men's refusal to allow Jackson's wife, Leticia, to accompany him while he tended to his shop. Throughout most of my fieldwork, Leticia spent very little time on the corner. When she did stop by to bring Jackson lunch or money or to pass along a message, she seldom stayed longer than a brief conversation. This changed, however, after an unexpected turn of events forced Jackson to keep closer tabs on his wife. A few months earlier,

Jackson had been arrested while trying to steal textbooks from the bookstore at a nearby community college. Pleading down from commercial burglary to theft, Jackson ended up serving a total of ninety-three days in county jail. Still wrestling with his addictions, he suffered debilitating withdrawal symptoms throughout his first couple weeks inside. By the end of his sentence, however, he had sobered up and was determined to finally get his and Leticia's lives back on track. This would not be easy. He had lost all contact with his wife. He had also lost his housing and all of his material possessions. Without the income provided by Jackson's various hustles, Leticia had been unable to pay the rent on their SRO room. Building management forcibly removed Leticia from the unit and put a mark of "abandonment" on their rental history—a stain that would make it even more difficult to secure housing in the future. With nowhere to turn, Leticia followed her addiction out into Skid Row's streets. Jackson spent his first month on the outside scouring the neighborhood for his wife, spending a few hours a day scraping together cash on the corner. Much to his relief, he soon received word from friends that Leticia had been spotted at the Union Rescue Mission. Jackson was overjoyed to reunite with his partner of seventeen years, and the two were inseparable in the following weeks. I now rarely saw Jackson without Leticia.

His fellow vendors, however, were less enthusiastic about the reunion. Their discontent came to a head one afternoon. I arrived on the corner in the middle of the dispute. I greeted the couple and noticed Jackson shoot a concerned glance toward Larry, Craig, and Terrance, who had all set up their shops a noticeable distance away.

"What are *you* looking at?" Craig called out to Jackson.

Jackson did not hesitate before answering. "Not much, apparently." But he avoided looking directly at the other men.

Terrance also yelled at Jackson. "What's that, little man? Did you say something?" He sounded like he was trying to pick a fight.

Instead of responding directly, Jackson turned his back to the two. "These assholes," he said under his breath.

"What's going on?" I whispered.

"They're just being assholes," Jackson replied softly, trying to appear unconcerned. "They're pissed off that I got Leticia out here helping me out, trying to say she's the reason we all got tickets a couple days back."

Over Jackson's shoulder, I saw Craig walking quickly toward us, with Terrance in tow. "You talking more shit? You got something to say to my face?" Craig peered down at Jackson, fists clenched.

I tried my best to intervene. "It's all good, man. Nobody's talking shit. It's all good."

"No, *man*," he scolded me. "It ain't all good. This little nigga's fucking it up for every one of us. He knows he can't have her hanging around all damn day." Craig turned back to address Jackson. "We told you that last time. Or don't you remember?"

Jackson stood tall. "I can have anybody I . . ."

Craig's fist caught Jackson midsentence, thudding into his stomach. Jackson buckled over. Leticia ran to his side.

Craig took a step back and turned toward me, as though expecting me to attack. Instead, I froze, at a loss.

Craig continued to lecture, though almost reluctantly, as if surprised at his own punch. "I done warned you. I'm done playing with y'all. You need to take this bitch and dip."

"Who you calling bitch?" Leticia screamed, taking a step toward Craig, raising her fist.

Jackson grabbed her other arm, pulling her back. "Naw, baby."

Craig stood staring at us for a moment, then turned away. He and Terrance walked back to their shops. I reached down and began gathering Jackson's inventory and loading it back into his duffle bag. Leticia helped me as Jackson propped himself against the fence, catching his breath. The three of us headed toward their friend's SRO room, where the couple had been spending their nights, sleeping on the floor. They did so in a clear violation of the building's rules, but Leticia had been barred from the mission for showing up high.

I pieced together the details of Craig's attack as Leticia ranted for two blocks. She flailed one arm in explanation, but kept her other arm firmly around Jackson's waist as she huddled close to his body. This was, apparently, precisely the kind of behavior that had been catching the officers' attention. Over the course of the previous week, Leticia and Jackson had been detained twice while they stood on Fifth Street.

"We was just standing here minding our own business," Leticia complained, "when two of them came up and asked me if I was 'working.' At first I didn't know what they meant. I thought they was asking if I needed a job or something. But then I realized these assholes was asking if I was trickin'! I said, 'This is my husband right here.' Like I'm turning tricks? But they didn't even believe me. They made us take out our IDs and show them we had the same last name. Then they asked us if we were on probation or parole, if we had any warrants on us. Just for standing here talking. After all that, they still told me to take off."

"Not before they wrote us all up," Jackson added. "Craig too." Jackson's sobriety made him seem reserved next to Leticia's constant fidgeting.

We arrived at the SRO building, where Leticia ran inside to use the bathroom. Jackson and I leaned against the wall. "Those guys really fucked me," he said after a short lapse in the conversation. He gazed out at the street, deep in thought. "I mean, I know she makes it harder for me, and for them. I understand. But I don't have a choice, man. That's my wife." His voice quieted. "Next week. I'm fucked."

"Why? What's up?" I asked.

"It's Mother's Day," he replied.

"Mother's Day already happened." I chuckled, but quickly caught myself.

"No. The *other* Mother's Day. That's what they call it when the checks come in. The GR [General Relief] checks. Her pick-up date's on the fourth, but I can't leave her alone at all that week. Last time she damn near smoked up her whole check before I could get her to give me her money. And she fought me on it. When I got out, she was using even worse. I can't make her stop completely. She ain't strong enough to go cold turkey like me. I said we gotta wean her off it in a rational way. It kills me, man. That's my wife. That's the mother of my child."

He sighed, concluding his stream of thoughts. "I gotta make sure she don't kill herself, or up and disappear or something. We're broke, Forrest. How am I supposed to keep my wife alive *and* keep saving enough money to get a place? We can't be in the mission no more!"

I offered what I assumed to be the most obvious solution. "Dude, why don't you just move? Set up somewhere else and then you don't have to worry about Craig or anybody."

"Yeah, I'm gonna have to. That's the only way I can have her out there with me. But that was the good spot. That's the first place all my regular customers go when they get paid. Nobody wants to go nowhere else for movies 'cause they don't wanna spend their money on a disc that don't work. Ain't no refunds and returns in this business." Jackson sometimes satisfied customers who doubted the quality of his bootleg movies by previewing them on one of the other men's portable DVD players—one of the resources the vendors readily shared. "Customers don't wanna take a risk on a movie that don't work. That means I gotta sell them for less. Probably half price! That three-dollar movie I got is gonna end up going for a buck fifty, if I'm lucky."

The two of us stood in silence. We both understood Jackson's difficult choice. Returning to Fifth Street would require leaving Leticia unsupervised. Abandoning Fifth Street to support his wife through her recovery would immediately reduce the couple's already meager income. This, in turn, would mean they would not be able to move off the streets and into their own room for the foreseeable future. As research on homelessness consistently demonstrates, Jackson's chances of keeping Leticia (and himself) away from crack and crack-addicted peers would be extremely low if the two remained unhoused.[33] Banished from Fifth Street, the couple faced a no-win situation.

||||||||||||||||

A week after Craig punched Jackson, I stood with Jackson and his wife on Seventh Street, on the opposite side of Skid Row. I watched Jackson finish selling one of his DVDs at half price, just as he had predicted. He turned to me, defeat in his eyes. "You wanna know what living in Skid

Row's really like?" he asked, referring back to our very first conversation more than a year earlier. "Trying to make a living down here, getting done the way Craig and those guys did me, you know what it's like? It's like hustling backward." Jackson's succinct phrase captures how the vendors' militancy about cooling off the block could directly obstruct their peers' efforts to secure sufficient incomes, find stable housing, and generally improve their lives.

At least at first, the vendors' regulatory behaviors facilitated Jackson's abstinence. Their hostility to Leticia's recovery, however, serves as a vivid illustration of how exclusively their system of informal control focused on avoiding the police. The vendors' system of informal control protected certain people from detrimental police encounters but exposed others to yet more miseries. Acting as surrogate officers and drawing on cop wisdom to punish their peers, the vendors' attempts to cool off the block introduced an additional source of anxiety, fear, violence, and marginalization into the daily lives of residents they excluded from their protection. For Sam, Jackson, Leticia, and others who ran afoul of the vendors, interactions with the eyes on Fifth Street could be just as detrimental as interactions with the police. Whatever moral ambivalence the vendors might have felt toward the dealers, addicts, unhoused people, whites, women, and others who surrounded their sidewalk shops, aggressive law enforcement and the informal social controls that it generated had the effect of reinforcing the territorial stigma that accompanies residence, or even presence, in Skid Row. The vendors' regulatory behaviors coalesced with formal police activities to uphold inner-city apartheid by reinforcing the prevailing notion that only poor black men and severely impoverished whites belong in Skid Row.[34]

The vendors' systematic tactics for cooling off the block carry important theoretical implications. A wealth of sociological and criminological research seeks to understand what factors and mechanisms increase or decrease the prevalence of informal control in impoverished neighborhoods. The vendors' punishment and expulsion of Jerome, Sam, and Jackson and Leticia are cases in point. The intensification of policing does more than merely increase or decrease the prevalence of residents' voluntary regulation of neighborhood problems and disturbances. It also has important qualitative effects. It reshapes precisely who and what residents come to define as a problem or disturbance in the first place. Informal controls may increase, but they may do so to the ultimate detriment of the larger community. We end up with eyes on the street, but are they the kind of eyes we want?

Back on Seventh Street, Jackson pulled out his wallet to count the day's disappointing profit. Noticing that it was jammed with unpaid citations, I made a suggestion. Since he was no longer benefiting from the protections provided by his former companions, Jackson needed to find alternative ways to shoulder his near-daily encounters with the police. By this time, I had taken my fieldwork into the offices of the Los Angeles Community Action Network (LACAN), which operated a free weekly legal clinic for Skid Row residents. Through a hard-fought organizing campaign, LACAN had worked out an arrangement with the local courts to dismiss citations issued to those financially unable to pay their fines. After a month of cajoling, Jackson followed my advice, consulted the LACAN clinic, and allowed the organization to wipe his fines from his record. This proved to be the first step in getting back on his feet. Spending time with LACAN, Jackson joined a group of residents engaged in a form of resistance that departed significantly from those taken up by Steel's crew or the Fifth Street vendors. Rather than merely attempting to deflect, avoid, or preempt police interventions, those involved with LACAN deployed their cop wisdom as part of an overt and formal effort to undercut therapeutic policing and reform police policy. I detail their strategies of resistance in the next chapter.

CHAPTER FIVE

Policing the Police

One late afternoon, as the sun retreated below the downtown skyline, I sprinted furiously down Skid Row's Sixth Street, trying to keep pace with a man known in the neighborhood as "Commander Malcolm." Clad head to toe in green military fatigues, Malcolm was in hot pursuit of an LAPD squad car streaking toward the corner of Sixth and San Julian Streets. The camcorder hanging from his arm flailed as he athletically sidestepped several men sitting on the curb. Behind me, I could hear the faint footsteps and panting breath of three other members of Malcolm's "Community Watch" team as they too struggled to keep up.

Police sirens grew louder as we approached the intersection, now illuminated by pulsating red and blue lights. I followed the Community Watch team as they began to push past a group of huddled onlookers, who welcomed them with excited shouts.

"Move out of the way," one man ordered. "Here comes LACAN!"

"Turn on those cameras quick," a woman yelled. "Don't let them arrest that man."

Within seconds, we had pushed our way to the front of the small crowd. Malcolm's group raised their camcorders and trained them on six LAPD officers who were surrounding a black man in handcuffs. As two officers emptied the contents of the man's pockets onto the hood of a squad car, Malcolm and another team member inched closer as the officers began their interrogation. Suddenly noticing the cameras, one of the officers stopped the body search, turned to Malcolm, and called out to him.

"Hey look, it's the Commander," he said mockingly. "And he's got his little army with him."

The other officers followed suit. One stuck his tongue out while another began taking pictures of Malcolm using his personal camera-phone. "Smile!" he called out.

After a minute or so of this, they turned back to the man in hand-cuffs. They ran his name for outstanding warrants. After deeming the man "clean," they eventually removed the handcuffs and sent him on his way.

Malcolm immediately approached the officers and launched into a barrage of questions, as one of the other team members kept a camera pointed at the officers over Malcolm's shoulder. "Why did you hand-cuff and search that innocent man?" he asked. "Is that how you treat *everyone* in downtown?"

One of the officers responded without hesitation. "He was jaywalk-ing in a high-crime area. He might have been a drug dealer or a parole violator. We couldn't tell until we put him against the wall first."

Malcolm smiled faintly as he heard this. He turned and exchanged satisfied glances with the rest of his team. "Is that right?" he asked as he turned back to the officer.

"That's right," the officer replied as he moved to get back into his cruiser.

We stood in silence, watching the squad car pull away from the curb. Malcolm squinted as he watched the car travel further down Sixth Street. After five blocks, the car suddenly stopped. The offi-cers flung open their doors and immediately pressed a pedestrian up against a nearby wall. Without exchanging another word, Malcolm took off. As he streamed down the sidewalk toward the officers, he prepared his camcorder to begin recording once more.

||||||||||||||||

The tense interactions between Commander Malcolm and Central Di-vision officers have become a familiar sight in Skid Row. These con-frontations fit within a larger, ongoing campaign by the Los Angeles

Community Action Network (LACAN)—a progressive, grassroots community organization comprised primarily of impoverished Skid Row residents—to end the Safer Cities Initiative and its related policies. Under Malcolm's leadership, the Community Watch team records officer interactions to increase accountability, mitigate police aggressiveness, and generate evidence for use in civil litigation, criminal defense, and political organizing campaigns. Whereas "Neighborhood Watch" groups, popular in more affluent neighborhoods, seek to mobilize residents to assist law enforcement and increase the police's reach, Community Watch attempts to de-escalate enforcement and constrict police influence.

Community Watch's orientation toward and interactions with Skid Row officers present a striking contrast to those detailed in the previous two chapters. Unlike Steel's crew and the Fifth Street vendors, each of which labored to evade, deflect, or preempt police contact, Malcolm and his team actively sought out as much police contact as possible. Where Steel's crew and the Fifth Street vendors primarily sought to protect *themselves* from detrimental police contact, usually at the expense of others, the Community Watch team increased their own police contact and risked arrest to protect *others*. What explains such contrary responses to policing? What led some residents to literally run toward the nearest officer while others worked diligently to stay off the police radar? What impacts did this alternative approach have on policing?

As I accompanied Malcolm on his daily patrols for over two years, I discovered that residents' divergent responses to policing were best explained by how they viewed, or "framed," the neighborhood. Frames, as described by sociologist Erving Goffman, refer to the schema of interpretation governing the subjective meanings we assign to events and occurrences.[1] Urban sociologists have recently extended this concept to the idea of "neighborhood frames." Neighborhood frames filter our perceptions about the neighborhoods in which we live.[2] We view and experience a neighborhood not "as it is," but through a neighborhood frame that highlights some aspects of the neighborhood and not others. So while one resident may proudly view her neighborhood as a beautiful place to live, another may perceive the same neighborhood as a dilapidated ghetto.[3] By shaping perceptions of a given area, neighborhood frames condition how residents act in and toward their physical and social surroundings.

In Skid Row, variations in neighborhood frames led to different forms and consequences of resistance to policing. While both Steel's crew and the Fifth Street vendors accepted (and even perpetuated) Skid Row's territorial stigma, Malcolm and the Community Watch team rejected the area's infamous reputation and stereotypes. As a result, they applied their acquired cop wisdom in a very different manner. Rather than draw on their folk ethnography of policing to evade and deflect police contact, the members of Community Watch leveraged their indigenous knowledge about policing to generate collective strategies of resistance and formal opposition capable of bringing about significant police reforms.

Neighborhood Frames and the Development of Collective and Overt Resistance

I met Malcolm a little over a year into my fieldwork, when I visited the LACAN office, at the time located near the corner of Fifth and Main Streets. During my time in Skid Row, I had come across several editions of the organization's newspaper, *The Community Connection*, which detailed its efforts to de-escalate policing in the neighborhood. As time went on, I became increasingly interested in hearing the organization's take on the policing practices I had now experienced firsthand.

Arriving at the LACAN office early on a weekday morning, I entered the small, cluttered lobby and approached an elderly, stern-looking black man seated at the front desk. When I told him I was hoping to speak with someone about policing, he told me to wait for "the Commander" to arrive. I took a seat on a weathered couch and opened up a copy of *Seize the Time*—Bobby Seale's autobiography about the formation of the Black Panther Party—that I had grabbed as I left my house an hour earlier. I sat reading, listening in on a conversation between the man at the front desk and a group of similarly aged men regarding the upcoming professional football season.

I remained quiet until Malcolm—tall, muscular, and confident— burst into the office. He had tattoos on his neck, arms, and hands with phrases like "Black Power" and "Caucazoid 187." His freshly combed hair jutted out from beneath a black beret loaded with small pins depicting outstretched fists and revolutionary slogans. Around his neck was a red, black, and green medallion in the shape of the African continent, which swayed back and forth with his smooth gait.

As he walked through the doorway, he raised his fist in the air and yelled, "All power to the people." Without solicitation, he announced to everyone in the lobby that he had just finished giving testimony at the monthly LAPD Commission meeting. In his words, he had "put all the pigs on blast."

I stood up and introduced myself, trying to explain my research as quickly and convincingly as possible. Before I could finish, however, Malcolm looked down and noticed my book. He smiled enthusiastically. It turned out to be a fortuitous choice of reading material. "You're reading about the Panthers, huh?" He dove into a lengthy description of the Community Watch program. "You see, we're trying to do this like what the Black Panthers were doing back in the day. We gotta keep an eye on the pigs and stop them from doing their pig shit." He continued to speak as he ushered me into his small cubicle office, where he showed me his photographs from a recent Black Panther reunion in northern California. We developed an instant connection.

Despite our immediate rapport and his interest in my research, Malcolm imposed an ultimatum: if I intended to study Community Watch, I would have to contribute to its efforts. In time, the organization allowed me to participate in its training sessions, which consisted of a "know your rights" curriculum, military calisthenics, and role-play exercises in which residents prepared for future police interactions. Several months after making contact with the group, I donned a dark green shirt and military fatigues, grabbed a clipboard, and trekked out with the team on my first patrol. During this initial "probation period," Malcolm limited my involvement to General Support, one of four assigned roles. General Support is in charge of writing down officers' badge numbers, witness names, and short descriptions of police interactions. I was more than happy to carry the clipboard, as it gave me even more opportunities to jot down my own notes. Once I had a better grasp of street names and landmarks in the neighborhood, Malcolm allowed me to fill the role of Communications, charged with constantly radioing in to a team member at the office and updating them on our location. I occasionally served as Videographer, recording police interactions. I did not, however, take on the fourth and final role, Point Person, which was performed exclusively by Malcolm or another veteran team member.

I spent a significant amount of time getting to know Malcolm as I shadowed him on as many as three two-hour patrols per day. As we walked through the neighborhood, we conversed at length about his biography, which was strikingly similar to Steel's. Like Steel, Malcolm grew up near the Pueblo del Rio housing project in South Central Los Angeles. As a member of the Denver Lane Bloods gang, Malcolm began using and dealing crack cocaine as it washed over the city during the 1980s. He also began robbing banks. Following a number of short jail and prison sentences, Malcolm botched a stickup in Burbank, California. Convicted on several counts of armed robbery, Malcolm remained in prison for over a decade, from 1991 to 2004. Similar to Steel, Malcolm left prison a changed man. Whereas Steel escaped his gang affiliation by devoting himself to the weight pile, Malcolm exited gang life as a result of the mentorship he received from a lieutenant in George Jackson's Black Guerilla Family, the prison arm of the Panthers. During the large portion of his sentence that he spent in solitary confinement, Malcolm devoured books on Egyptian history and Black Nationalist thought. When he returned to the general prison population, Malcolm began teaching revolutionary black history to his fellow inmates. He punctuated his transformation by shedding his legal name in favor of one that reflected his new ideology and his commitment to staying away from gangs, crime, and drugs.

Following their releases from prison, neither Steel nor Malcolm intended to return to their former South Central neighborhood. Instead, each made his way to Skid Row. On arrival, both quickly became subject to the ubiquitous nature of Skid Row policing. At that point, however, their paths diverged. Steel sought to reduce police contact by distancing himself from those who "belonged" in Skid Row, eventually fleeing the area to escape increasing police contact. In contrast, Malcolm embraced his identity as a Skid Row resident, growing more committed to collective resistance with each police interaction.

These divergent stances cannot be explained by the men's distinct ideological commitments alone. Rather, they reflect opposing neighborhood frames, informed by the different roles that the neighborhood held for either man over the course of his life. Recall that Steel and most of the men at the weight pile had largely avoided Skid Row throughout their early lives. Steel remained reluctant to identify as a resident throughout his time there. Malcolm, on the other hand, reveled in the experience. He often joked that he had felt "at home" in Skid Row from the time he was conceived in one of the neighborhood's SRO hotels. His mother and father had met and fallen in love in Skid Row when both held jobs at the Bullock's department store on Seventh and Broadway. Although his parents separated in his youth, every week Malcolm made the trip from his mother's house in the Pueblos to downtown, where he spent quality time with his father and explored the city streets.

"Pops would give me a couple dollars, or he would give me a bunch of free tickets to the theater," Malcolm told me one Saturday evening as we sat talking in the empty LACAN office. He sat next to a shopping cart full of speakers and other car audio equipment that he planned to sell later that evening. "I've always loved downtown since I was a kid. During the day, with all the businesses, you have all these people shopping, it was exciting. At night, when the stores closed, all the ballrooms and nightclubs opened and the fancy lights would light up like Vegas. There was an energy, a whole style about it. If I went out at two in the morning in South Central it would be dead. Plus, in downtown there was always money to be made. I would always do little shit for money. When I was twelve years old, I got my very first job, working at a huge toy store over on San Pedro Street. My first job. That was a big deal for me!"

Throughout his early life, Malcolm viewed "downtown" and "Skid Row" as a single neighborhood, through which he and his family moved with ease. It was to this neighborhood that he returned after his lengthy incarceration. What Steel and his crew saw as a wasteland filled with desperate addicts, Malcolm remembered as the place that entertained, employed, and sheltered him.

"This was my territory," he said proudly. "This place was always a haven for me where I could lay low and get my shit together. After I pulled a robbery, or if somebody had a hit out for me, this is where I would come. If I needed to get away for a bit, this is where I would come. When I got out, I knew this was the only place I could address my addiction without going back to the old hood."

After enrolling in and quickly absconding from a Skid Row recovery program, Malcolm moved into a subsidized SRO room on Main Street, where he eventually got sober. From this vantage point, he began noticing significant changes to his treasured neighborhood. The most noticeable change was what Malcolm frequently referred to as the growing "militarization" of Skid Row. "I look around and there's all these pigs and BIDs [business improvement district security guards] stopping people crossing the street, jacking them up. When I used to spend time down here, they weren't down here at all. Now they're on every corner. It's like they're the biggest gang around."

Malcolm found himself compelled to act when the militarization came, quite literally, to his door. One Sunday afternoon, he was sitting in the common room of his SRO hotel watching television when he heard screams coming from just outside of his building. He rushed outside with several other residents to intervene as a BID security guard detained a woman, twisting her arm behind her back. The group of neighbors forced the guard to let go of her arm and back away. Apparently the guard had grabbed the woman to confiscate what he assumed to be a crack pipe. When the woman opened her hand, it turned out that she had only been holding a small tube of eyeliner.

"Where the hell else is it OK to treat a random lady like that?" Malcolm complained as he retold the story. "When I saw that, I knew this shit had gone too far. I knew right then I had to do something. I had learned all this powerful shit in prison, but when I got out I didn't know exactly what to do with it. What I knew after seeing the way this asshole treated this lady was that I needed to start patrolling these motherfuckers before that shit happens to more people around here." Malcolm did not know exactly what to do next. But when he retold the story to a former cellmate the next week, his friend suggested that he take his idea to LACAN. The next day Malcolm made the short walk to the organization's office.

Since the launch of the Safer Cities Initiative, LACAN has been its most vocal opponent. Two longtime Skid Row community organizers established LACAN after growing dissatisfied with the "social service" and "advocacy" models that predominate in the majority of organizations in the area, most notably the mega-shelters.[4] To the co-founders, it seemed that such organizations had long and problematic histories of making decisions and advocating on behalf of area inhabitants without seeking input or participation from the individuals they purported to be assisting. Rather than advocate on behalf of Skid Row inhabitants, LACAN attempts to teach them to advocate for themselves and each other. LACAN began pursuing this resident-driven organizing model by working on issues surrounding civil rights, housing, health, food access, and gender equity.

LACAN has grown significantly since its founding. A nine-member board of directors steers the actions of the approximately seven hundred members, almost all of whom reside within Skid Row's boundaries. The organization employs four full-time and one part-time staff organizers, as well as two interns, nearly all of whom also live in Skid

Row. Mirroring the demographic characteristics of the neighborhood, roughly 70 percent of LACAN members are black, and three-quarters live in one of the nearby SRO hotels. Like many of their neighbors, a number of those involved with the organization experienced periods without stable housing, faced incarceration, and struggled with addiction throughout the duration of my fieldwork.

Given the organization's makeup and approach, Malcolm felt an instant connection. He spent several hours speaking with staff members and returned the following day. LACAN leaders received Malcolm's idea about monitoring officers with enthusiasm. They gave him a disposable camera and a clipboard and told him to begin taking pictures of overly aggressive officers. Over the next months, Malcolm assembled a group of like-minded residents. In November 2005, when enough team members had been amassed to conduct daily patrols, LACAN formally announced the launch of the Community Watch program. Finding new purpose, Malcolm devoted his waking hours to documenting police behavior. A year later, LACAN hired him as a full-time organizer.

Not all of those who joined Community Watch or LACAN shared Malcolm's black militant politics. Members' views spanned a broad ideological range, with Malcolm's at the most radical pole. All of these individuals, however, shared a neighborhood frame that envisioned Skid Row as a viable and "real" community. As it had for Malcolm, this frame originated in what we might think of as "moments of community"—that is, key biographical junctures in which individuals recognized similarity and solidarity with fellow residents and, as a result, developed a personal connection to, and stake in, the neighborhood and its inhabitants.

The story of Herb, a stubborn white man in his seventies who frequented the LACAN office every day, epitomizes this phenomenon. Having lived in LA for most of his adult life, Herb had always assumed the worst about Skid Row's impoverished, predominantly black population. On several occasions, he recalled having difficulty understanding why blacks "complained so much" about their lot in life. This all changed in 2000, however, when Herb found himself penniless and unhoused after falling into an unexpected coma. While he was in the coma, his former life unraveled. Unable to pay his mortgage, he lost his home. His wife became suicidal, and the county took away his children. His hospital stay maxed out his health insurance. Kicked out of the hospital and lacking other options, he made his way to Skid Row and began sleeping in Pershing Square Park.

"Something really crazy happened while I was down here," Herb told me in his gruff tone, as we rested on one of the couches following a tiring Community Watch patrol. "All the people in the park, who had been there and knew the area, all these people that I used to look down on, they became my best friends. And they looked after me. They told me where and when to sleep and helped me get food. I realized that these are good people, just like me. They didn't deserve to have the police coming and clearing them out of the park all the time." Once he began receiving SSI payments, Herb secured a room in a nearby SRO hotel. Yet he did not turn his back on his newfound friends. He continued spending several hours in the park each day, bringing sandwiches and other food to share. As police harassment escalated following the launch of SCI, Herb joined LACAN in part to better protect those who still slept in the park.

In fact, LACAN originated in just such a moment of community. Two months after I began participating in Community Watch patrols, one of the founding members of LACAN accompanied me on a walk through the neighborhood. When we reached the corner of Fifth and Crocker Streets, he pointed to a building across the intersection, which had been the scene of a life-altering tragedy.

"Way back," he began, "my cousin was shot down right there. He and a friend were coming out of the treatment center and two guys rolled up to rob them. They tried to defend themselves. One of them shot my cousin a few times. The man ran off, and he turned this corner right here. What happened next was that a bunch of members of the community chased this guy down. He had a gun and they chased him and they caught him. They jumped on him and held him down until the police came." We continued along the route as he retraced the events. "I think that really shows what I'm always talking about. This community was looking out for him. The city and the LAPD always want to argue that there is no community down here. But, in reality, all you have to do is come down here and if they actually got out of their squad cars and talked to people, they'd see there is a strong community. I see it all the time."

Whereas the peer groups profiled in the previous two chapters understood community in exclusive terms, as something accomplished *in spite of* the neighborhood's defining conditions, those involved with LACAN adhered to a far more inclusive ideal, extending bonds of community even to those who might strike a casual observer as deviant and criminal. Members like Malcolm, Herb, and others refused to accept the dominant, derogatory stereotypes of their neighborhood.[5] "They look at Skid Row like it's the pits of hell," Malcolm complained once, speaking of no one in particular. "They can't see anything good coming from out of here. Just all negative. They think everybody is on parole or probation; that everyone is a dopefiend." The statement describes the outlook of city officials and Central Division officers as well as that of Steel, Big Ron, and the other men who gathered at the weight pile.

According to those involved with LACAN, negative assumptions about the neighborhood existed in a mutually reinforcing relationship with policing. Blanket stigmatization facilitated the city's decision to flood the neighborhood with officers. The massive number of citations and arrests that resulted served to confirm outsiders' notions of the inherent deviance and criminality of those living in Skid Row. This in turn facilitated more policing. Malcolm described this feedback loop as a kind of self-fulfilling prophecy. "Do you know why people use drugs and alcohol in the first place?" he asked me on an evening patrol after passing a group of intoxicated men sharing a bottle of whiskey. "It's because they're bored. And they're depressed. They don't have any jobs so they just have to sit around. Or they end up homeless. But! They can't get those jobs because of all these bullshit arrests! That kind of shit holds us back. How is anybody supposed to survive with all these pigs jacking everybody up? How are you supposed to get a job now that you've got a criminal record? They come by and arrest everybody for stupid little shit, then they just say, 'Look! They really are just a bunch of criminals. Just a bunch of animals!'"

Rather than accept the popular image of Skid Row as an anarchic jungle, LACAN members viewed Skid Row as a legitimate residential neighborhood. Given their meager incomes, low levels of education, and tumultuous biographies, these residents recognized Skid Row—with its saturation of affordable housing, inexpensive food, and emergency resources—as the only neighborhood in which they might ever find some semblance of stability. Like Malcolm, these residents sprang to action when new policing policies began to threaten this possibility.

Fighting Criminalization and Stigma through Community Watch Patrols

As they embarked on their collective effort to combat ubiquitous and aggressive policing, LACAN members found themselves hampered by the exact territorial stigma they rejected. In their earliest campaigns, they attempted to convince local political leaders about the detrimental effects of ubiquitous criminalization. The organization's contentions, however, fell on deaf, or at best skeptical, ears. To begin with, visible signs of its members' low status handicapped their attempts to make their voices heard. Physical signs of poverty, including missing teeth and mismatched clothing, combined with marginal levels of education, limited public speaking experience, and criminal records in ways that confirmed their audiences' preexisting assumptions about Skid Row inhabitants. I witnessed this denigrating process firsthand when LACAN members testified during the public comment period of LA City Council and the LA Police Commission hearings. Residents' appearances during "normal working hours" not only produced skepticism about their claims but opened them to ridicule and lectures by council members on the moral uplift of looking for work (instead of complaining to public officials).

Malcolm lamented the compounding effects of Skid Row's territorial stigma as the two of us walked out of a particularly hostile city council meeting. "You've got all these people down here yelling and screaming about what the LAPD is doing to them," he complained. "But these phonies up in city hall just look at us like, 'Oh, what's that? You're black? *And* you live in Skid Row? Get the hell out of here, you bunch of crackhead bums!'"

The design of Community Watch explicitly addressed this skepticism by capturing unwarranted detainments and the resulting searches, citations, and arrests on tape. LACAN members anticipated that objective video evidence of such practices would make up for their lack of credibility. Much to their frustration, however, they learned that the spatial vilification of Skid Row and its residents carried more weight than they had imagined. Even with hundreds of hours of video recordings, assumptions about Skid Row and its residents continued to delegitimize what the organization saw as clear-cut examples of police mistreatment and abuse.

An incident in the summer of 2007 brought this dilemma home. LACAN members recorded a video of several officers punching, kicking, and tackling an elderly resident named Joe Nelson. Rendered unconscious by multiple blows to his head, Nelson had to be removed from the scene in an ambulance. Working with Nelson's defense attorney, LACAN introduced the footage in Nelson's criminal trial. The organization also provided several residents as eyewitnesses. The recording and testimony, however, was overshadowed by the contrasting narrative provided by the arresting officers. They argued that Nelson had proactively invited them to converse with him, and then he unexpectedly began throwing small pieces of crack cocaine into his mouth as part of a sudden psychotic episode. The officers testified that their use of force was intended to dislodge the narcotics from Nelson's mouth, both to ensure his safety and to preserve physical evidence. Their use of force was not only justified, they claimed, but carried out for Nelson's own good.

In providing this alternative account, the officers introduced crucial contextual information that LACAN's video could not counter. This meant that even though LACAN had been able to introduce brutal and disturbing footage, the dispute once again hinged on the credibility of the contesting parties. Unsurprisingly, the officers' narrative won the day. The court found no misuse of force and convicted Nelson on drug possession charges, despite multiple residents' eyewitness testimony that Nelson had been tossing sunflower seeds into his mouth, not crack cocaine.

The Nelson trial proved to be a critical juncture in the development of Community Watch. The team learned that passively recording unconstitutional, unwarranted, or inappropriate police behaviors would not be enough, no matter how glaring or obvious those actions appeared. To increase the credibility of their footage, Community Watch developed two new patrol practices intended to curtail officers' opportunities to offer effective counternarratives. First, the team made new efforts to document police interactions from start to finish. This meant following officers throughout their patrols, chasing after police cruisers driving toward potential crime scenes, anticipating likely locations for police stops, and generally "being in the right place at the right time." Doing so would put the team in a better position to capture the precipitating events and contextual information surrounding a given instance of police contact. Community Watch members reasoned that if they had captured such information in the Nelson case, they would have been able to prove that contact with the officers was nonconsensual, that Nelson had not behaved erratically, and that Nelson had indeed been eating sunflower seeds. Second, Community Watch members became more proactive in interrogating officers while the cameras were rolling, asking them to provide contemporaneous and potentially incriminating narrations of events that would be difficult to alter or amend at a later date. Such footage would, essentially, appropriate police officers' elevated credibility to make up for residents' own discredited status.

These practices would likely have proven difficult, if not impossible, for residents hailing from middle- or upper-class neighborhoods, where ubiquitous policing and surveillance do not define daily life. The ability to record contextual and precipitating events depends on accurately predicting when and where officers will make contact with inhabitants. Compelling officers to self-impeach on camera requires a deep familiarity with officers' interactional tendencies and patterns. But much like Steel's crew and the Fifth Street vendors, LACAN members possessed an immense amount of cop wisdom by virtue of their residence in the neighborhood. Instead of using their folk analyses of policing to circumvent or preclude police contact, however, Community Watch members leveraged their cop wisdom to intensify and exploit interactions with officers.

In the hands of residents like Malcolm, Herb, and others, cop wisdom became the foundation of what social movement scholars call "tactical innovations."[6] Tactical innovations are creative strategies that social movement actors and organizations devise to "overcome the basic powerlessness that has confined them to a position of institutionalized political impotence."[7] As the Community Watch case demonstrates, however, such innovations often provide only a temporary advantage. In chesslike fashion, Central Division officers responded with a series of countermeasures, or "tactical adaptations," to neutralize Community Watch's efforts and reinstitute the original power disparities. Given this back-and-forth dynamic, Community Watch's ultimate success hinged largely on its ability to consistently innovate and stay one step ahead of officers.

Capturing Precipitating Events and Contextual Information

The Community Watch team initially struggled to document police detainments, citations, and arrests from start to finish. Traveling Skid Row's fifty blocks on foot, they often arrived on a scene only after an officer had detained a suspect. As the Nelson trial demonstrated, the decontextualized footage they produced had limited influence.[8] In the months following that verdict, however, the team began to generate more comprehensive footage by employing its members' cop wisdom. By reading the surrounding street scenes in light of the disruptions caused by police interventions, the team literally tracked officers through the neighborhood—an activity that Malcolm sometimes referred to as "pig hunting." Engaging in this practice allowed the team to better predict future police contact and thereby position themselves in the right place at the right time.

During one typical afternoon patrol, Malcolm and I walked out of the LACAN office on Main Street and headed toward the center of Skid Row via our normal route along Fifth Street. Two additional Community Watch members, in matching green T-shirts, walked at a slower pace several yards behind us. Mark, a soft-spoken black veteran of the Vietnam era, limped slightly as he descended the gradual slope that led into the neighborhood from the adjacent downtown. He was flanked by Patti, a black woman in her late sixties, who took great care to always walk on the side of the street that provided the most shade from the glaring summer sun. As usual, Malcolm struggled to contain his annoyance at the fact that Mark, Patti, and other team members had a hard time keeping up with him. Like most days, he and I walked well ahead, engrossed in our usual conversation about policing.

As had become his custom, Malcolm paused when the two of us reached the intersection of Fifth and San Julian Streets. He stood in silent concentration, carefully surveying the block. Directly behind us, San Julian Park overflowed with activity and the sound of heated games of dominoes and spades. The empty sidewalks outside, on what was typically one of the neighborhood's busiest thoroughfares, stood out in contrast.

"You see this?" Malcolm asked me, while continuing to stare down San Julian. "You can tell the pigs were just here."

"Yeah? It is pretty quiet," I responded.

"See that wall?" he said, gesturing toward half a block of sidewalk next to the entrance to the Union Rescue Mission, currently shaded by a tall warehouse building. "Right now, at this time of day, there should be a grip of people posted up right there. But ain't nobody there now. You can tell they all ran over here into the park. It's usually safe in there. The pigs let the security guards handle that jurisdiction."

Mark appeared at my side. "The cops were just here," he said, unaware that Malcolm had made the exact same observation only moments earlier. "You know how I know?" he asked us, in an instructional tone. Malcolm sighed in annoyance. Mark was fond of finding opportunities to prove his authority, whether on policing, politics, or football. "How many people do you see sitting down?"

I looked up and down the street. A lone man sat on the curb, eating takeout from a small restaurant on the next block. "Just that dude," I answered with a shrug.

Mark continued. "He must have just got there. Everybody else is waiting to see if they're coming back. What they do is give everybody a warning. They tell them to get up, then they circle the block and arrest the ones that sat back down. That's how they got Tim [one of Mark's friends]." Looking at the conditions on the street, Mark suspected that officers had recently engaged in an instance of prowling—a patrol practice (described in chapter 2) in which officers drive up and down the street ordering everyone to stand up and vacate the sidewalks adjacent to the mega-shelters.

Malcolm chimed in with his own opinion, entering into the kind of collective analyses that unfolded on nearly every Community Watch patrol. "Naw," he began authoritatively. "I think it was *more* than that. It was a *big* bust. Shit, it's dead out here. You know what they probably did?" he offered. "They probably blocked off the street at both ends so they could do their investigation, making sure everybody cleared out of the crime scene. That's why they're all bunched up on the ends of the street. This was bigger than just some bullshit harassment."

As if on cue, a young man in a long white T-shirt and baggy jeans emerged from the park and approached Malcolm. "Commander," he said quietly as he positioned himself at Malcolm's side.

"Sup wit it?" Malcolm replied, greeting him with a nonchalant fist bump.

The man went on to confirm Malcolm's suspicion of a large drug bust. "You guys just missed the whole thing," he said. "The narcs came out of *nowhere*. They arrested about eight niggas. Man, they got a *gang* of shit on all these motherfuckers. You should have seen what they pulled out their pockets, G. That's some promotion type shit right there." I noticed that he and Malcolm remained standing shoulder to shoulder, keeping their eyes forward as they spoke. They both appeared intent on masking the fact of their conversation. To me, it felt eerily similar to the kinds of interactions that officers have with their confidential informants. "I'm thinking they must have had some undercovers in the crowd setting up the buy," the man concluded in a satisfied tone. "That's how they knew exactly who to go after."

Malcolm perked up upon hearing this. "Undercovers, huh?"

"Yep."

"That means they got the jump-out crew running today," Malcolm said. By this, he meant the undercover narcotics squads deployed under SCI to conduct buy/bust stings (see chapter 2). "You say that was about ten minutes ago?"

"Less. Like five," the man replied.

"Damn," Malcolm said as he stepped off the curb and quickly began walking eastward on Fifth Street, toward the Bottom.

As I walked quickly to catch up with Malcolm, I marveled at what had just unfolded. The young man's information confirmed that Malcolm had accurately discerned the specifics of police activity merely by assessing the distribution of people, behaviors, and general conditions in public space. On other occasions, I had witnessed Malcolm piece together past police activity based solely on the droppings left by officers' horses. Malcolm frequently followed trails of droppings, working from the oldest to the freshest, to sneak up on mounted officers and film their interactions with residents before officers noticed the cameras. By paying attention to the spacing of the droppings, Malcolm could also predict the tenor of the interactions that awaited him at the end of the trail. Closely clustered droppings signaled aggressive enforcement, with officers stopping frequently to detain, interrogate, and issue citations to pedestrians.

"If we hurry, we'll catch them," Malcolm told me as I walked to his side. He glanced behind us and noticed that Mark and Patti had fallen behind. "Damn. Always this shit," he complained. "If they could just walk a little faster, we could get over there before the jump-outs start trying to make their buys."

After another five minutes of walking, the two of us approached an intersection and Malcolm lowered his voice. "See this over here?" he asked me, subtly motioning toward a police cruiser parked a half block down the street. From our vantage point I saw two officers sitting in the front seats. "That's a chase car," Malcolm said. "It's all part of the jump-out squad. They send dudes in, dressed like addicts, to make a buy. Then, when the other guy comes back with the shit, he calls on the radio to the chase cars. These guys come in and make the actual bust so the guy on the inside doesn't blow his cover. He just walks off and starts up the next buy. If that chase car is right there, then that means they got an operation going down somewhere close, on one of these other blocks." He increased his pace once more. "Come on," he said over his shoulder.

Malcolm came to an abrupt stop when he reached the next intersection. He stood with his back pressed against a nearby brick wall and peeked around the corner. "I bet this is where they sent the guy in," he said in a hushed voice. "Check it out." I followed his lead, poking my head out from the cover of the wall to peer down the street. Among the various pedestrians walking up and down the sidewalks, I noticed roughly twenty people congregating on the shady part of the block. "That's a big group," he said. "If the jump-outs aren't already in there, they're about to be." He stepped out from behind the wall. "Wait for Patti and Mark. I'm gonna go do some recon. Get the camera ready in case they make their move. I'll get them from up close." I watched as Malcolm walked down the sidewalk and nonchalantly blended into the group.

Over the previous months, Malcolm had increasingly engaged in these "reverse stings," as he called them, lying in wait at the site of likely undercover narcotics operations. The Community Watch team embedded itself into street corner groups and watched the police as the police watched residents. A few minutes later Patti and Mark arrived and, without a word, fell in next to me as I continued to hide behind the wall. They knew this technique well enough not to ask what Malcolm was doing.

Less than five minutes later, Malcolm's predictions were borne out yet again, as two patrol cars sped down the street, sirens blaring. Two unmarked cars, driven by plainclothes officers, followed behind. The three of us hustled down the street to join Malcolm with our cameras. The officers slammed their vehicles to a halt in front of the group, jumped out, and immediately placed four men in handcuffs.

"Did you see him?" Malcolm asked us as I arrived, keeping his eye on the commotion.

"See who?" Patti asked in response.

"Did you see a undercover?" Malcolm clarified, growing annoyed.

"Naw," I replied.

Malcolm shook his head in frustration. "Damn! Me neither. I didn't see nobody that looked like a pig. It was just a bunch of residents standing around. That means they just rolled up on these guys without no real evidence or nothing. Be sure to get this whole thing on tape. We can use this to show that they're just jumping out on people for just standing here. That's some bullshit search and seizure right there. They just make their arrests and then figure out their probable cause afterward."

While there was no way to be certain in that moment, I had faith in Malcolm's assessment. Over the past few months, Community Watch had compiled a binder containing photos of all the undercover narcotics officers and their unmarked cars. They continued to update the book as the division added new officers and vehicles. If Malcolm had not recognized any of the pedestrians as undercover officers, there likely were not any there.

The team stood recording the incident for the next twenty minutes, until the officers loaded the suspects in the back of their cars and sped westward on Fifth Street in the direction of the Central Division station. Like San Julian Street had been earlier, the block was now deserted except for a few pedestrians who had remained to watch the arrests from a safe distance. "We got these motherfuckers," Malcolm said as he watched the last patrol car round the corner. Pleased with the team's ability to capture what appeared to be an unwarranted detainment, Malcolm called an end to our patrol and led us back to the office to debrief and complete the postpatrol paperwork.

Over the course of the next year, it became apparent that Community Watch was not the only party refashioning its strategies. As Community Watch became more successful in anticipating police contact, officers tactically adapted. They sowed unpredictability into their routines and intensified their acts of intimidation. On one occasion, for instance, two undercover officers in an unmarked car led the team on a frustrating game of cat and mouse through the streets of the Bottom. The events unfolded as the Community Watch team turned a corner and spotted an undercover narcotics car that Malcolm recognized from the photographs in his binder. Walking single-file, pressed closely to the wall, the team quietly approached the car in hopes of recording the officers' next interaction with residents. When the team was a half block away, the driver peeled off. Rather than leave the area, however, the driver parked on a nearby cross street, just within our view. Confused, the team jogged to the car's new location. When the team got close, the driver sped off again and parked on the next block, still within our view. The team followed the car again, only to have it speed away. This continued for the next forty-five minutes, with the team zigzagging up and down various streets in pursuit of the car. Just as we were about to give up, the car made a sudden U-turn, raced toward us, and slammed to a stop only feet away.

The two officers sat laughing hysterically. "Hey guys," the officer in the driver seat called out of his open window. "Why don't you just hop in the back?" He motioned to the back seat, where arrestees sit.

"You'll get some better shots. It'll be faster, and you won't have to walk so much!" He grinned widely, spun the tires, and sped off once more.

Disheartened, Malcolm terminated the day's patrol on the spot. No one said much on the walk back to the office. For the team, it was a humiliating end to an aggravating afternoon. The team's spirits lifted, however, when I informed them that I had been able to record the incident on camera. I knew that Community Watch had been collecting instances like these to substantiate their claims about officers' repeated acts of intimidation. So while no one on the team could say they enjoyed these kinds of exchanges, Malcolm and the team actually began encouraging them.

"Catching Them Slipping"

As the team stood recording police stops, they deployed interactional techniques intended to, in the words of those associated with Community Watch, "catch the cops slipping." On the most basic level, catching officers slipping meant engaging, confusing, and at times provoking officers in such a way that they offered up self-incriminating information and narratives. Ironically, the Community Watch team borrowed this technique from the police. The team had begun mimicking the very interrogation style to which neighborhood residents were constantly subjected.

During one of Community Watch's monthly "know your rights" training sessions, attended by a half dozen residents, Gerald, a quiet resident in his early thirties, described how police consistently attempted to catch him and his neighbors slipping. "All the cops down here got these little tricks," he told the group sitting around a large table in the back room of the LACAN office. "I'm always telling everybody in my building they don't gotta say *nothing* to these cops. *Nothing.* Just give your name and that's it. And then ask if you're under arrest. If they say you ain't, then you're really free to dip!" He held out a slender finger as he lectured. "Now," he continued, "everybody knows this, but when they get hemmed up by the cops, they start singing like a bird. The cop's going to always start with simple questions. But in reality they're not simple at all. They do that to put you to sleep, to trip you up, and then they got you." His voice dropped an octave as he impersonated an officer asking a barrage of questions. "'Where do you live? Where are you going? You on parole? You got anything on you I need to know about? Can I pat you down just to make sure?'" Gerald did a cutting motion across his neck with his hand as he posed this last question. "And that's a wrap! Guess what? You just consented to a search. Now they see that the address on your ID is different from the one you gave them. Now they say you lied to them. Now they say they gotta take you down to the station. Now you're sitting there in handcuffs in booking. All because you didn't shut your damn mouth. That whole time, they were just waiting for you to open your mouth so they could catch you slipping."

Having been subjected to this savvy interrogation technique themselves, the Community Watch team appropriated the method and turned it back on officers. Like officers' line of questioning, catching officers slipping proceeded through a particular sequence. First, team members drew officers into what appeared to be an innocuous exchange. Once they had adequately engaged officers, they gradually escalated the conversation, shifting the interaction toward something that resembled a cross-examination. Then they pressed officers with unexpected questions and accusatory statements to elicit responses that confirmed the organization's long-standing accusations.

The team's efforts to catch officers slipping became readily apparent when they began collecting video evidence to support their claims that Central Division continued to violate a recent court order. In 2008, LACAN and the American Civil Liberties Union (ACLU) won a federal injunction—known as the Fitzgerald Injunction—that prohibited Skid Row officers from handcuffing and searching pedestrians cited for jaywalking and other minor offenses, and from inquiring if pedestrians were on probation or parole.[9] The court also mandated division-wide training on constitutionally permissible forms of search and seizure. Despite the ruling, residents complained that officers continued to handcuff and search them at the same rate.

I accompanied Malcolm and three other members of the team during one of the subsequent patrols. About a half hour in, the team came across two mounted officers searching a man in the course of issuing him a citation—a clear violation of the Fitzgerald injunction. As the officers remounted, the team discreetly turned on the cameras as Malcolm tried to catch them slipping.

"Hey, can I ask you a question?" he called out in a polite, nonconfrontational tone. With the cameras rolling, Malcolm intentionally attempted to sound like someone requesting help or directions. This subtle opening did more than simply grab the officers' attention. By accepting Malcolm's initial request, the officers opened themselves to subsequent and more damning questions. If they outright denied the initiating question (officers who recognized Malcolm did this quite often), or departed without responding to the subsequent question, the interaction provided evidence for LACAN's claim that Central Division disrespected and disdained Skid Row residents. This type of footage ran counter to the division's desired image as community liaisons.

After the officers nodded their heads, giving Malcolm permission, he launched in. "Now, don't you know it's illegal to search for minor offenses and ask people if they are on probation or parole?"

The officers appeared genuinely confused. They both squirmed a bit in their saddles and looked to one another for help. After a long silence, both shook their heads. "No," one of them finally said. They looked at Malcolm as if waiting for him to fill them in.

Instead, Malcolm only gave them a sarcastic chuckle. "So your sergeant has never told you about the Fitzgerald Injunction?" he asked.

"Nope," the officer replied, his confidence returning. Malcolm asked the question again. "Naw . . . nope," the officer responded once more.

With this, the officers led their horses away from us. As the clatter of the hooves faded up the street, Malcolm turned to me with a widening smile. "Man," he said. "They're supposed to be trained and briefed in this stuff! Obviously they're not. And we got them on tape saying that shit too."

Through his repeated questioning, Malcolm not only documented that Central Division officers continued to violate the injunction; he also produced footage indicating why. The officers' reactions on tape suggested that Central Division had not yet trained its officers, in direct defiance of the court order. Malcolm added this video to the growing collection of footage that the organization planned to present to the court to demonstrate lack of compliance.

While subtle, the production of this kind of evidence has important consequences in addressing police misconduct and brutality. Officials' ability to individualize misconduct and brutality as the problem of a few "rogue cops" presents a perpetual challenge to marginal groups attempting to gain redress and press for police reforms.[10] The rogue cop narrative explains unconstitutional policing as an anomaly that can be addressed through normal departmental channels, without larger structural changes to policy or departmental culture. In coaxing officers to offer up information about their (lack of) training, Malcolm generated evidence for a "systemic claim" showing that officers' unconstitutional behavior is a patterned problem, endemic to Central Division's organization and management.[11]

Yet, as with the team's tactical innovation in predicting and tracking police movements through the neighborhood, Central Division officers eventually caught on and adapted to Community Watch's efforts to catch them slipping. Their most immediate and overt countermove was to curtail Community Watch's ability to record police behavior altogether by arresting members of the team and confiscating their cameras and clipboards for "interfering with a police investigation." While California law permits citizens to film police officers in public, the law does not specify how far observers must stand from an incident. Officers capitalized on this ambiguity by accusing the team of not providing a wide enough berth and thereby putting officers in danger. Under threat of arrest, officers forced the team to maintain a distance that precluded their capturing statements on tape.

Walking this thin and arbitrary line every day, team members knew that any given patrol could potentially end in a jail cell. During my time with Community Watch, a handful of team members were arrested while on patrol. The constant threat of arrest created an incredible tension that did not dissipate when team members hung up their cameras for the day and ventured back out into their neighborhood. As residents, they were subject to increased surveillance and detainments when they went about their daily lives. For instance, Malcolm, Mark, and the man who filmed the Nelson incident were all arrested on suspicion of narcotics distribution while merely hanging out with friends and neighbors. The charges were eventually dropped. During the trial, however, the arresting officers indicated that they had recognized the men primarily on account of their activities on Community Watch.

Officers further capitalized on their law enforcement powers to intimidate team members into putting their cameras down. In one common technique, officers "reminded" those on Community Watch that they had personal knowledge of their places of residence, histories of addiction, criminal records, and other intimate biographical information. For several months following one of Malcolm's arrests, officers *not* involved with the case repeatedly approached the team, addressed Malcolm by his legal name, and loudly publicized various private details about his pending trial. During one particular patrol, I walked with Malcolm and the team down a quiet street in the Bottom. Three squad cars slowly pulled behind us. As each car passed, the officers sitting in the passenger seats called out to us.

"Hey John," the first yelled in an overly friendly tone.

"Good morning, Mr. Washington," called the next through a grin.

"Good luck with your trial, John," the officer in the final car said, with a delicate Ms. America wave.

Despite the fact that the team had near-weekly interactions with these officers during Community Watch patrols, there had been no occasion for them to learn Malcolm's legal name. Their sarcastic and coordinated greetings were clearly intended to let Malcolm know that Central Division officers were actively sharing his personal information among their ranks.[12]

While Malcolm saw these thinly veiled threats of retribution as proof of Community Watch's effectiveness, and of officers' growing fear of the patrols, I counted three team members who stopped participating in Community Watch due to their anxiety about retaliation. I myself felt pressured to terminate my fieldwork when officers began directing their intimidation techniques toward me. When a few of the officers with whom I had become friendly in the early stages of my fieldwork saw me with LACAN, they accused me of "switching sides." When they encountered me in the neighborhood, particularly when I was *not* flanked by the Community Watch team, they frequently called out to me by name via their squad cars' PA systems. On one occasion, I stood conversing with a man waiting in line for a bed at the Midnight Mission when a police cruiser pulled up. The driver called out to me. "Forrest," he said, his voice crackling over the speaker. "Yes, you. Forrest. In the blue shirt. Forrest. You're *still* down here? Let me know when you want to hear the truth about Skid Row." The officer capped his statement with a short, piercing blast of his siren before driving off. I turned back to resume my conversation, but the man refused to continue speaking with me. The officers' familiarity with and animosity toward me clearly made him uncomfortable.

At times, officers took this move one step further by provoking fellow residents to lash out at the Community Watch, and thus force the team to cease filming. The two undercover narcotics officers that had led the team up and down the streets in the Bottom particularly favored this approach. On an evening Community Watch patrol, the team had begun recording these officers rifling through the pockets of a man they had detained outside of the Union Rescue Mission. As soon as the team turned on its cameras, one of the officers walked closer to the suspect and whispered in his ear. "Smile," I heard him say, too quietly to be picked up on tape. "Your video is going on the LAPD website for your friends and family to see."

The man's eyes immediately grew wide. "Turn that fucking camera off," he yelled at the top of his lungs. "You heard me," the man continued, growing more irate. The officers laughed quietly behind him as he continued. "Turn off that god-damned camera. Get the fuck out of my face with those cameras." The team immediately stopped recording. They knew that scenes of residents lashing out at the team would tarnish the organization's claims that it worked on behalf of the community. For Community Watch, this footage had become unusable.

When officers could not force Community Watch to put down its cameras, they resorted to a far more subtle countermove that served to contaminate any images Community Watch might present to future viewers. Officers reclaimed the perceptual field by bringing attention back to particular individuals, behaviors, and conditions that accentuated LACAN's crisis of credibility. This gave rise to a kind of conversational tug-of-war in which both parties wrestled to graft a desired narrative onto the videos produced on patrol.

A prime example of these kinds of struggles unfolded between the Community Watch team and a pair of horse-mounted officers. For the duration of my fieldwork, LACAN consistently viewed the mounted patrols as emblematic of the hypocrisy underlying SCI. The city often justified this policing policy as a remedy to the filth, disorder, and unhealthy conditions characterizing Skid Row. Yet, as LACAN argued, by failing to clean up after the horses, thereby leaving feces all over the sidewalks, the department had a hand in creating those conditions. On this particular afternoon, Malcolm set out to collect evidence of officers' willful negligence. The team followed a trail of horse droppings from outside of the Central Division station to a quiet corner in the Bottom, where we found the mounted officers wrapping up a narcotics arrest. As the officers snapped on their black latex gloves and loaded the arrestee into the back of a police van and remounted their horses, Malcolm called out to the closest officer.

"So officer," he said, pointing to the mound of feces on the sidewalk that one of the horses had left. "You gonna clean up that crap or what?" Malcolm was attempting to call attention to the precise moment in which officers make the decision *not* to clean up after their horses.

The officer paused for a second. He glanced at the camera and

Video still of officer sweeping horse droppings.

seemed to be weighing his options. He apparently came to a decision and let out a begrudging sigh. He dismounted and began using the inside of his boot to sweep the brown pile into the nearby gutter.

The officer made a few passes before looking up at Malcolm. Rather than respond antagonistically, however, the officer used the opportunity to graft new contextual information onto the recording. "You're trying to get me to say something inappropriate on camera," he said confidently. "You're not gonna catch me saying anything inappropriate on camera." With this statement, the officer offered an alternative explanation for the events at hand. He raised the possibility that Malcolm's underlying motive might not have been to improve neighborhood cleanliness, but rather to bait officers into *uncharacteristically* lashing out.

The officer continued on this course as he reversed scrutiny back onto the Community Watch team. He made two more passes with his boot before abruptly stopping, looking at Malcolm, and then back at his partner. "You see that jailhouse tattoo he's got?" he called out in a conspicuously loud voice, drawing everyone's attention to the scratchy prison tattoos on Malcolm's neck. "You like that?" he asked out loud. "It says 'Death to Whitey.'" With this move, the officer not only reminded future viewers of Malcolm's status as an ex-convict, but also raised the possibility that racist desires fueled Malcolm's attempts to humiliate a white officer. Casting Malcolm as the aggressor, the officer further implied that the antagonisms caught on tape might be more accurately attributed to Malcolm's interference. These possibilities cut deep into LACAN's claims that they were acting on behalf of Skid Row residents. From the streets to the courtroom, LAPD personnel and representatives attempted to portray the organization as out of touch with the true interests and needs of Skid Row. When officers made this claim successfully, video evidence lost its representativeness. If this happened, Community Watch could no longer use footage of officers' hostility toward the team as proof of officers' treatment of Skid Row inhabitants more generally.

In response, Malcolm attempted to wrestle control of the narrative back from the officer, reasserting his motivations and connection to fellow residents. "Thanks for keeping my community clean," he said through a wide smile.

"What?" the officer snapped back at him. He seemed to be uncertain whether Malcolm had said something confrontational.

"Thanks for keeping my community clean," Malcolm repeated in an even more affable tone. By thanking the officer *on behalf* of the community, Malcolm deflected the officer's attempt to separate him from his neighbors. He also countered the race-baiting claim. The response clearly tripped up the officer. He paused at Malcolm's unexpected politeness. After a moment of silence, he shot the team one final disapproving look and spurred his horse away.

The team walked back to the office in high spirits, comically recounting the events. The presence of the cameras had compelled the officer to treat them with a level of deference that they rarely experienced. The team had forced the officer to alter his behavior. They took pleasure in watching the officer use his boots to shovel horse feces.

It did come at a price, however. While the officer submitted to the team's rather embarrassing request, he had nonetheless been able to undermine the efficacy of the footage by casting doubt on the team's underlying motives. Thus, despite celebrating the incident over the following weeks, Community Watch never once presented the video in a public forum. They instead relied on more "obvious" footage that contained less damning personal information about team members.[13]

As the tug-of-war over video footage ensued, Community Watch and Central Division officers increasingly implicated suspects and bystanders in their attempts to graft their contesting narratives onto footage. By enlisting nearby pedestrians as "props" in their performances, they offered proof about the way Skid Row "really was," while creating dissonance in their opponent's desired narrative. For Community Watch, this meant cultivating favorable responses from residents that portrayed the team as the representative defender of the community. Unsurprisingly, this posed little difficulty. I did not encounter a single resident who enjoyed being detained, searched, cited, arrested, or jailed.[14] Many protested loudly, hurling profanities at officers. A smaller number put up physical resistance by refusing to spread their legs for a search or by moving their arms in a manner that made them difficult to handcuff. Throughout my fieldwork, I witnessed five detainees who attempted to flee, bolting from the scene when officers returned to their squad cars to run the suspect's name through the police database.

Given the reputation of LACAN and Community Watch throughout the neighborhood, most suspects tended to grow bolder when Community Watch appeared on the scene. Some cried to the team for help, pleading for them to continue recording. Suspects and bystanders sometimes filled in the contextual information that Community Watch aimed to collect. These individuals provided the team with their names and addresses, to be passed along to the public defender's office or the ACLU.

In response, officers frequently threatened to arrest Community Watch members if they spoke with suspects. When officers failed to make good on these threats, they pursued an alternative strategy of refocusing attention on the wrongdoings of those who became excited by the team's arrival. For example, during an afternoon patrol the team encountered a mounted officer arresting a disheveled, unhoused woman. Sitting in handcuffs next to a collection of suitcases and bags, the woman perked up when she saw the team approach.

"Hey," she beckoned in a quiet voice. "Hey. Hey. Tell him I didn't do anything. Hey."

The officer had been busy radioing for a van to transport the woman to booking when he heard her calling out to us. "Hush," he sternly ordered, as he pulled an iPhone from his pocket and began taking his own video of Malcolm's team.

The two sides spent the next few minutes awkwardly filming one another. After a brief exchange, the officer smiled slightly, snapped on a black latex glove, and picked up a small hypodermic needle that had been resting at his feet. He held it up high for us to see it as he continued to record with his camera phone.

Behind me, one of the other team members sighed in defeat. "Ah shit," he complained under his breath.

The officer slowly shook the syringe in the air. "Did you get the picture of the syringe over here?" he called out sarcastically. "Be sure you get this on film too. I know how much you guys like to film the real truth around here. I don't want you to leave this one on the cutting room floor!"

By displaying the syringe and "reminding" the team to film it, the officer effectively infused the team's footage with a narration of the events that justified his actions. He presented proof that, rather than unconstitutionally detaining and arresting innocent residents, as LACAN contended, he was merely upholding the law, apprehending guilty offenders. He also repeated the all-too-frequent insinuation that Community Watch edited its footage to misrepresent officers' actual behaviors.

In court hearings, city council meetings, and other public forums, officers regularly argued that LACAN condoned and, through Community Watch patrols, actively *protected* addicts, dealers, and other criminals from prosecution. A number of Central Division officers made a point to interrupt filming and state this particular contention on camera. I once stood with the team recording an arrest when a senior officer very familiar with the organization's legal and political campaigns parked behind us and quickly approached. He positioned himself directly between the camera and the unfolding incident, blocking our view. He paid no attention to the arrest taking place behind him. He had clearly come to corrupt the footage.

"So can I ask you a question," he said to Malcolm, mirroring the team's method of initiating exchanges. Over the preceding weeks, the team had three other interactions with the officer that began in this same manner. Malcolm acquiesced with a deep sigh. The officer began leveling his now-familiar questions toward the camera. While indirect, his underlying message—that Community Watch facilitated criminal behavior—was clear. "I mean," the officer reasoned out loud, "you guys have all these cameras. You guys have the power to say, 'Hey, look what's going on in the streets.' And you guys can bring us the video. I mean, you're out here more than we are and you guys have the videos. You know exactly who the drug dealers are, and what they do. You can help us clean up these streets, but you guys refuse to be a part of the solution."

"Oh come on, man!" Malcolm complained. "We don't gotta go through this *again!*"

Emboldened by Malcolm's frustration, the officer pressed on. "It's a valid question. Why don't you guys help us? You've got all the video!"

Rather than answer the question, Malcolm simply threw his hands up, turned on his heel, and started walking away. The rest of the team followed closely behind.

The officer stood smiling. "All right then," he called out in a mocking tone. "You don't wanna talk? God bless you, Commander. You have a nice day!"

Malcolm remained quiet until he rounded the corner. "I can't stand that motherfucker," he said through gritted teeth. "He's getting to be

POLICING THE POLICE **239**

a real problem, standing in front of the camera like that, knowing we can't do shit to make him move. And even if we did get the shot, we'd have him all up on the tape talking about 'Why don't you stop the dealers?' We can't give that tape to the lawyers! Like we need *that* up in court? We'll have the jury sitting there asking why we're not stopping crime. Shit! We would love to stop it, but that's the police's job! Maybe if they'd stop harassing everybody, they could actually do their job!"[15]

While the officer's subtle countermove clearly frustrated the team, they did not relent. Instead, they continued to deploy further innovations. To neutralize attempts to obstruct filming or contaminate footage, the team began bringing an additional camera (or two) on patrols. This proved fruitful two weeks later when the same officer interrupted the team once more as the team stood filming an arrest. Rather than leave the scene, as they had on the previous occasion, one of the team members willingly accepted the officer's invitation to debate. As the conversation heated up in front of the "decoy camera," another team member slipped away from the group, using the spare camera to record the arrest without further interference.

As I watched these chess matches unfold over the course of my fieldwork, it became clear that, while Community Watch suffered from an immense power disadvantage, it was nonetheless the nimbler party. Debriefing after each patrol, the cohesive group devised new moves more quickly than officers could agree on consistent and uniform countermoves. Given the sheer number of officers who patrolled the neighborhood in a given week, the team could also direct its methods toward those who were new to the beat or otherwise slow to adapt. Over time, this kind of strategizing yielded tangible results.

Community Watch Propels Major Reforms and Disables Therapeutic Policing Practices

By consistently leveraging the group's collective cop wisdom, Community Watch successfully generated visual evidence that overcame residents' lack of credibility and ultimately forced the LAPD to revise its policing practices. In fact, one of LACAN's first major civil rights victories resulted directly from the team's proficiency at anticipating police interventions and catching officers slipping. Relying on these two techniques, Community Watch recorded a series of particularly damning videos that clearly demonstrated Central Division's systemic, unconstitutional treatment of residents.

In the course of its daily patrols through the neighborhood, the Community Watch team noticed that Central Division had taken up a new, highly intrusive and destructive practice intended to push residents into the mega-shelters and rehabilitation programs by making life in the neighborhood more uncomfortable and inhospitable. In partnership with the city's Bureau of Street Services (BSS), Central Division officers began confiscating massive amounts of property— including tents, clothing, bags, bicycles, shopping carts, and milk crates. Each morning, a convoy made up of Central Division cruisers, skip loaders, dump trucks, and BSS crews drove up and down Skid Row's streets in systematic fashion. First, the convoys blocked off each street by parking a dump truck at either end of the block. Next, officers flanked BSS workers as they walked along the gutter, using rakes to pull property from the sidewalk, often directly out of the hands of pedestrians, and into the street. If the owners of the confiscated property stepped out into the street to retrieve their items, officers threatened them with citation and arrest. Next, BSS workers drove a skip loader along the gutter, scooping up all the property and loading it into the back of the dump truck. When they completed the process, the entire convoy moved on to the next block. The crews were remarkably efficient. They appeared suddenly, which meant they consistently caught residents unaware. The crews were able to clear an entire block in less than ten minutes.

Over several months, the Community Watch team dedicated its daily patrols to videotaping Central Division's property confiscations. Throughout these patrols, a local documentary filmmaker and organizational ally accompanied the team, using his professional equipment to record high-quality audio of officers' statements. One

The daily LAPD-BSS convoy.

particular piece of footage, which LACAN referred to as the "Sanford and Son video," proved instrumental. The video documents a group of officers seizing personal property despite residents' screams for help. It also captures a number of incriminating admissions as officers attempted to justify their actions to the team. As officers and BSS workers loaded confiscated items into an LAPD truck, the team approached and explicitly asked the officers why they were confiscating milk crates and what they planned to do with them. The nearest officer, clad in white latex gloves, responded quickly. He stated matter-of-factly that he and the other officers would be "storing them in a temporary warehouse, to return them to their owners." The officer looked directly into the camera and stated that he had "already been in contact with those companies. They want them back."

With the officer's explanation firmly documented on the video, the team decided to track whether the officer made good on his word. To do so, they continued filming the convoy throughout the day. At nightfall, the team followed closely behind the convoy as it concluded its sweep of the neighborhood and made its way to just outside the borders of Skid Row, to a secluded area under the Sixth Street bridge. The video captures the officers playfully singing the theme music from the 1970s television show *Sanford and Son*—a racially charged sitcom portraying the hijinks of a black junk collector—over their PA loudspeakers. The video then shows officers indifferently dumping all the property they had confiscated over the course of the day onto the sidewalk (hardly a "temporary warehouse"). At one point, the video even shows the officers enlisting nearby homeless pedestrians to assist them in unloading the trucks, and compensating them with small items (which LACAN claimed to be either money, cigarettes, or narcotics). While the homeless pedestrians worked, the officers leaned comfortably against their nearby cruisers, smoking cigarettes and engaging in lighthearted banter.

The Community Watch team moved in once again, hoping to document the inconsistencies in the officers' story. The filmmaker asked what the officers planned to do with the confiscated property. The officers' response was striking. Instead of maintaining the previous story that the items would be returned to their owners, the officers now described the items as "all trash." Despite the earlier scene of pedestrians pleading with officers to return their items, one of the officers claimed, "The people who were on the sidewalk didn't want it so they put it in the truck." With this, the group of officers dispersed, clearly abandoning the items.

Of all the footage Community Watch had gathered up to that point, the Sanford and Son video chronicled the most egregious discontinuity in officers' statements and behaviors. Shortly after recording the footage, LACAN and a group of affiliated attorneys publicly released the video in a press conference and meeting attended by representatives from the city council and the mayor's office. The organization used the footage to support its claims that Central Division consistently engaged in unconstitutional and cruel policing practices. LACAN additionally argued that, by merely dumping the confiscated property in a different (but relatively nearby) location, the officers were actively creating the grounds for future arrests while reinforc-ing the neighborhood's infamous reputation. While the organization had had difficulty generating credible evidence for these claims in the past, the Sanford and Son footage utilized officers' own words as definitive confirmation. By documenting the sheer scale of resources and manpower devoted to this recurring operation, the team also curtailed the department's ability to explain away the incident as the actions of a few bad apples.

Upon viewing the tape, city leaders pledged to reform property confiscation practices in Skid Row. Much to LACAN's dismay, how-ever, these pledges proved short-lived, and Central Division covertly returned to its former practices. Malcolm and several other LACAN members noticed that the convoys had begun clearing the streets much earlier in the morning, before Community Watch patrols typ-ically began for the day. In response, the team began its own patrols earlier to obtain fresh evidence of Central Division's noncompliance. To assist in this effort, the organization recruited Jeff Dietrich, Cath-erine Morris, and others affiliated with the Catholic Worker to record any incidents that occurred near the Hippie Kitchen. With the help of the Catholic Worker, Community Watch quickly amassed an im-mense amount of video and photographic evidence. The team also redoubled its efforts to contact and record statements from residents whose belongings had been seized.

This brought the team in contact with Tony Lavan, an unhoused man who slept on the sidewalks adjacent to the Union Rescue Mission. One afternoon, Mr. Lavan ventured into the facility to take a shower, leaving his belongings in the care of several of his friends. While he was away, and despite protests by his companions, a Central Division convoy cleared the sidewalk of all pedestrians and property. Lavan's friends could only look on as a skip loader picked up and destroyed all of Lavan's possessions, including his medical records, prescription medication, clothing, cellular phone, laptop, tent, and other valuable items. Familiar with Community Watch on account of their daily pa-trols, Mr. Lavan agreed to join with seven similarly impacted individuals in a federal class action lawsuit—*Tony Lavan, et al. v. City of Los Angeles*.

I traveled to the federal courthouse with a group of residents to watch the proceedings unfold. It immediately became apparent that the court took LACAN's visual evidence seriously. The measures undertaken by Community Watch counteracted the legal handicap caused by Lavan and the other residents' social and economic standing. Indeed, the team's filming practices had tipped the scales, making the LAPD the party that suffered from a lack of credibility. As had been the case at the Nelson trial, the city attorney attempted to cast doubt on Community Watch's recordings. According to the attorney, the evidence lacked necessary contextual information that could only be filled in by the officers in question.

"The idea of the pictures is," the city attorney argued at one point regarding a series of photographs taken by Community Watch and the Catholic Worker, "it's a totality of circumstances. . . . When you talk to officers . . . the officers who were there . . . it's not exactly at all what the photographs show. There's more to the story."[16] In an attempt to cast doubt on the comprehensiveness of the evidence, the city requested a full evidentiary hearing, which would have forced Mr. Lavan, the other plaintiffs, and the officers to all take the stand and testify. This was a clear attempt to exploit the asymmetrical social statuses of Skid Row residents and the LAPD officers assigned to patrol them. As the city attorney openly acknowledged, "Hearing live testimony gives the court an opportunity to see and hear the people themselves, to make some credibility judgments as to how they come across."

Having learned from the Nelson case, LACAN had anticipated the city's strategy and had restructured its recording practices. In an unprecedented move, the judge promptly (and harshly) declined the city's request for the full evidentiary hearing. The judge asserted that "the affidavits, declarations, and evidence attached to the [plaintiff's] declarations are sufficient for the court to hear argument and make a ruling." Breaking even further from the usual course of action, the judge repeatedly castigated the city attorney, stating that images generated by Community Watch and the Catholic Worker directly contradicted the city's claims. The judge went so far as to question whether the city had committed perjury in the course of its defense.

Focusing on the evidence rather than on the stigmatized individuals presenting that evidence, the court ruled in favor of Mr. Lavan and the other plaintiffs. The judge based his decision primarily on the capacity of the plaintiffs to demonstrate that officers had violated their Fourth Amendment rights against unlawful search and seizure, as well as Fourteenth Amendment assurances of due process. The court ruled that Central Division officers had indeed violated residents' constitutional rights by confiscating private property against residents' wishes, while simultaneously threatening to arrest them when they attempted to reclaim their belongings.

The court underscored its decision by issuing a federal injunction immediately barring the city from continuing its property confiscation practices. The Lavan Injunction, as it is now called, orders Central Division officers and BSS crews to follow specific guidelines regarding all property in Skid Row. First, the injunction requires officers and BSS workers to allow residents ample opportunity to claim their items before removing them. Second, if no one claims a particular piece of property, officers and BSS workers must post a notice on a nearby wall, fence, or other visible surface describing their actions and providing a location where property can be recovered. Third, all confiscated property must be stored in a nearby facility for a minimum of ninety days to provide residents the requisite time to locate and recover their items. Despite three years of intense legal contests in which the city brought multiple petitions to the Ninth Circuit Court of Appeals, and even to the US Supreme Court, the Lavan Injunction remains in effect to this day.

A New Approach to Skid Row?

I participated in Community Watch patrols in the months immediately following the *Lavan* ruling. Like neighborhood residents, I was eager to see whether Central Division officers would obey the court orders. Given the aggressiveness with which officers and BSS workers had previously confiscated residents' property—literally raking it out of their hands as they stood on the sidewalk—Central Division's incredible level of compliance astonished me. While the LAPD-BSS convoys continued their daily rounds, they only picked up items that were obviously refuse and that were already in the street. Not once did I observe workers in the convoys attempting to seize any property from its owner. In fact, the officers and BSS workers regularly bypassed what looked (from my vantage point) to be abandoned property on the chance that its owner might eventually return.[17]

Observers both in Los Angeles and beyond shared my surprise at Central Division's dramatic retreat from what the *New York Times* had described as "a merciless seize-and-destroy policy on the most vulnerable population."[18] The *Los Angeles Times*, certainly the most consistent witness to the various transformations in Skid Row since the district's birth in the nineteenth century, declared that the Lavan Injunction marked the beginning of a "new approach to Skid Row," in which officers and city workers "interact[ed] more sensitively with people who live on skid row."[19]

More recently, the city took an additional, historic, and unexpected step toward ensuring police accountability. In January 2014, the LAPD outfitted thirty Central Division officers with body-worn cameras to better monitor their patrol practices and interactions with the public. After a brief, favorable testing period, the city allotted $1.2 million to purchase six hundred additional cameras. While Los Angeles represents one of the first cities to use body cameras, pilot programs in other cities have produced impressive results. A randomized controlled experiment conducted by the nearby Rialto, California, Police Department found that over the course of a twelve-month study period, use of force by officers wearing cameras fell by 60 percent, while citizen complaints fell by 88 percent.[20] For those at the *Times*, Central Division appeared to be restoring the "decades-old, albeit uneasy, truce" with the Skid Row population that had been broken during the early 1990s in the run-up to the Safer Cities Initiative.[21]

The city has supplemented these policing reforms by improving living conditions and increasing amenities in Skid Row. This began with a $3.7 million plan to install additional public bathrooms, trash cans, and storage facilities, as well as a mandate that the mega-shelter facilities provide greater access for individuals not currently enrolled in rehabilitative programs.[22] While these improvements may seem minor at first glance, to a neighborhood characterized by such an overwhelming number of people using public space every day, they are vital. In an earlier era, the Catholic Worker successfully compelled the city to install exactly these amenities (see chapter 1), but many were removed or relocated inside the newly built mega-shelters in the 1990s. In recent years, LACAN and the Catholic Worker had appealed to the city to reinstate them in public spaces. For these two organizations, these sorts of resources anchor their larger efforts to transform and rebrand Skid Row as a welcome home for the region's poorest citizens.

Four decades after the Catholic Worker put forward its plan to improve Skid Row's livability, and two decades after this work was overturned in favor of aggressive policing policies, Skid Row's small collection of progressive organizations have begun to turn back the clock. They have made significant strides in actualizing their vision of Skid Row as a permanent, "real" community. While the dominant conception of Skid Row as a recovery zone remains intact, neighborhood transformations in the wake of *Lavan* indicate that the century-long struggle to define and govern Skid Row is far from over. At a minimum, recent events have reinvigorated a coalition increasingly capable of challenging the punitive paternalism ushered in by the mega-shelters.

IIIIIIIIIIIIIIIII

Media reports on the about-face in Skid Row policing and living conditions point to the *Lavan* decision as the primary catalyst. Yet, as I discovered on Community Watch patrols, the Lavan Injunction was merely the most visible expression of a much longer struggle. Those living beyond the streets of Skid Row rarely noticed the five-plus years of daily, street-level resistance by Skid Row residents, without which the recent transformations would not have materialized.

Like residents in most impoverished neighborhoods, Skid Row inhabitants' denigrated status undermines their claims of injustice and the possibilities of redress. Residents carry their territorial stigma with them as they venture into various seats of power to exercise their rights as citizens. These groups routinely find themselves outmatched in contests of credibility with the police, which pit their words—as arrestees, defendants, and ex-offenders—against those of officers. Consider the Nelson trial a case in point. As had the 1992 Rodney King trial, the Nelson case featured brutal video footage and several resident eyewitnesses who attested to excessive use of force.[23] Despite what residents thought to be clear and obvious video evidence, the officers' account of the incident ultimately won the day. The courtroom merely amplified and reproduced the institutionalized powerlessness that the urban poor experience every day in the street.

Yet, through Community Watch, a growing number of Skid Row residents have developed an effective remedy. Across thousands of interactions with Central Division officers—whether on Community Watch patrols or simply going about their daily round—residents like Malcolm, Patti, Mark, and Herb acquired the knowledge and skills necessary to begin reversing the asymmetrical power dynamics handicapping marginal groups. These residents capitalized on their cop wisdom to gain a surprising amount of control over police interactions. By systematically anticipating and manipulating these exchanges, they generated new, more credible evidence for their claims of injustice. By offsetting the taint of place, they have begun to level the playing field and strip officers of their ability to pursue therapeutic policing practices.

Unlike the deployments of cop wisdom detailed in the previous chapters, Community Watch rejected outright the popular view of

Skid Row as a Hobbesian, self-destructive world. Instead, those af-filiated with LACAN framed the neighborhood as an altruistic and self-reflective community. Rather than settle for individualistic tac-tics that bring protection from police at the expense of their neigh-bors, LACAN members built on their neighborhood frame to generate collective and often self-sacrificing strategies designed to protect the community as a whole. Through daily Community Watch patrols, residents then made this neighborhood frame a reality. In protecting fellow residents, they confirmed the presence of a supportive and re-sponsible community. Through their daily actions and the eventual large-scale legal victories, they have begun to ensure equal constitu-tional protections while reducing the moral blemishes worn by Skid Row residents. They have also provided communities beyond Skid Row with an effective, actionable, and replicable model for achieving hopeful community change from within, from the bottom up.

Conclusion

On a balmy September evening in 2010, I joined five hundred or so other Angelenos as they anxiously filed into a stuffy auditorium at Westminster Avenue Elementary School, located some seventeen miles west of Skid Row in the bohemian beach community of Venice, California. While Venice and Skid Row sit opposite one another on the literal and figurative edges of the city, the two neighborhoods' approaches to poverty governance were rapidly converging. On this night we gathered to hear city council member Bill Rosendahl announce the launch of the "Vehicles to Homes" program—a highly aggressive policing and social service campaign targeting the roughly three hundred individuals and families who have lived in RVs parked along Venice's palm tree-lined streets for decades. In recent years, business and home owners' complaints about the unsanitary conditions, noise pollution, and crimes purportedly caused by the RV dwellers had reached a fever pitch. That night, they made their voices heard even before Rosendahl called the meeting to order. A man in a blue polo shirt and khakis yelled "Get a job" at a bearded RV resident wearing a tie-died shirt and a hemp necklace. Two young children hoisted a hand-painted sign with the phrase "Our Streets Are Not Toilets." Much to the home owners' chagrin, the RV dwellers and their allies returned fire with their own class-based insults. In the middle of the room sat a gray-haired woman in military fatigues holding a sign reading, "The Spirit of Venice Will Leave if You Exile the Poor."

After nearly fifteen minutes of shouting between the two sides, the roughly thirty LAPD officers lining the walls moved into the crowd, silencing the most vocal individuals with the threat of arrest. Amid the temporary lull, Rosendahl stepped to the dais, introduced himself, and began outlining his "relocation and rehousing plan," which, he insisted, would be beneficial to *all* parties involved. Directly inspired by the Safer Cities Initiative, Rosendahl detailed a two-pronged approach for solving Venice's "RV problem." First, a new municipal ordinance (LAMC 80.69.4) would prohibit any vehicle taller than seven feet or longer than twenty-two feet from parking on Venice's streets between the hours of 2:00 a.m. and 6:00 a.m. The city would deploy an additional twenty-one LAPD officers to the area to ensure strict enforcement of the new oversize-vehicle law. Second, a set of designated "safe lots" would be created to accommodate those displaced from parking (and thus living) along Venice's roadways. To access the lots, however, the RV dwellers would have to submit to a handful of stipulations: they would be required to provide proof of "economic deficiency," sign behavioral contracts, meet regularly with caseworkers, and agree to abide by a rehousing agreement that would culminate in their moving out of the RVs and into conventional housing.

Despite the punitiveness of the plan, Rosendahl's tone throughout the night was one of fatherly guidance. He was acting, he said, for the RV dwellers' "own good." Echoing the words of officers, government officials, and service providers in Skid Row, Rosendahl described living in an RV as a "lifestyle choice." "There are a lot of people on the beach, in those cars and campers, that don't want help," he said at one point during his speech, "but those who want help, we want to be able to help them." When several RV dwellers let loose a chorus of boos, Rosendahl held firm to his message of tough love. "If you want help," he repeated, "then we'll help you. If not, then get out of our face!"

Policing and Poverty Governance in the Twenty-First Century

Venice is certainly not alone in adopting this new stance. A growing number of cities up and down the California coast, including Santa

Barbara and San Luis Obispo, have launched nearly identical programs, proposing the same coercive ultimatums to their most disadvantaged residents: alter your behaviors, change your attitudes, enter services, and develop self-discipline, or else face harsh criminal penalties. When Central Division captain Charlie Beck replaced William Bratton as LAPD chief in 2009, he solidified the place of such ultimatums as a core tenet of policing in one of America's largest and most influential cities. As ground zero to one of the most naked expressions of this disciplinary mode of law enforcement, Skid Row provides an ideal site for uncovering the causes and consequences of the paternalistic regulations that are spreading throughout Los Angeles and beyond. This book has focused on the Safer Cities Initiative and its related policies and programs to provide an in-depth, multiperspectival account of one (though certainly not the only) mode of poverty governance that we are increasingly deploying against America's most truly disadvantaged.

Understanding this emerging brand of social control requires that we rethink urban policing. A range of criminal justice scholars has proposed that we are witnessing the rise of a "new punitiveness," in which the ideals of rehabilitation and reintegration have been replaced by the goals of retribution, neutralization, and exclusion.[1] These accounts tend to construct a sharp dichotomy between punitiveness and rehabilitation, regarding them as mutually exclusive goals. The popularity of this narrative is unsurprising, particularly given the long shadow cast by the prison over discussions about the role of the criminal justice system in regulating marginal populations. Over the last four decades, researchers have interpreted the increasingly harsh and austere conditions found inside prisons—including lengthier sentences, increased use of solitary confinement, the return of chain gangs, and the elimination of education and counseling programs—as evidence of a turn to destructive and nonrehabilitative forms of punishment. As criminologist John Pratt and colleagues contend, today's punishments suggest that "no improvement is sought or expected from the inmate. From a social laboratory designed with the purpose of improvement, the prison has been reborn as a container for human goods."[2] Wacquant similarly concludes that if there are agents of rehabilitation left in the criminal justice system, "they surely are not employed by departments of corrections."[3]

Today, our conversations about nearly *every* aspect of the criminal justice system—whether police, courts, jails, probation, or parole—customarily proceed from a discussion of "mass incarceration" and a ceremonial retelling of the United States's staggering imprisonment statistics. It is an obligatory point of departure. Yet this term (mass incarceration) and these numbers (2.3 million inmates) grossly underestimate the reach of the criminal justice system and misrepresent the modal criminal justice encounter.[4] Indeed, incarceration is but the tip of an iceberg. Below the surface are millions of street-level police stops, infraction citations, and low-level arrests. In 2008 alone, 40 million people had face-to-face contact with police. Excluding routine traffic stops, police involuntarily detained 5.5 million people, the majority of whom were released without charge.[5] Unfortunately, our prison fetishism has led scholars to interpret these policing statistics, and the growing regularity of contact between the police and the urban poor, as yet more straightforward evidence of a turn away from rehabilitation. The resulting accounts assume that the urban poor are brought *into* contact with the criminal justice system by the exact same impulses and logics that keep them behind bars for prolonged periods of time, under increasingly cruel conditions.

Yet imprisonment is not policing. While the two are undeniably coupled—the police create the "inputs" for prisons—we must not confound these two regulatory institutions and their constitutive processes. Local police departments are political actors in their own right, operating within particular political environments and amid other actors within the organizational field of poverty governance. The police face particular municipal demands, public influences, and community partnerships that differ from those faced by departments of corrections.[6] Further distinguishing policing from imprisonment, police officers represent the quintessential example of street-level bureaucrats.[7] That is, they possess a significant amount of discretion and autonomy while on patrol. How officers concretely implement policy and interact with the citizenry necessarily hinges on how they understand their larger mandates in relation to the demands of their daily work, the dynamics of the areas they patrol, and the characteristics of those with whom they regularly come into contact. They do so without much regard for what is occurring inside penitentiaries.

Against this backdrop, this book reexamined the rise of strict quality-of-life laws, zero-tolerance enforcement policies, and the climbing rates of detainment, citation, and arrest in a new light, and beyond the shadow of the prison. As it turns out, the notion of a new punitiveness rests on too narrow a definition of *both* punitiveness and rehabilitation and, as a result, obscures the complexity and collaborative nature of contemporary poverty governance. Punitiveness and rehabilitation are, in fact, far from antithetical. In some contexts, they are mutually dependent. In Skid Row, for instance, policing has been at its most punitive precisely when it has been most concerned with reintegrating the poor. Wacquant's agents of rehabilitation may no longer pace the halls of the prison, but they have clearly begun to patrol the streets of impoverished urban neighborhoods.[8] Corrective and reintegrative interventions have not disappeared. Instead, they have increasingly been taken up by organizations and actors operating at the *front end* of the criminal justice system.

To be clear, this book is not merely describing a change in venue. Rehabilitation has not simply moved to a different arm of the criminal justice system. Rather, therapeutic policing represents an important shift in the rationale and techniques by which the state attempts to bring marginal populations back into the social and economic fold. Firmly rooted within a larger neoliberal project, this form of poverty governance places a primary emphasis on the role of the self-governing individual operating within a market of potential actions. Under this rubric, the poor, like all citizens, can and should make "rational choices" and must take personal responsibility for those decisions.[9] Poverty can be most effectively alleviated, then, by forcing the poor to "recover" the skills, abilities, and attitudes necessary to weigh the costs and benefits of future behavior.

To grasp the primacy of choice as both cause of and solution to urban poverty, we need only consider the titles of the programs instituted in Skid Row alongside the Safer Cities Initiative—programs like Streets or Services, and Homeless Alternatives to Living on the Street. Skid Row policing couples these programs with aggressive and constant enforcement of minor laws to restructure residents' range of potential decisions, deincentivize behaviors deemed irresponsible, and compel the self-discipline that residents have supposedly shirked. Ironically, this mode of social control seeks to govern poor residents as free and responsible subjects at the same time that it constricts their behavioral options and forcibly funnels them into more approved ways of living.

This ideological shift is a contingent outcome of concrete struggles between identifiable historical actors. In the second half of the twentieth century, neoliberal welfare reforms not only reduced the quantitative amount of social support available to the urban poor, but also restructured the qualitative administration of programs and services in a manner intended to elicit better market decisions from the poor. Both in practice and by design, the privatization of vital support services increased the role and influence of nonprofit, voluntary, religious, and other "shadow state" organizations in overseeing marginal populations.[10]

Facing new contract stipulations and increased competition for funding, these organizations have forgone the more accommodative models of poor relief characteristic of the mid-twentieth century. More than ever, organizational longevity depends on these actors' ability to control surrounding neighborhood conditions and thus ensure a continuous stream of clients (and the dollars that these clients represent). These organizations have explicitly called on the police—as the maintenance men *par excellence* of the local spatial order—to assist in reducing the "temptations" that exist beyond the doors of their facilities.[11] In return for funneling new clients through their doors, these organizations, as the presumed representatives of the poor, provide the police with incredible legitimacy and political support. As a result, the police now maintain a close and symbiotic relationship with the local welfare organizations they opposed for most of the twentieth century.

Although the discussion in this book derives from my fieldwork in Skid Row, this collaborative program of coercive benevolence has become firmly ensconced in a host of cities throughout California and the country. At the time of this writing, local police departments and prosecutors in at least fourteen of California's fifty-eight counties have partnered with private organizations to operate pre-booking and pre-plea misdemeanor diversion initiatives that closely parallel Central Division's SOS program.[12] In Santa Barbara, for example, eligible misdemeanants are given the option of avoiding jail by enrolling in anger management, life skills, or drug and alcohol abuse classes run by the nonprofit Pacific Education Services. Atlanta's aptly titled Gaining Opportunities and Living Smarter (GOALS) program; Wicomico County, Maryland's Phoenix program; and Tucson's "diversion and life skills" program all present low-level (and predominantly impoverished) offenders with the same ultimatum: start making better life choices, or go to jail.

Given the faulty dichotomy so often constructed between punitiveness and rehabilitation, those on both the left and the right continue to celebrate these police-service partnerships and their resulting diversion programs as a more cost-effective and compassionate alternative (or at least accompaniment) to aggressive zero-tolerance policing policies.[13] My fieldwork alongside Skid Row officers paints a more complicated and, I would argue, more troubling picture. The partnership between the LAPD and the mega-shelters has resulted in daily patrol practices characterized by an unprecedented level of repression. By fusing punitive enforcement with rehabilitative programs, the Safer Cities Initiative converted street-level police contact into an official form of social services intake. This development radically transformed not only how street-level officers understand

and go about their daily work, but also how these officers view, interact with, and process (potential) offenders. Skid Row officers now see themselves as performing a kind of outreach social work function, not only on behalf of partner organizations, but also on behalf of Skid Row residents, who, in officers' opinions, desperately require their authoritative guidance. This approach led to a perverse development: the officers *most* committed to rehabilitation and reintegration, whether because of their own biographies or a more generalized sympathy for the downtrodden, often acted the most punitively toward residents.[14] When criminal justice contact is reframed as a therapeutic intervention in and of itself, coercive and sometimes violent measures become deployed as a perverse form of care.

This irony is one of this book's central findings. Until now, despite increasing concern over mass incarceration, the punitive turn, and the proliferation of zero-tolerance policing, we have made remarkably little effort to incorporate the voices of the men and women charged with carrying out these policies and practices on a daily basis. Perhaps even worse, some accounts attempt to make claims about officers' underlying motivations based almost solely on the experiences and statements of the policed. In contrast, the time I spent with officers engaged in zero-tolerance policing allowed me insight into a key aspect of the punitiveness currently on display on the streets of America's most impoverished communities: its powerful emotional component. At least some officers intend harsh punishments to communicate a larger commitment to social justice. By curtailing the amount of free food available in the neighborhood, coercively separating vulnerable women from potentially oppressive partners, or arresting homeless people for sitting on the curb, Central Division officers felt that they were doing their best to solve poverty and its associated problems, one resident at a time.

Using threats of citation, arrest, and incarceration, these officers demanded that residents (re)enter the formal labor market, secure conventional and permanent housing, and obtain necessary health care, despite the fact that these "options" do not exist in any real sense.

Contrary to the narrative proffered by police, therapeutic organizations, business interests, and local officials, the problem is one of supply, not demand. Unfortunately, the spiral of legal entanglements that result from these criminal justice interventions only compounds residents' supposed "unwillingness" to take up the lifestyle choices demanded by the police. While a citation for blocking the sidewalk or littering might cause momentary frustration for residents in more well-to-do communities, for the urban poor, it frequently results in insurmountable fines; disqualifications from work, housing, and services; and the constant fear that the next run-in with police may end behind bars.

Cop Knowledge

In addition to its dire material impacts, the aggressive, disciplinary form of policing discussed in this book produces important sociological effects. As society's premier guardians of the social order, the police possess a great deal of *symbolic power* to diagnose, classify, and authorize particular ideas about neighborhoods, their residents, and their problems.[15] The police not only provide our society with data on crimes and law enforcement; the police supply us with a great many of our taken-for-granted ideas about poverty, crime, and disorder.[16] As the police increasingly interact with and intervene against the urban poor as if poverty results from improper behavioral and lifestyle decisions, they help to produce and reproduce broader stereotypes that blame the poor for their current predicament. These ideas about the poor effectively alleviate the responsibility of the nonpoor to care for society's most disadvantaged members.

These ideas can even turn residents within poor communities against one another. Implicit and widely available stereotypes (like those circulated about the undeserving poor) tend to alter the judgments not only of those in the mainstream, but of the very individuals who are the objects of the stereotypes.[17] Throughout the twentieth century, poverty researchers documented residents in stigmatized neighborhoods engaging in practices of lateral denigration, trying desperately to distance themselves from their denigrated neighborhoods and the "typical" inhabitant. The police's regular and intrusive presence in these same urban areas has raised the stakes of proving one's difference and decency. In Skid Row, where therapeutically oriented officers try to distinguish and transform irresponsible and self-destructive residents into self-disciplining and productive citizens, some residents feel compelled to double-down on efforts to distance themselves from those they perceive as the former. In their attempts to avoid unwanted police interventions, residents end up (if only tacitly) accepting, actualizing, and accentuating the very stereotypes they seek to escape.

The weight of this symbolic power indicates the need to rethink the collateral damage caused by aggressive policing. In discussing law enforcement in marginalized neighborhoods, we often fixate on the disintegrative capacities of the police, on how the police remove vast numbers of people (typically young black men) and vital resources (income, social capital, and familial support). Yet, the police also play a *generative* role—that is, they play an active part in creating the cultural frameworks though which residents make sense of and live within their immediate social milieu. The threat of constant unwanted police contact forces residents to develop and refine cop wisdom—a new interpretive schema in which they reread the various people, behaviors, and spaces of their neighborhood from the perspective of onlooking officers. In Skid Row, where officers functioned as recovery managers, a majority of residents' concrete tactics to sidestep police contact centered on outwardly communicating their commitment to rehabilitation (like James's tendency to flash his mega-shelter badge), their sobriety (like Tyrell's modified daily round), or their lack of involvement in narcotics sales (like the vendors' constant assaults on dealers). At the same time, residents' choice of tactics to evade police contact carried the potential for individual and community ruin. These tactics often led to isolation, an erosion of social capital, and a noticeably hostile public order.

While the omnipresence and aggressiveness of policing in Skid Row certainly helps to illuminate the development of cop wisdom among its targets, the response is hardly unique to this neighborhood. Precisely *how* residents in other neighborhoods and cities mobilize their cop wisdom depends in large part on how they are policed and on what particular appearances and behaviors officers deem suspicious and worthy of intervention. This is ultimately an empirical question that demands further research. Based on my fieldwork, I would anticipate that residents living in other therapeutically policed locales—Venice and Santa Barbara, for instance—would deploy cop wisdom in ways that closely resemble those of Skid Row residents. While we would need to observe everyday life in, say, the Bronx, East St. Louis, or Detroit to uncover the *specific* tactics of resistance that police targets develop in those places, we will almost certainly find that (the threat of) unwanted police contact intimately shapes residents' perceptions of and interactions with peers and community. We are also likely to find that cop wisdom constricts certain social relationships and activities while emboldening others.

Preliminary data collected in Chicago demonstrates this much. After completing fieldwork in Skid Row, I joined the faculty at the University of Chicago. Located on Chicago's South Side, the university sits adjacent to the neighborhood of Woodlawn—one of the city's poorer and more heavily policed areas. From my first walks to and from campus, I was struck by the ubiquity of the Chicago Police Department, as well as the University of Chicago Police Department, whose officers cruise slowly up and down Woodlawn streets, detaining, interrogating, and searching young black pedestrians. Curious about the transferability of my Skid Row findings to other settings, I put together a small team of graduate and undergraduate students to interview teenagers in the area about their experiences with police. In one interview after another, the teens conveyed that their preoccupations about being stopped altered how they dressed, how they wore their hair, which streets they walked down, and who they associated with in public. Like those in Skid Row, Woodlawn teens have learned to reexamine their own appearances, behaviors, and associates through the eyes of passing officers, in hopes of subtly communicating that they do not warrant further police scrutiny. Unlike Skid Row residents, Woodlawn teens did not necessarily mobilize their cop wisdom to demonstrate a commitment to rehabilitation. Rather, they developed a set of concrete tactics designed to convince officers that they were not involved in gang activity. These strategies directly reflected the model of policing the teens encountered.

On Chicago's South Side, where the fragmentation of "super-gangs" has led to territorial violence between block-level cliques, patrol officers and gang units primarily use street stops and interrogations to search for guns, gather information about escalating conflicts, intercede prior to retaliatory violence, and check for parole and probation violations.[18] Fully aware of local police priorities, young men in Woodlawn make use of a number of "props" to enhance their performances of innocence. Many of our male respondents reported that they make a conscious, and sometimes exhausting, effort to recruit female companions to walk with them during nearly every step of their daily round—to and from school, football practice, the corner store, and other neighborhood locations.

Antoine, a charismatic and popular young man, explained why young women are so instrumental in deflecting police scrutiny. "They [the police] think girls are mostly neutrons [gang-neutral]," Antoine reported. "They think that they don't be beefing as much as we [guys] be. It's like this: If I'm hanging out with a girl, they aren't gonna come up and start asking me questions. They're gonna think I'm just kicking it with my girlfriend on a date or something. Especially if it's late at night. They're thinking I'm probably not on the way to start something. It's like, girls are safe, you know?"

Young women confirmed the prevalence of this tactic. They recounted instances in which, upon noticing an approaching squad car, young male acquaintances (or even strangers, in some instances) would throw their arms over young women's shoulders to suggest a romantic involvement. Once patrol officers passed, the young men would return to their previous activity, rejoin their male companions, or simply walk away without further word.

Whereas Skid Row's therapeutic model of policing led residents to avoid (and at times even lash out against) women in public spaces, given officers' concerns with prostitution and drug use, the gang-oriented patrols in Woodlawn appeared to have a reverse effect on gender relations. Rather than view women as a liability, young men in Woodlawn gravitated toward their female peers. And yet a similar process unfolds in both settings: the meanings that residents ascribe to gender are continually mediated by the manner in which *officers* understand and act toward gender.

Beyond Chicago's South Side, recent national events provide further evidence of the proliferation of cop wisdom. Over the last few years, the American public has become all too familiar with the names of an alarming number of young black men killed at the hands of police officers during routine investigatory stops—names like Oscar Grant (Oakland, California), Tamir Rice (Cleveland, Ohio), and Eric Garner (New York City). In August 2014, a police officer in Ferguson, Missouri, shot Michael Brown, an unarmed eighteen-year-old black man, at least six times in the course of a street stop. In a parallel to the civil unrest that set the streets of Los Angeles ablaze in 1992 following the beating of motorist Rodney King, residents in Ferguson took to the streets, where they protested, looted, and confronted riot gear–clad officers for several weeks. As tensions on the streets continued to boil over, black leaders and residents throughout America reflected openly on their own arbitrary and abusive experiences during police stops.

One of the more striking insights to emerge from this public discourse has come from black parents, who have vocalized their daily fear that their own sons could easily become the next Michael Brown. In the hopes of avoiding this fate, these parents have been compelled to engage their sons in what has come to be known simply as "the talk."[19] Unlike many of the routine teaching moments that parents feel compelled to share with their children, the talk is not about the birds and the bees or the perils of drug use. Rather, the talk conveys a set of concrete instructions about how to behave when police officers might be watching, or simply nearby. Much like the catalog of "dope-fiend" behaviors compiled by Steel's weight-lifting crew, the talk lists "don'ts" for young black men as they move through the world: Don't walk through unknown residential neighborhoods after sundown. Don't carry any dark or metallic item that can be mistaken for a knife or gun. Don't leave any store without a receipt. Don't fidget with your hands in your pockets. Don't put your hoodie up. Perhaps most important of all, don't run.

In warning against these potentially perilous behaviors, parents supply their children with instructions on how best to decrease the risk of misrecognition by officers. Parents have come to learn, often through firsthand experience, that these are the behaviors most likely to lead officers to assume that a young black man is criminally inclined and therefore deserving of detainment, interrogation, or worse. As parents engage in the talk, they, much like the residents of Skid Row, strive to reinterpret mundane appearances and behaviors through the eyes of onlooking offers. In doing so, they must not only see their sons as a cop might, they must also take note of, and ask their sons to account for, the racist and classist stereotypes that might color an officer's perceptions. As they tell their children to avoid acting like "real" criminals, parents unwittingly provide an early lesson in lateral denigration and distancing. The ubiquity of the talk across the country alerts us to the fact that a whole segment of the American population has been forced to become copwise (with all its advantages and disadvantages) as a rite of passage into adulthood. It is not an exaggeration to say that it is often the difference between life and death. These citizens know that, given the neighborhoods they live in, the color of their skin, and their class background, officers will assume their sons guilty until they can prove (or at least perform) otherwise.

Through the intergenerational socialization of cop wisdom, residents of marginalized communities develop the necessary interpretive skills to navigate the new urban reality they increasingly confront whenever they set foot in public space. This is, in some ways, a contemporary variation on street wisdom, the cultural frame that residents used to counter the systematic *lack* of police vigilance that prevailed in these neighborhoods less than a generation ago. Impoverished urban residents have long called for more adequate police protection and for their cries for help (and calls to 911) to be addressed more quickly and genuinely. Lacking this, they have been pressed to take matters into their own hands. Street wisdom offers a means to navigate neighborhood streets safely. By reinterpreting the world through the eyes of potential assailants, streetwise individuals can better anticipate and thus avoid criminal victimization. The arrival of the police en masse in many of these same neighborhoods has only transformed, rather than eliminated, residents' need to engage in a folk criminology, now coupled with a folk ethnography of policing. At times, the two can be complementary: anticipating what a criminal might do in a given situation helped Skid Row residents better anticipate what passing officers would do. At other times, however, street wisdom and cop wisdom appear grossly incompatible. Someone like Leticia, who attracted unwanted police attention when she traveled the neighborhood accompanied by Jackson, put herself at far greater risk of crime if she traveled alone, without the protection of her husband. In situations like these, residents are forced to chart a precarious course between the Scylla of victimization and the Charybdis of criminalization.

Despite this book's focus on the daily dilemmas faced by Leticia and other residents, it should not be read as fatalistic. Recent developments in Skid Row suggest that, at the same time that omnipresent and aggressive policing has made life in disadvantaged neighborhoods more tenuous and treacherous, it has also inculcated its targets with the skills necessary to engage in formal and effective strategies of resistance. Given their regular contact with officers, residents involved with LACAN and its Community Watch program have learned to leverage their cop wisdom to better predict impending police stops, track patrols through the neighborhood, and draw officers into potentially incriminating interactions. In moves that are reminiscent of the Catholic Worker coalition's strategies in the mid-twentieth century, residents involved with LACAN have taken crucial first steps toward (re)cementing Skid Row as a viable and permanent low-income neighborhood that can offer safe harbor to the city's most dispossessed. The actions of LACAN demonstrate that residents have found, and will continue to search for, innovative means for making their voices heard. While they certainly proceed from a disadvantaged position, they are anything but hapless victims.

In fact, the organization has provided a model for effectively challenging zero-tolerance policing that can be put into use elsewhere. LACAN's seemingly unlikely legal victories illustrate that litigation represents a potent, if difficult, means for neutralizing aggressive law enforcement and mitigating the symbolic power of the police to envision the urban poor as irresponsible, untrustworthy, and in need of paternalistic discipline. In order to replicate the organization's class action lawsuits and secure injunctive relief from unwarranted searches and seizures, other communities must heed LACAN's hard-learned lesson that courtroom battles over truth claims and expert knowledge are always stacked in favor of the police and their allies. Disadvantaged litigants must therefore embrace new techniques for constricting police narratives that would otherwise justify harsh treatment as appropriate and even beneficial. As LACAN has shown, one of the most powerful techniques must be carried out not in the courtroom, but in the routine interactions between officers and residents along the streets of urban America.

Taking the Community Watch program as a model, residents in heavily policed communities must begin meticulously recording these exchanges. As they do so, they must focus on capturing events from start to finish and intensify efforts to document officers' motivations, sentiments, and explanations in the moment. Only then will marginalized communities be capable of generating the legal evidence necessary to challenge officers' courtroom declarations. Having observed the humble origins and daily operation of Community Watch, I believe that local grassroots organizations could equip and train sufficient numbers of residents in a relatively short time and at little cost. Small handheld cameras are cheaper and more user-friendly than ever before, and video camera functions have become standard on even inexpensive cellular phones. Through increased texting capabilities and publicly available wireless internet connections, these videos can be instantly disseminated, hosted online, and prepared for use in court. In fact, the ACLU recently created a smartphone program that allows citizens to upload their recordings of police behavior directly to the organization's online repository, thereby preserving the footage in the event of arrest or officer retaliation.

Such organized efforts to record police behavior have beneficial effects that can extend across large swaths of a community. By policing the police and risking their own arrest on behalf of others, LACAN members have begun to move past the individualistic, zero-sum, and often self-destructive tactics of resistance that other residents marshal to protect themselves from police contact. In contrast to their neighbors who only hope to deflect police attention onto others, LA-CAN members embrace a neighborhood frame that rejects the widespread vilification of Skid Row and its inhabitants. Through notable moments of community, these individuals have come to feel a close connection with their neighbors, deviant or not.

Where Do We Go from Here?

Despite their antagonistic relationship on the streets of urban America, the police and the policed have something important in common: both have been forced to adapt to the sustained neoliberal attack on the Keynesian welfare state, albeit from very different structural positions. By reprioritizing, cutting, and outsourcing social protections, our state, federal, and local governments have not only unraveled the support system but have forced local police departments to take up the primary responsibility for managing those who inevitably fall through the cracks. The problem, of course, is that police officers make abysmal social workers. Yet, ill equipped as they are for the job, we continue to ask them to address large-scale social and economic problems like unemployment, homelessness, and mental illness using the only tools at their disposal: handcuffs, batons, handguns, and other violent means. Not only is the task impossible; it also pulls police attention away from more serious and harmful crimes.

How can we relieve the police of their current and incongruous responsibility over America's poor? How can we empower officers to address more dangerous offenses and respond less forcefully to minor ones? How can we build poverty-reduction strategies that are compassionate not just in motivation, but in practice and outcome?

In some respects, the answer is straightforward. It requires rebuilding the American social safety net, reviving protections against market vagaries, and recognizing that poverty and inequality are not the result of irresponsible choices and wanton morals. It requires undoing neoliberal reforms that seek to alter the lifestyle choices of the so-called undeserving poor. It requires renewed support for those caught at the bottom. To some, such calls for structural change appear hopelessly idealistic, if not naive. They certainly do not mesh well with America's current devotion to piecemeal policy initiatives. They cannot be accomplished with a single congressional bill. Yet, today's mode of poverty governance is rooted in too complex a web of historical legacies, structural forces, and political imperatives to respond to moderate and isolated reforms. Even the most cursory look to the past confirms the necessity of macro-level transformations. During some of America's proudest years, the social safety net provided by welfare bureaucracies and social support mechanisms helped protect Americans from the downward, often insurmountable spiral now virtually guaranteed in the event of an eviction, job loss, serious illness, and other unfortunate life event.

This is not to say that there is no place for concrete, short-term policy solutions. Just as neoliberal reforms eroded the safety net over the course of several decades, a large-scale revamping of our public support structure will not be accomplished overnight. In the meantime, we cannot overlook the needs of those who are suffering, this very minute, in poor neighborhoods across the country. A major lesson from this book is that any realistic attempt to address these communities' needs must be rooted in rehabilitative and reintegrative interventions that *do not* rely on the coercive power of the police. We must find ways to shrink the jurisdiction and role of the police in the lives of the poor. Fortunately, budget shortfalls and fiscal austerity measures have created new opportunities for the adoption of alternative social service models.

In recent years, two particular models—called "housing first" and "harm reduction"—have emerged as viable alternatives to therapeutic policing and its disciplinary logic. The housing first approach posits that secure and stable housing is among the most important prerequisites for addressing issues related to poverty, such as unemployment, mental health problems, or substance abuse.[20] The harm reduction model holds that many deviant behaviors, including substance abuse, sexual commerce, or participation in illegal economies, are but symptoms of deeper, structural problems.[21] Harm reduction advocates argue that until these macro-level shortcomings are addressed, the most realistic policy approach is to lessen the harms associated with deviant behaviors, rather than continuing futile attempts to eliminate them.[22] At their core, both housing first and harm reduction reject the notion that the receipt of social supports and continued freedom from punishment should be contingent on an individual's ability to demonstrate self-improvement, whether through abstinence, formal employment, or some other performance of morality. Both also recognize that aggressive policing is an inappropriate and counterproductive response to most social and economic problems. They stress that it is impossible to arrest our way out of inequality.

It is hard to imagine a more fitting crucible for housing first and harm reduction programs than LA's Skid Row. Fortunately, I am not alone in this thinking. In 2007, the Skid Row Housing Trust—an outgrowth of the Catholic Worker coalition and a longtime advocate of these alternative models—collaborated with local organizations and agencies to launch Project 50. To date, this program remains one the most explicit counterweights to the therapeutic policing carried out by the LAPD and mega-shelters. In contrast to recent welfare reforms that constrict support for the most poverty-stricken, Project 50 makes such individuals its priority. Over the course of several months, Project 50 outreach workers fanned out across Skid Row to identify the neighborhood's fifty most destitute, vulnerable, and chronically homeless individuals, a number of whom had severe illnesses and were mere months from dying. The program first ensured adequate housing, providing each of the fifty with an apartment room in an SRO hotel, then assisted them in accessing health care and other social services. In short, Project 50 removed the task of outreach social work from the police and put it back in the hands of caseworkers with direct access to noncoercive services and resources.

While the idea of providing housing, with virtually no strings attached, to individuals who may be unemployed or actively abusing drugs and alcohol is controversial, the success of the program is undeniable.[23] After the first full year, forty-three of the fifty remained fully housed and stabilized. Only four had been arrested and incarcerated. Those with histories of substance abuse continued to participate in counseling and rehabilitation. Those with mental illnesses continued to receive treatment and medication. All participants continued to receive preventive medical care.[24] With the help of Project 50, this seemingly hopeless lot, made up of the exact individuals envisioned by therapeutic policing as *least* capable of managing their own lives, have done precisely that. And they have done so without the use of coercive threats. Equally impressive, these results have come at a significant savings. After two years, and even after an expansion to 133 participants, the program had more than paid for itself, yielding a surplus of $4,774 per housing unit provided. These savings primarily stemmed from the fact that participants were no longer cycling in and out of jails and emergency rooms. Compared to nonparticipants, incarceration costs for program participants fell by 28 percent in the first year alone. Medical costs dropped by 68 percent.[25]

This is a hopeful start. But it is not enough. Barring a meaningful reconceptualization of poverty, a society-wide movement toward noncoercive social services, and a serious revitalization of the safety net, we will be forced to continue relying on a destructive, hurtful, and expensive brand of police regulation as our primary means for addressing poverty. Thankfully, our future is not set in stone. We have a choice. We can instead invest in our fellow citizens. They certainly deserve our confidence. Facing the injuries and obstacles caused by unrelenting criminalization, America's urban poor display an unmatched level of creativity, ingenuity, and resilience as they navigate tumultuous conditions. We must enable these communities to redirect their cognitive and emotional energies—now so often focused on evading the police—toward more collective and beneficial pursuits. Our poorest communities can begin to rebuild trust, stability, and dignity on their own terms, backed by the knowledge that if they stumble, we will no longer let them fall. If we can be brave enough to put faith in our lowliest neighbors, we can build this future together.

Methodological Appendix
An Inconvenient Ethnography

In the tradition of urban ethnography, I immersed myself in the daily lives of those who live and work in Skid Row.[1] This up-close, participatory method necessarily precludes the possibility of remaining a detached and dispassionate observer. As I hope the preceding chapters illustrate, I (like all ethnographers) inevitably became a part of the scenes and interactions that I witnessed and analyzed. This is the outcome whether the fieldworker intends it or not. While I am highly dubious of the notion that certain attributes and statuses yield inherently "better" data, I do believe that different researchers inevitably generate different interactions in the field. A host of concerns—from access, to the research questions asked, to the "data" encountered— are necessarily conditioned by the ethnographer's point of entry, position, and personality.[2] With this in mind, it is necessary to describe how this project developed, how I cultivated relationships with both the police and the policed, and how they understood, responded to, and even exploited my extended incursion in their worlds. This appendix also provides a candid meditation on the dilemmas of doing fieldwork in heavily policed settings and articulates some of the practical concerns of the multiperspectival framework I employed.

Ethnographer or Narc?

As I indicated in the introduction, I did not set out to study policing when I began daily fieldwork in LA's Skid Row district. Rather, I intended to study residents' informal economic survival strategies. In my first few exploratory visits to the neighborhood during a graduate ethnography seminar at UCLA, I had been particularly intrigued by the collection of disheveled street vendors hawking an assortment of goods along Skid Row's sidewalks—from clothes and canned food to pirated DVDs and individual cigarettes. While I expected that the topic of policing would occasionally arise (I had read several *Los Angeles Times* columns describing the launch and intensity of the Safer Cities Initiative), I naively anticipated that I would be able to keep the topic of law enforcement tucked neatly at the margins of what I saw as my "real" focus of research. My first few months of fieldwork, however, disabused me of these assumptions. I quickly found it difficult to push the topic of policing aside long enough to sustain focus on much else.

The Safer Cities Initiative, and the anxiety it generated among residents, presented the first major obstacle to initiating my fieldwork. Indeed, the omnipresent threat of police contact made it difficult even to strike up preliminary conversations with vendors. In the hopes of getting to know some of these men, I spent my first week in the neighborhood introducing myself to nearly every vendor that I came across. Most treated me with suspicion and abruptly shrugged me off, insisting that they were "too busy to talk." After a handful of failed attempts, I eventually met an older black gentleman who was willing to chat with me. He invited me to stand with him while he sold cigarettes out of a duffle bag along one of the neighborhood's main thoroughfares. The conversation was off to a satisfying start when, less than five minutes later, a Latino man of similar age abruptly interrupted us, pulling my new acquaintance away from me by the arm.

"Don't talk to him," the man ordered through a thick Cuban accent. "Don't talk to him, papi. He's a cop."

"No, no," I managed to answer through my surprise. "I'm not a cop." Judging from the scowls that crept over the men's faces, my answer had not convinced them. Hearing my own shaky words as they left my lips, I could hardly blame them.

"Look at him," the Latino man instructed, seemingly emboldened by my unsatisfactory response. He pointed at me, tracing his finger from my shoes to my face and back down to the small spiral-bound notebook I held in my hand. "Look, papi. That's a cop." Without another word, the two men fled up the sidewalk, briefly shaking hands before the Latino man jogged across the street to catch an approaching bus.

This process repeated itself once more that same week. The week also produced two instances in which pedestrians sounded an alarm before I even had the chance to strike up a conversation. On one of these occasions, I was merely standing on a corner observing the street scene when a nearby man called out to me.

"Hey dog," he yelled. "Why you eye-hustling?" Apparently I had been watching those around me a bit too intently. His voice grew more agitated when I did not respond quickly enough. "I said, why you eye-hustling out here, dog?" The man raised his voice, grabbing the attention of everyone within earshot. "Five-oh right here, yo!" He nodded his head in my direction. "Five-oh right here! Look out for his wire." Hearing this, everyone nearby began clearing the area while shooting me hateful glares. "I see that wire you got," the man yelled at me as he walked away. "I see that wire." I found myself standing alone on the block.

While I knew that forging relationships in Skid Row would require significant time and energy (this is true of any ethnography), I had not expected such hostile reactions to my mere presence. If anything, I had assumed that my own biography would work to *alleviate* residents' concerns about my identity and intentions. I grew up sixty miles east of Los Angeles in the city of San Bernardino, which consistently ranks as the most impoverished city in the United States outside of Detroit.[3] I spent my childhood amid urban poverty, gangs, and violence. I consider myself streetwise and generally feel comfortable navigating Skid Row's streets. Prior to graduate school, I worked in California prisons as a prisoners' rights activist. I also spent time as an investigator for the public defender's offices in Washington, DC, and San Jose, California. During that time, I became skilled at discussing sensitive and illegal matters with both victims and perpetrators.

None of this mattered much in those first weeks, however. My initial interactions proved the start of a pattern, in which residents' suspicions that I was an undercover officer precluded my even beginning to make personal connections. Whatever "insider" knowledge I thought I possessed or assumed I exuded, residents fixated instead on my more immediate and physical attributes, particularly my racial identity (or at least, their perceptions of it). In terms of my background, I am mixed. My father is black and my mother is Mexican. My skin is darker than a few of my friends and family members whose parents are both black, but I inherited my mother's thinner lips and nose. While I often self-identify as black, Skid Row residents overwhelmingly read me as either white or Latino. This not only set me apart from most residents (Skid Row's population is estimated to be more than 70 percent black); it also aligned me, at least demographically, with the predominately white (35 percent) and Latino (44 percent) LAPD.[4]

Some of my other physical attributes also served to increase residents' suspicions that I might be a cop. When I first entered Skid Row, I was twenty-five years old, I had a short military-style haircut, and I had the muscular frame of someone who spent considerable time in the gym. Later, when I had established close friendships with the vendors, some of the same men who initially shrugged me off told me that I had looked "fresh out of the police academy."

While I could not readily change my racial background, phenotype, age, or physical frame, I could at least try to mitigate their repellent effects as I struck up conversations with strangers and spent hours idly hanging out. As part of this effort, and as I described in chapter 4, I began selling cigarettes. In time, my consistent presence on one of the neighborhood's busiest streets enabled me to meet a host of Skid Row residents, including a few of the vendors. Over the next two and a half years, roughly sixteen of these men integrated me into their social world and vouched for my identity when customers and other pedestrians cast doubts on my identity or reasons for being in the neighborhood. I soon stopped selling cigarettes and spent my time assisting the vendors in displaying and managing their inventory. I shared cans of malt liquor after long days standing in the heat. I ran errands that allowed them to maintain their place along the sidewalk. I accompanied them to court dates. I wrote letters of support for employment applications and sentencing hearings.

I also began spending more time in Skid Row's two "pocket parks," where I worked out on metal exercise equipment and eased my way into dominoes games. As described in chapter 3, the pocket parks have become home to a workout culture based on innovative uses of the pull-up bars, metal fences, electrical boxes, picnic tables, or really any physical structure available.[5] These activities provided a convenient excuse for jotting down field notes as I logged my workouts and tallied scores. My outward appearance, particularly my physical build, also seemed to strike residents as far less "out of place" as I hung from pull-up bars alongside other shirtless park users sweating in the sun. I frequently turned to others to ask for workout tips, and I found it relatively easy to strike up casual small talk within this bounded context.

My regular presence and continual curiosity about unfamiliar exercises eventually produced a number of key friendships, as well as an invitation to begin exercising alongside Steel and his crew. Given my cool reception from other residents, I found the excitement with which Steel's group welcomed me somewhat surprising. I imagine their response had a lot to do with the fact that I greeted them alongside their informal leader. I immediately assumed the role of willing student. I joined the rotation of exercises and listened to the stories and jokes they told as they waited for their turns. In the beginning I remained relatively quiet, though I frequently spoke up to ask the men to elaborate on various tales they shared. They seemed happy to oblige my requests. I got the strong impression that my presence and constant questions provided them with a heightened sense of dignity. Big Ron made the biggest deal of my ongoing interest in them. During one session, as I dropped down from the pull-up bar, Big Ron made his feelings about my presence explicit.

"See," he said to the others, while patting me on the back. "Young buck saw us out here doing our thing and he knew. He *knew*, right off the jump, that we're doing something positive, you feel me?" For Big Ron, my interest confirmed the group's involvement with something special. Despite the other fascinating and sensational events occurring in Skid Row, he rationalized, I had decided to focus sustained academic attention on them.

Whereas my skin tone and phenotypical characteristics prompted some residents to push me away, these attributes became the grounds on which Steel's group pulled me closer and attempted to keep me involved. My racial background became particularly salient as the men leveraged my presence to reinforce the legitimacy of their activity. During my third session with the group, several of the men inquired about my race. After confirming that I was half black, the conversation soon turned to other matters. Yet the topic returned an hour later, as the workout came to a close, when several of the men joked that I would need to continue "working on my pump" to preserve my blackness, as well as my masculinity. This occurred as I failed to complete my final set of bicep curls. When he saw this, Dante showed little sympathy and launched into a bout of shit-talk, aimed directly at me.

"What was *that*, young man?" he asked skeptically as I lowered the homemade barbell to the ground.

Big Ron came to my defense before I could even respond. "Naw, he all right," he said to Dante. "I saw him do about twenty of those the other day when you weren't here."

"Is that right?" Dante said, looking past Big Ron, directly at me. "You sure you're not spending too much time hitting those books? We don't want you to forget how to get down. Gonna lose that pump for good."

"Yeah," Reggie agreed. "You'll be walking around here like, 'Um, hello sir, how are you doing, sir?'" He raised his voice by an octave and adopted a slight southern, "white" accent as he spoke. "You'll be like, 'Can I borrow a cup of sugar?'"

The entire group erupted in laughter. Except me. I felt insulted and humiliated. Like the rest of the men, I recognized this as a quotation from the 1990s movie *Bad Boys*. In this particular scene, the main characters (played by the black actors Will Smith and Martin Lawrence) are conducting a police investigation in a lavish mansion. Fearing that they will be viewed as burglars, they alter their voices to mask their race, convince the occupants that they are white, and thereby signal that they pose no threat.

As he collected himself, Reggie noticed my embarrassment. He backed off a bit and resumed his normal voice. "Hey, I'm just fucking with you," he said apologetically. He took a few steps forward to shake my hand. "But seriously, though. I've seen some niggas from the block go off to college, turn all uppity, and shrivel up. I'm just looking out for you, dog. I don't want you falling off once you go and get that degree. I just want you to keep it real."

In the face of the disparities in our economic and social statuses, the men repeatedly used their own physical size and devotion to weightlifting as a signifier that they "kept it realer" than I did. In so doing, they reclaimed a position of power in our interactions. The men provided a clear warning that as I continued to pursue my education and potentially enlarge the social gap that separated us, I ran the risk of betraying the "black side" of my heritage. The solution, of course, was to defer to these men's authority despite what my own credentials or wider society might suggest.

Shifting Focus

Looking back on the decision now, it feels almost inevitable that I eventually made policing the primary focus of my research. My first-hand observations in the field revealed the short-sighted and sometimes entirely off-base nature of many of my preformed theories, hypotheses, and research designs. Anthropologists Mary Black and Duane Metzger (1965) explain why this is such a common experience: the field confronts the ethnographer with *responses*.[6] When ethnographic subjects and informants make routine statements, engage in repeated behaviors, and enter into patterned interactions, they are ultimately providing answers to some set of looming questions that are important to, though often taken for granted by, those within the local context. Everyone in the site "just knows" the unspoken questions that elicit these responses. The problem, of course, is that the researcher does not share that knowledge, at least at the outset of fieldwork. The fundamental task of ethnographic analysis, then, is to work backward, to discern and articulate the questions to which informants are constantly responding. "Unless you know the question," Black and Metzger warn, "you can't know many things about the response."[7] Because these questions are often quite different from those we formulate in the cozy confines of the ivory tower, ethnographic research is frequently characterized by unanticipated detours and sudden turns.

My own shift in course occurred as I began noticing that throughout the vendors' interactions with me, their peers, and their customers, they seemed obliged (nay, forced) to provide a coherent answer to what Wiseman calls the "etiological question of Skid Row," which asks, "What are you doing here?"[8] I had made a conscious decision from the outset of my work *not* to ask the vendors how they "ended up" in the area. I resolved to let this information flow naturally from interactions, and on others' terms. For me (coming from a clear position of privilege), this line of questioning felt condescending and awkward. It seemed to imply an assumption about these men's personal (and moral) failure to bootstrap themselves out of their current predicament. Nonetheless, from our initial introductions through even the most mundane exchanges with one another, the men continuously found ways to work in unsolicited stories that explained their "skid" to the bottom. In the same breath, they articulated their current efforts to improve their lot and to emphasize, importantly, how they differed from the "typical" Skid Row resident. It was as though they feared that casual observers, or even close observers like me, might miss these critical distinctions.

Consider the symbolic significance of the men's inventory choices. When I first met Jackson, for instance, his sidewalk shop prominently featured college textbooks, school supplies, and small clock radios. As Jackson rarely failed to remind fellow vendors and customers, these were the kinds of items that residents would need to advance their education and pull themselves out of poverty. These items conveniently resonated with Jackson's explanation of his own presence in the area—a story that quickly flowed from customers' inquiries into the price of his items. He had been evicted from his South Central apartment, and the Los Angeles transit strike in 2000 left him unable to continue taking vocational mechanical engineering classes at a nearby community college, which led to the cancellation of his Pell Grant and his inability to recover financially.

Another vendor, Stevie, engaged in a similar signaling process when he made the unexpected decision to cease selling lighters. This struck me as incredibly odd and counterproductive from a business standpoint, especially considering that Stevie primarily sold homemade incense. Despite the fact that incense customers had a clear reason to buy lighters, Stevie insisted that selling lighters contributed to crack use. A recovering addict himself, Stevie began using his inventory as an opportunity to criticize what he saw as a lack of self-control on the part of Skid Row's drug-using residents. He offered his own decision to forgo additional profits as evidence that he himself had acquired extreme levels of control.

At first glance, these episodes appeared to reflect the processes of internal differentiation that poverty researchers have long documented among residents of impoverished and "ghetto" neighborhoods.[9] I assumed that I had uncovered yet another instance of how residents attempt to convince others of their own moral decency. In time, however, I came to see that I had misjudged the audience for these performances. Through a series of peculiar interactions, I realized that many of the vendors' displays were intended for an ultimately more powerful audience: police officers. If residents were answering a taken-for-granted question, it was the police who were asking it.

One afternoon, I sat against a chain-link fence on Fifth Street with a handful of vendors as they tended their shops amid bustling sidewalk traffic. In one sale after another, Stevie loudly narrated his transactions with customers. "Here we go, sir," he announced as he began the sale of a portable CD player to a retirement-age man leaning on a black aluminum cane. "I'm selling you this Walkman. It's a good one, you're going to enjoy it. And, in return, you're handing me a twenty-dollar bill." Stevie paused as he dug in his pocket. He resumed his narration when he pulled out a small wad of bills. "Here we go. You gave me twenty bucks for the Walkman. And now I'm giving you your change." He counted out the bills loudly. "One, two, three, and five makes eight. This is eight dollars in change for your new Walkman. Thank you sir, it was a pleasure doing business with you."

I was perplexed as I watched and listened. Why was Stevie announcing his business to anyone within earshot? I stood up from my milk crate and asked Stevie what he was doing. He candidly explained that he was *intentionally* overdramatizing his hand-to-hand transactions with customers. According to Stevie, police officers expected drug dealers to try to *conceal* their interactions with customers. Stevie hoped to mitigate officer suspicion by making his own, *nondrug* sales even more conspicuous.

"Let's just say there's an undercover sitting right there on the corner," he explained to me, in one of the first of many hypothetical exchanges with police. "You probably won't be able to see him. Maybe you've got your back to him, but he's watching you. You're not doing anything wrong, though. You just made a good, honest sale. Unless you want to spend the night in jail just based on some bullshit hunch he's got about you, you better not let there be any confusion about what the hell you're doing out here."

It turned out that Stevie had begun this practice at the same time that he removed lighters from his inventory. The move came on the heels of a particularly traumatic arrest at the hands of an undercover officer, in what Stevie claimed was a case of mistaken identity. Following a short jail stint, during which he stewed about how he might have avoided the arrest, Stevie turned to these new measures, not so much to communicate decency to his fellow vendors and his customers as to prove innocence to the police. It seems unlikely that Stevie would have deployed these tactics in the past, when a far less vigilant style of police surveillance and intervention predominated in Skid Row. I suddenly recognized that a host of the vendors' practices were deeply conditioned by their anticipation of officers' reactions. Seen in this new light, behaviors I initially deemed contradictory or senseless now appeared coherent and instrumental. The vendors' actions lessened the probability of misrecognition and detainments, while also building in small bits of evidence that they could present to officers in the event of a detainment. It was evidence that might convince officers that the men were not, in Larry's words, actively "contributing" to drug activity.

One of my own early detainments, in which officers singled me out and presumed me guilty until I could prove myself innocent, provided the final push necessary for me to make policing the central focus of my research. As I stood jotting notes next to the vendors one late evening, two passing officers forcibly detained, searched, and interrogated me. As I describe in chapter 4, the officers rifled through my backpack and told me that I "fit the description" of a young male suspected of selling narcotics in the vicinity. After discovering my identity and the real reason for my presence, the officers ordered me to leave the neighborhood at once. Still a bit shaken up, I followed their instructions without complaint. This particular police interaction yielded two important developments. First, despite my fears that the event would cause the vendors to view me as jeopardizing their performances of innocence, it had the opposite effect. Having witnessed my ability to quickly deescalate the interrogation, escape without a citation, and cause the officers to become more deferential, the vendors insisted that I *increase* my involvement on the corner, as well as in their other daily affairs and routines. In fact, the men began calling me several times a week to synchronize our time out on the streets. I became a prop that the men used to perform their decency and innocence for officers.

Second, and more immediately, the late-night police stop laid bare my own inequitable position vis-à-vis the residents I was studying. That evening I easily followed the officers' orders, left Skid Row, and took refuge in my home in the nearby Echo Park neighborhood. For the most part, I had the ability to avoid police contact for the foreseeable future. The vendors, like the majority of other Skid Row residents, had no such recourse. They had no such escape route. Any time they stepped into public—whether to walk to the store, speak with friends, or simply enjoy a moment of sunshine—they risked yet another tense and intrusive police stop. As I drove back to my house that night, I became convinced that an adequate understanding and explanation of life in poor neighborhoods required me to think more seriously and systematically about this new urban reality. In the coming months, I began engaging residents in more explicit conversations about their experiences with police. Thinking about my position also led me to recognize the need to incorporate officers' accounts alongside those of residents.

Calling Officers to the Stand

In a provocative essay titled "How Not to Lie with Ethnography," sociologist Mitchell Duneier argues that, to ensure a reliable and honest rendering of how a social phenomenon under study *actually* works, ethnographers should engage in what he terms "inconvenience sampling."[10] In much the same way that a judge might call potentially hostile witnesses to the stand, inconvenience sampling directs fieldworkers to broaden their observations to include those people and perspectives that are the *least* convenient for the impressions developed in the initial phases of fieldwork. Typically, these are the actors most difficult for the ethnographer to get to know given her entry point into the field and relationships with primary contacts. Given my own entry point, I could imagine no more inconvenient set of actors than Central Division officers. The need to include officers in this kind of "ethnographic trial" became increasingly clear as I continued to compile residents' stories about the dire consequences of their seemingly minor interactions with police. These tales, often heart-breaking, appeared to provide straightforward evidence for the ex-planations of urban policing currently found in academic and policy discussions. Using terms like "war," "active pogrom," and "genocidal politics," such writings describe the police as leading a vindictive at-tempt to clear the destitute from the urban landscape, while willfully neglecting their social, economic, and health needs.[11]

While my early fieldwork produced little evidence to refute these accounts, my own biography led me to question these prominent and emotive narratives. My colleagues are often surprised to learn that a number of my close family members work in law enforcement. My cousin is a deputy sheriff. My younger brother was a military police officer. My mother and uncle are members of the sheriff's medical re-serve corps. Listening to my informants' experiences and reading ar-ticles about vindictive police treatment, I had a hard time imagining my loved ones engaging in these practices. When my family gathers for holiday dinners and special occasions (sometimes joined by other deputy sheriffs, and even members of the LAPD), they share stories of rescuing victims and stopping bad guys, not the genocide and annihi-lation theorized in academic accounts.[12] I also had a hard time imag-ining that those sitting around our family table differed that much from most officers. And yet, detainments, citations, arrests, and their dire consequences persist at a historic pace. How could this be? The question was as personal as it was academic.

Fortunately, I was poised to begin finding answers. I had unexpect-edly gained access to Central Division officers during my late-night detainment along Fifth Street. Once the officers identified me as a graduate student, their demeanor changed drastically. They provided me with a business card listing the names and contact information of their supervisors and Central Division's senior lead officers (SLO). As they warned me about the dangers of walking around the neigh-borhood at such a late hour, they suggested that these senior officers could answer any further questions I might have. They insisted that I needed to speak with officers, *not* residents, if I "really wanted to know what's going on" in Skid Row. It was a phrase that officers repeated throughout the remainder of my fieldwork.

Beginning in 2008, I supplemented my existing research with fieldwork alongside the Central Division officers. I took my notebook into the bunkerlike Central Division station, where I conducted informal interviews with Central Division leadership, observed training modules, and attended various meetings. Out on the streets, I shadowed and observed patrols. Much to my surprise, Central Division personnel greeted me with a surprising openness. As I became closer with a handful of officers, I had to acknowledge that, for the most part, these men and women woke up every morning resolved to make the world a better place. I want to note that, among the range of findings presented in this book, this is one that consistently draws skepticism. I had surely expected residents, who struggle to shoulder the weight of fines and incarceration, to doubt my assertions about police officers. But even some of my academic colleagues seem to have difficulty eschewing popular stereotypes that portray officers as heartless foot soldiers looking for any opportunity to harm the poor. I suppose that my family's relationship with law enforcement may have restrained my willingness to castigate individual officers too readily. Whether or not this is the case, I believe that I have nonetheless avoided an overly simplistic account that obscures a more troubling empirical reality, in which "good" people perpetrate harmful acts.

I attribute officers' immediate willingness to entertain my constant questions and lingering presence to several factors. First, my "fresh out of the academy" look led officers to casually assume that I was a military veteran. The question "Which branch?" opened many of my conversations. As a result, officers tended to presume that I was familiar with firearms, understood the chain of command, and shared in their working-class, blue-collar ideology. Some of the division's younger officers saw my physical build as an indication that I was a fellow "gym rat." They engaged me in discussions about protein powders and preworkout supplements.

Second, my institutional affiliation with UCLA seemed to put officers at ease, particularly Central Division brass. Few police chiefs have
done more to embrace and incorporate academics in police administration than William Bratton. As head of the New York department,
Bratton drew heavily on the writings of James Q. Wilson, at the time a
faculty member at UCLA. Bratton continued this trend when he took
over the LAPD. Internal documents indicate that the chief's esteem
for police researchers flowed down to the divisional level. George
Kelling, Wilson's coauthor on the broken windows thesis, made regular appearances in Skid Row in the years preceding the launch of the
Safer Cities Initiative. Because I had arrived in the neighborhood only
a few months after Kelling's departure, I entered a divisional culture
that viewed police scholars more as collaborators than critics. For instance, following a meeting with several local organizations, a senior
officer took liberties with our affiliation while introducing me to a
newly hired staff member at one of the neighborhood's prominent
social service facilities. "This is Forrest," the officer told the woman
as we filed out of the conference room. "He's getting his PhD at UCLA.
He's spending time with us, and you'll see him at more meetings like
these. We're trying to keep finding ways to help you do what you do
best." Statements like these implied a far closer level of collaboration
between me and Central Division than actually existed.

Third, and perhaps most critically for the analysis that ensued, I
attribute much of officers' openness to the deeply held, therapeutic
meanings with which they imbued much of their daily work. As far
as I could tell, officers did not try to hide their routine practices from
me. Instead, they appeared to view my presence as a means for documenting and disseminating a more holistic and, for them, more "realistic" account of Skid Row. Even the greenest officers grasped that
the division's aggressive patrol practices had produced vocal critics.
Yet, officers insisted that these detractors did not realize that detainments, citations, and arrests served a greater good. Indeed, officers
rested their claims of moral superiority on the fact that they recognized the underlying altruism of their actions while selflessly suffer-

ing the misinformed backlash that resulted. As with Steel's crew and some of the vendors, officers seemed to interpret my intense interest in Central Division's daily practices as further confirmation of their monopoly of the moral high ground. In the early periods of fieldwork, I occasionally questioned whether officers' proclaimed commitment to rehabilitation was simply a grand public relations performance, maybe a story spun just for me. Yet the consistency of the rehabilitative agenda throughout internal documents and across ranks indicated the central role of therapeutic policing in the organizational culture. I also witnessed the rehabilitative agenda in action—in repeated exchanges with residents, as senior officers schooled rookies, and during the humorous banter that unfolded between partners. If it was all just an act, it was perfectly rehearsed, executed, and sustained among a diverse cast of players.

"Switching Sides?"

I enlarged my inconvenience sample yet again when I reached out to the Los Angeles Community Action Network (LACAN). I planned to observe their community organizing activities around police misconduct and abuse. Alongside the Catholic Worker, LACAN voices the loudest opposition to the Safer Cities Initiative in the neighborhood, if not the city. I was caught off guard, yet again, when access to LACAN proved difficult and lengthy. Despite the warm reception I received from Commander Malcolm from the very first day I set foot in the LACAN office, the rest of the organization's leadership exercised more caution. Like the residents I encountered on the streets, some in LACAN feared that I might be an undercover officer, perhaps sent by the LAPD to infiltrate the organization. If nothing else, their wariness of me illustrates the fierce antagonisms that rage between LACAN and Central Division.

When I returned to the office a second time to continue my conversation with Malcolm, he informed me that they "needed to check me out first." For the next two months, I showed up to the office multiple times each week, only to be told that they had not yet confirmed my identity and purpose. Finally, the organization contacted a UCLA professor who corroborated my enrollment status and vouched for my intentions. Over the next months, LACAN allowed me to fully participate in organizational activities, attend planning meetings, and accompany the Community Watch team during its daily patrols. LACAN's various organizing campaigns resonated on a personal level, often reminding me of my previous activist work. I assisted the organization with a host of tasks, from updating member rosters to staffing its free legal clinic. Over the course of 2010, I also instructed a small group of members on interview and survey methods. Using this training, they began collecting and analyzing data regarding their own neighborhood. After a rocky introduction, LACAN provided me with close friends and collaborators.

My increasing involvement with LACAN, particularly my affiliation with the organization in public, dramatically altered my position in the field. Most significantly, it transformed my previous relationship with, and access to, the police. I was thrust into the middle of an ongoing struggle. Officer Andrews—a veteran of Central Division with whom I had become friendly—once noticed me walking comfortably among the Community Watch team, clipboard in my hand. His initial look of surprise turned into visible frustration. As the team neared, Andrews called out to me. "Hey," he beckoned, waving me over. "Come check this out. I want to show you something." I paused, and looked to the members of the team for some guidance on what I should do next. They simply stood shaking their heads, unsurprised by the officer's actions. The tension was thick in the air. I felt torn. I knew that whatever choice I made next might carry serious consequences for continuing my research with either party.

"Come on," Andrews continued, acknowledging my hesitation and waving me over more forcefully. "It's all good. I want to show you what they're *not* going to show you." I finally obliged and made my way over to him. He turned and leaned into the trunk of his cruiser, pointing to a thick, rusty steel pipe inside. "See that?" he asked me. "I just pulled that off a guy. You're an educated man, let me ask you this: What do you think he was going to do with that? Plumbing? Fix a sink? No. This is a weapon right here. This could *kill* somebody. And *that's* what he was going to do with it." He motioned back to the Community Watch team, who were talking among themselves, just out of earshot. "But if you listen to them, we're just going around taking everybody's stuff. What they *won't* show you is the woman lying in the hospital bed after this guy attacks her. No. If you ask them, *he's* the victim. They're trying to protect *him*! They're out of touch with reality."

At this point, a member of the Community Watch team called out to me. They likely heard this last statement and wanted me to end the conversation. They had begun to walk away, so I made a move to catch up with them. "Can we talk more about this later?" I asked the officer, walking backward to prolong the conversation.

Andrews waved me off dismissively.

"No, seriously," I called out, still walking backward.

"I'm trying to give you the truth," he replied with disdain. "But I can see that's not why you're down here. Apparently you just want a juicy story." He motioned to the clipboard. "Go ahead, write down all the lies they're feeding you."

"*Seriously*, I want to hear what *you* have to say."

"That's why you're walking away," he replied, as he gave me a final dismissive wave and turned his back.

After that, my interactions with Officer Andrews were never the same. When we encountered each other on the street, he ignored me while he carried on with his patrol tasks. Andrews was not alone. After seeing me on Community Watch or sitting with LACAN members during community policing meetings, several other officers similarly gave me a cold shoulder. A collection of meetings and interviews I had scheduled were mysteriously canceled. I imagine these officers felt as though I had switched sides and, in so doing, was providing a new level of legitimacy to their opponents. While I was (and remain) confident that I improved my research by integrating multiple and competing voices, it was clear that officers felt betrayed.

As I described in chapter 5, a few Central Division officers went so far as to retaliate against me, making my research "inconvenient" in a different way. These officers interrupted my conversations with residents and tried to intimidate me by calling out my name on their PA systems. Their strategy worked. I grew paranoid whenever I walked through the neighborhood alone, and whenever I drove near downtown. I feared that one of these officers might notice me, pull me over, write me a frivolous ticket, or maybe worse. I constantly worried that these officers had flagged my profile in the police database. My paranoia only increased when a resident relayed that he had overheard two officers talking about me while he sat in booking following an arrest. He could not recall exactly what they said, but insisted that they referred to me by name and did not mince words about their frustrations with me. Hearing this, I briefly considered terminating the project.

Fortunately, not all officers responded like this. In fact, my visible presence alongside LACAN led some officers to *increase* their openness and their attempts to involve me in their work. These officers seemed to view me less as a traitor, and more as a reasonable go-between who, being willing to listen to their perspectives, might potentially "take the truth back to LACAN." For example, Officer Morgan invited me to observe his team's panhandling stings following an uneasy meeting I attended alongside LACAN. When the organization's leadership declined his invitation outright, Morgan turned to me as a substitute. I was more than happy to oblige, and Morgan made the most of the opportunity. He capitalized on our subsequent time together to not only communicate the necessity of deincentivizing informal economic enterprise, but he also tried to discredit LACAN by detailing its most prominent members' criminal backgrounds.

Despite the difficulties it caused me, I believe that my inconvenient and multiperspectival approach yielded significant benefits. Most notably, it allowed me to turn up genuinely surprising findings and reveal underexamined and counterintuitive processes. If I had limited my research to only those on the receiving end of policing, I would have remained blind to the rehabilitative impulses undergird-ing Skid Row policing. Or worse, I might have fallen into the trap of explaining officers' motivations and aims solely based on residents' statements and opinions. Conversely, my time with officers enhanced my understanding of residents' behaviors. Uncovering the therapeu-tic qualities of Skid Row policing better positioned me to understand which specific tactics and strategies of resistance tended to be most effective and why. While the resulting account may read as less damn-ing of individual officers than some readers might have anticipated (or wanted), I believe that it provides a more honest and nuanced ren-dering of how the policing of marginality actually unfolds. If noth-ing else, I hope that it encourages researchers to at least consider the possibility that the police and policed are thinking, feeling actors si-multaneously struggling to find their way amid large-scale transfor-mations in American poverty governance.

Acknowledgments

One of my sociology heroes, Howie Becker, famously wrote that every piece of artwork is the product of a vast, often invisible network of collaborators, consorts, and supporters. While some might question a comparison between art and sociological research, anyone who has tried to write a book knows that it is impossible without the guidance, assistance, and support of a small army. Certainly too many to name in a few pages of acknowledgments. And yet I'll try.

I conducted the research for this book during my time in the UCLA Department of Sociology. I could not have asked for a more exciting intellectual home than Haines Hall. Words cannot express my gratitude for my mentor, Stefan Timmermans, whose methodological rigor, sarcasm, and seemingly endless generosity kept me both productive and sane over the course of six years. Now, as an assistant professor, I've tried to emulate his model of scholarship and advising. I find myself in greater awe of the man each day. Bill Roy's consistent encouragement and deep feedback mattered enormously. I laugh a little to myself every time I channel Bill, asking my own students, "But what is sociological about that?" As an aspiring ethnographer, I could not have asked for a more brilliant instructor and critic than Jack Katz. Jack has a way of deconstructing and reimagining a project—always for the better—that would leave my head spinning for weeks. I benefited tremendously from the insights and counsel of David Snow, who pushed this book in new, unexpected directions and rekindled my commitments to symbolic interactionism.

Edna Bonacich played an immense role in my development as an intellectual and activist. I am eternally grateful for our near-weekly lunches, where she always reminded me why I chose this path in the first place. I discovered her work as an undergraduate at UC Santa Cruz, and now I pinch myself at the thought that we plant strawberries and squash together in her backyard. I thank the universe for bringing me into contact with Gary Blasi, whose relentless style of fact-finding and advocacy opened the door for my own research in Skid Row. Gary had superhuman levels of patience as I learned the ropes of graduate school, and of Stata statistical software. Maurice Zeitlin's classes on sociological theory and case studies of revolutions impressed upon me the importance of linking claims and evidence. His "Four Questions" now haunt my students' dreams. David Halle convinced me it was OK to fall in love with cities and urban sociology. Abigail Saguy was a steadfast supporter, mentor, and coauthor. I never told her this, but I blame her for creating my long-standing obsession with Google Calendar. Bob Emerson is the reason I chose UCLA, and he mysteriously provided funding that allowed me to make the move. And finally, every time I step in front of my class, I take comfort in the thought that Peter Kollock is smiling down on me.

My fellow graduate students at UCLA left more of an imprint on this book, and on my life, than they will ever truly know. I will remember the days I spent analyzing field notes, sharing ideas, and breaking bread with Laura Orrico and John O'Brien (my fellow Timmermaniacs). My years living in Venice with Laura were almost too good to be true, and I continue to benefit from John's deep thinking. Anthony Ocampo, the first student I met at UCLA, took me under his wing. He taught me about the passive voice and how to share in others' successes. Lorenzo Perillo taught me that the gym is as good a place as any to ponder hegemony and colonialism. Elena Shih's spark of light and endless Tupperware collection kept us all energized and fed when the going got tough. Through their dedication to fieldwork and close analysis, Iddo Tavory and Jooyoung Lee showed me what immersive ethnography should look like. My conversations with Amada Armenta helped propel the fieldwork down new roads. I hold a special place in my heart for Josh Bloom, who took time out of his own busy graduate studies to help me survive mine. I also owe thanks to Mike DeLand, Tara McKay, Neil Gong, Kjerstin Gruys, Dwight Davis, Gabriel Nelson, and the rest of the Bruin family. While conducting fieldwork, I met Nicholas Dahmann, who was a graduate student at USC at the time. Many of the insights in this book would have been impossible if Nick had not introduced me to geography and offered theoretical interpretations as we walked Skid Row's streets.

My colleagues at the University of Chicago have provided the intellectual intensity and support necessary for completing this book. Kristen Schilt has gone well beyond the call of duty as my friend, colleague, and unofficial mentor. She continues to answer her office door when I come knocking with random requests, and her homemade desserts are the best midday treat. Through his example and mentorship, Mario Small continues to challenge me to make ethnography theoretically relevant. Kate Cagney has become an unexpected advocate and mentor. Stephen Raudenbush, John Levi Martin, Andy Abbott, Lis Clemens, Bernard Harcourt, Cheol-Sung Lee, Rafe Stolzenberg, Richard Taub, Omar McRoberts, and Terry Clark have pushed me to think about the practice of sociology in new and different ways. Tianna Paschel was the perfect writing buddy, who, beyond making the best ice cream ever, reminded me to apply my sociological imagination to my everyday life. I'm proud to call Rafeeq Hasan one of my best friends. He inspires me never to lose sight of my political commitments. I've also been blessed with phenomenal students, who keep me sharp and excited about research. Andrew Miller read and edited several drafts of the manuscript. Alicia Riley, Melissa Osborne, and Ava Benezra have proven to be great collaborators. Their constant greetings of "How's the book coming?" pushed me to work even harder toward the day when I could simply answer, "It's done."

Throughout the research and writing, a number of people from other universities and disciplines made their mark on this book. I am particularly indebted to Steve Herbert, who entertained an e-mail request from a fan-boy graduate student years ago. I'm grateful for the work, friendship, and guidance of Victor Rios, who has always kept it real. Mary Pattillo and Katherine Beckett read chapters and gave valuable feedback and mentorship. Reuben Miller has become one of my favorite coconspirators. For the last five or so years, my work has benefited enormously from the brilliance of the members of an interstate writing group made up of Alex Murphy, Jacob Avery, Jeff Lane, Brandon Berry, and Patrick Inglis. I have also benefited from the community provided by a close network of ethnographers, punishment scholars, and generally amazing souls: Eli Anderson, Andy Papachristos, John Eason, Ben Fleury-Steiner, Mona Lynch, Armando Lara-Millan, Jon Wynn, Jennifer Reich, Nicole Van Cleve, Issa Kohler-Hausmann, Stephanie DiPietro, Alice Goffman, Colin Jerolmack, Andrew Deener, and Jamie Kalven.

Several institutions provided me with the time, space, resources, and forums that make scholarship possible. Fieldwork was supported by a number of sources: a minority fellowship from the American Sociological Association, a fellowship from the John Randolph Haynes and Dora Haynes Foundation, and a writing fellowship from UCLA. I wrote several chapters at the Racial Democracy, Crime & Justice Network's Summer Research Institute ("academic summer camp") at Ohio State University. I am indebted to Ruth Peterson and Laurie Krivo for the opportunity. Several research grants from the Division of the Social Sciences at the University of Chicago allowed me to pay for editorial assistance. A number of editors and reviewers provided sharp feedback on previous articles that I had written on Skid Row policing: parts of chapter 1 were previously published as "Race, Space, and the Regulation of Surplus Labor: Policing African-Americans in Los Angeles's Skid Row," *Souls: A Critical Journal of Black Politics, Culture, and Society* 13, no. 2 (2011): 197–212; parts of chapter 2 as "From 'Rabble Management' to 'Recovery Management': Policing Homelessness in Marginal Urban Space," *Urban Studies* 51, no. 9 (2014): 1909–25; and parts of chapter 5 as "Constructing Police Abuse after Rodney King: How Skid Row Residents and the LAPD Contest Video Evidence," *Law and Social Inquiry* 36, no. 2 (2011): 327–53.

Publishing with the University of Chicago Press has been a fantasy come true. I'm honored to have had the chance to work with Doug Mitchell, who is responsible for so many of the ethnographies that line my shelves and inspire my work. Doug's enthusiasm continually rekindled my faith in the book, and more than a few ideas in these pages emerged from our conversations over coffee. Thanks to Doug, I've also developed a newfound respect for jazz, the culinary world, Plato, and metaphor. Tim McGovern and Kyle Wagner deserve special thanks for their patience, and for keeping this book moving from proposal to publication. Levi Stahl found new ways to make the book interesting and exciting. Audra Wolfe, at the Outside Reader, provided editorial advice, encouragement, and counseling when I needed it the most.

My family and friends gave me the nourishment I needed to survive the research and writing process. My mom, Bobbi, has drawn on an endless well of patience and compassion as I share each incremental, often plodding, step forward. She is a rare treasure, and the world is a far better place because of her. I hope she feels that I have made Wade proud. My brother Matt provided his home for multiple writing retreats, read drafts of chapters, and dove into hours-long conversations about culture, the state, and human agency. Matt is the smartest human I know. My brother Nathan is a major inspiration. The thought of him and his fellow Marines coming home to places like Skid Row gave me the motivation to continue digging deeper into poverty's causes and solutions. Charlie and Kendra Collins have provided lifelong friendship, hospitality, and kindness that I can never repay. I owe some of my most heartfelt gratitude to my loving partner, Stephanie, who was by my side throughout much of this process. Our journey began while we were both working in Skid Row, so between the lines of the text is a story about us.

The most difficult part about writing this book was leaving Skid Row. While I cannot list them by their real names, I am beyond indebted to a number of Skid Row residents and Central Division officers who welcomed me into their lives and indulged my ceaseless questions. They taught me so much, about the social order and about myself. I am especially thankful for those on both sides of the badge who decided not to shun me when they saw me fraternizing with the "other side." This project would have been near impossible without "Malcolm," who was my steadfast teacher, guardian, and friend throughout my time in the neighborhood. His story of redemption and his dedication to social justice is a beacon of hope in a place where hope is often hard to find. Pete White and Becky Dennison gave up significant time and resources to facilitate my fieldwork. They provided me an education that was not being taught in Westwood. Jeff, Catherine, and the rest of the Catholic Workers at the Hippie Kitchen provided me with an oasis of cool water and smiles during the hottest days. Your conviction inspires me to forge ahead.

Notes

Introduction

1. Davis (1987, 65).
2. Wolch and Dear (1993); Blasi (2007).
3. Blasi and Stuart (2008).
4. Wolch and Dear (1993); Anderson (1990); Bourgois (1996); Venkatesh (2000).
5. Esping-Andersen (1990); Beckett and Western (2001).
6. Wacquant (2008, 2009).
7. Garland (1985, 2001).
8. Garland (2001, 43).
9. Harvey (2005).
10. Brown (2003).
11. Moffitt (2014).
12. Wolch and Dear (1993).
13. Wacquant (2009).
14. Jencks (1995); Beckett and Herbert (2010).
15. See Wacquant (2009).
16. Kohler-Hausmann (2013).
17. See especially Feeley and Simon (1992); Garland (2001).
18. Wacquant (2009, xxii; emphasis in original).
19. Ibid., 295–96.
20. See Smith (1996); Mitchell (1997); Beckett and Herbert (2010).
21. Wilson and Kelling (1982).
22. Kelling and Coles (1996, 15).
23. See Beckett and Herbert (2010).
24. Smith (1996, xviii).
25. See DeVerteuil, May, and von Mahs (2009).
26. Mitchell (1997, 311).
27. Katz (1997).
28. Polsky (1991, 4–5).
29. Ibid., 5.
30. Brown (2003).
31. Wilson (1997, 340–41).
32. Cruikshank (1999); Soss, Fording, and Schram (2011).
33. Soss, Fording, and Schram (2011).

34. See Lyon-Callo (2008); Whetstone and Gowan (2011); Gowan and Whetstone (2012).

35. Fairbanks (2009).

36. Foucault (1991); Dean (1999).

37. See Cohen (1985) on the concept of net-widening.

38. Foucault (1977, 24).

39. Herbert and Beckett (2010).

40. Blasi and Stuart (2008).

41. Garland (1990, 173).

42. Garland (1990).

43. See Swidler (2001); Harding (2010); Wilson (2010).

44. Swidler (2001).

45. See Anderson (1923); Shaw and McKay (1942).

46. For reviews, see Wacquant (1998, 2008); Goffman (2009); Rios (2011).

47. Bittner (1967).

48. Williams (1992).

49. Ibid., 82.

50. Goffman (2009).

51. Clark (1965, 86).

52. Citron (1989, B3); see also Davis (1990).

53. Wacquant (1998, 30).

54. Anderson (1990, 5).

55. Wacquant (2008).

56. Ibid., 169.

57. Bahr (1973, 287).

58. Drake and Cayton (1945); Anderson (1978, 1999); Jones (2010).

59. Los Angeles Community Action Network (2010).

60. Scott (1985, 1990).

61. Scott (1985, 29).

62. Thompson (1983); Gilliom (2001).

63. De Certeau (1984).

64. See Scott (1985, 28–37).

65. Scheper-Hughes (1992, 473).

66. Cohen (1999).

67. Rice (1918); Anderson (1923); Park and Burgess (1925). For a detailed discussion of the difference between the Skid Row district, the ghetto, and the slum as archetypical urban areas, see Huey (2007).

68. Bittner (1967, 705).

69. Estimates are based primarily on data collected by the Los Angeles Housing Department (LAHD), Los Angeles Homeless Services Authority (LAHSA), and the US Census.

70. DeVerteuil (2006).

71. Blasi (2007).

72. Deployment data are aggregated from the LAPD homepage: http://www.lapdonline.org (YTD 8/22/2009).

73. See Small (2007, 2008).

74. Zussman (2004, 362).

75. Small (2004).

76. Wacquant (2003, 5).

77. Anderson (1923); Liebow (1967); Anderson (1990); Duneier (1999); Gowan (2010).

78. Throughout the research, I followed the ethnographic convention of recording field notes in stepwise fashion (Snow and Anderson 1987). This method is unmatched for accurately representing statements and events in close and minute detail. First, I made detailed jottings at virtually all times while in the field, writing in a small spiral-bound notebook, in empty spaces of the newspaper, on the back of flyers for social services, or on any other inconspicuous piece of paper I could find. Initially, I worried that my incessant scribbling would interfere with the relationships I hoped to cultivate. However, I often found the opposite to be true. Once those working and living in the neighborhood had become familiar with my purpose, they sometimes encouraged me to take *more* notes. On several occasions, both residents and officers seemed discouraged when I was not actively taking notes on our interactions. Some even checked with me to make sure I had recorded an event they thought was particularly important. (In the methodological appendix I describe how some of my respondents exploited my presence.) When those in Skid Row gave me permission, I used a digital recorder to more precisely document interviews, conversations, and interactions. Second, I transcribed the resulting field notes and audio immediately after leaving the field. To improve my recall, I typically did this work in a 24-hour coffee shop, located just outside of downtown, before returning home. Third, I subjected my field notes to multiple rounds of coding in dialogue with relevant literature, roughly once every two to three weeks. Research questions and foci of inquiry were honed through theoretical sampling, as prominent themes and salient patterns emerged from the data.

79. See Blasi (2007); Blasi and Stuart (2008).

Chapter One

1. Business improvement districts, or BIDs, are formed by property or business owners to provide a heightened level of services, including security, street cleaning, and tourist assistance. In Los Angeles, a BID can only be established with the approval of at least 50 percent of owners within a geographically defined area, who pay an annual fee in exchange for services (Meek and Hubler 2006). By 1999, the majority of LA's downtown was overlain by BIDs. The CCEA BID alone encompasses 110 blocks, 575 property owners, and $1.34 billion in annual sales (Central City East Association 2005).

2. Central City East Association (2005, 6).

3. Soss, Fording, and Schram (2011).

4. See Wacquant (2009).

5. See Smith (1996).

6. DiMaggio and Powell (1983); Bourdieu (1984).

7. Marwell (2009, 3).

8. Becker (1963); Ruswick (2013).

9. See Anderson (1923); Hoch and Slayton (1989).

10. Inter-University Consortium against Homelessness (2007).

11. Katz (1996).

12. Ibid., 76; Gowan (2010).

13. Quoted in Katz (1996, 73).

14. Ibid.

15. See Ausubel (1951).

16. Boyer (1978, 140).

17. Booth (1890, 204–5).

18. Boritch and Hagan (1987).

19. Monkkonen (1981, 1982).

20. As police historian Eric Monkkonen (1981, 81) shows, during harsh winters and economic depressions, the number of lodgers exceeded the number of arrests.

21. Marquis (1992).

22. Beckett and Herbert (2010).

23. Katz (1996); Reich (2005).

24. Quoted in Monkkonen (1981, 127).

25. McLean (1965, 86–87).

26. Devine (1897).

27. *Los Angeles Times* (1901a).

28. *Los Angeles Times* (1901b, 12).

29. *Los Angeles Times* (1901c, 15).

30. *Los Angeles Times* (1905, 1).

31. Monkkonen (1981).

32. Quoted in Walker (1977, 81).

33. Ibid.

34. In 1915, drawing a link between immoral behavior and addictive substances, the LAPD experimented with an "anti-cigarette" clinic, treating over twenty-three hundred people in the first month (Walker 1977). According to LAPD chief Clarence E. Snively, "The nicotine poison which enters the body . . . has a tendency to make weak bodies, weak intellects and weak morals." http://www.lapdonline.org/history_of_the_lapd/content_basic_view/1108.

35. Riis ([1890] 1957, 207).

36. Anderson (1923).

37. See Hoch and Slayton (1989).

38. See Gowan (2010).

39. Walker and Brechin (2010, 48).

40. In fact, this was the first time in American history in which the end of a war did not increase the homeless population (Snow and Anderson 1993).

41. Hopper (1990).

42. Katz (1996, 44).

43. Morris (2009).

44. Snow and Anderson (1993).

45. Gowan (2010).

46. See Gowan (2010).

47. Beauregard (1991); Haas and Heskin (1981).

48. Haas and Heskin (1981).

49. Herbert (1971); Los Angeles Community Redevelopment Agency (1975).

50. Interview with Jeff Dietrich, Catherine Morris, and Catholic Worker members, March 4, 2011.

51. Ibid., 7.

52. Los Angeles Community Design Center (1976c, 12).

53. Los Angeles Community Design Center (1976a, 6–7).

54. Haas and Heskin (1981).

55. Goetz (1992).

56. Lamp was initially founded as the Los Angeles Men's Project (LAMP) in 1977, but was later renamed to reflect the services it provides for both men and women.

57. Interview with Mollie Lowery, February 13, 2012.

58. See Ferdinand (1976). Technological and administrative innovations further accelerated this trend. New forms of communication and transportation cut down on response times, which increased the possibility of catching offenders. Developments in forensic science and international information systems elevated the role of detectives in daily police work, while granting departments the ability to collaborate to solve an even greater number and range of crimes. Adopting a more professionalized, businesslike model, the new crime-fighting role also promised increased efficiency; because they were more adept at apprehending individuals who had actually committed crimes, departments devoted fewer preemptive resources toward entire groups in which only a fraction of individuals might become offenders.

59. Monkkonen (1981, 64).

60. Ibid., 158; see also Boritch and Hagan (1987).

61. Los Angeles Community Design Center (1976b, 5–6).

62. Ibid., 4.

63. Quoted in Beckett and Herbert (2010, 13–14).

64. Liddick (1976).

65. Interview with Dietrich, Morris, and Catholic Worker members, March 4, 2011.

66. Ibid.

67. Rosenzweig (2004).

68. Interview with Dietrich, Morris, and Catholic Worker members, March 4, 2011.

69. Clifford and McMillan (1987).

70. Interview with Dietrich, Morris, and Catholic Worker members, March 4, 2011.

71. Boyarsky (1987).

72. Wolch and Dear (1993).

73. See Goetz (1992).

74. Wolch and Dear (1993). A total of 12 million workers were unemployed, with 1.2 million discouraged from seeking employment. As a measure of the working poor population, 15 percent of Americans were living below the poverty line despite the fact that half of these people were in households in which at least one person worked (Wolch and Dear 1993, 7). Economic restructuring was particularly pronounced in Los Angeles.

75. Soja (1989, 201). Throughout the mid-twentieth century, southern California had the highest concentration of auto-related industries outside Michigan (Wolch and Dear 1993, 50).

76. Wolch and Dear (1993). While still a minority, women and children also became a more regular sight in the area.

77. The deinstitutionalization movement set the tone for much of the welfare restructuring that would follow. The passage of the 1963 Community Mental Health Centers Act began the process of closing state and local mental hospitals nationwide. California led the nation in this push, permanently closing state- and county-funded asylums. Initially springing from the same civil rights demands that overturned civility laws, the deinstitutionalization movement aimed to transfer psychiatric patients

out of custodial institutions into community mental health facilities (Wolch and Dear 1993). Unfortunately, alternative local services received little funding and largely failed to materialize. This meant that on discharge, former patients drifted to Skid Rows, where inexpensive accommodations and basic necessities could be found. Mentally disabled persons who were unable to navigate the housing market became homeless.

78. Wolch, Dear, and Akita (1988).

79. See Wacquant (2009); Soss, Fording, and Schram (2011).

80. Katz (1996, 296).

81. DeVerteuil et al. (2003); Wolch and Dear (1993).

82. Gowan (2010, 53).

83. Wolch and Dear (1993, 22).

84. Wolch (1990).

85. Katz (1996).

86. Gowan (2010, 49).

87. Katz (2002, 153).

88. Blasi (2007).

89. Gordon (1994, 1).

90. Already staggering when considered in isolation, the mega-shelters' organizational capacities and range of services are even more significant when compared to the typical mid-twentieth century relief organization. For instance, the Catholic Worker's long-standing soup kitchen operates out of a single-story, street-front building containing little more than a kitchen. Food distribution and dining takes place outdoors, in a modest courtyard behind the main building. The Catholic Worker serves meals only three days per week and can accommodate only eight to ten individuals in a communal house located two miles east of Skid Row. Since its inception, the soup kitchen has operated solely on unpaid, volunteer labor.

91. DeVerteuil (2006).

92. Coates (2005).

93. Harcourt (2005, 62).

94. Rivera (2003a, B1).

95. Interview with Dietrich, Morris, and Catholic Worker members, March 4, 2011.

96. Sparks (2012).

97. McMillan (1992, A1).

98. Martinez (1995, 3).

99. Mungen (1997, 3).

100. Ibid.

101. Ibid.

102. Ibid.

103. Ibid.

104. See Blasi (2007).

105. Blasi (2007, 14–19); also see Los Angeles Homeless Services Authority (2006).

106. During my fieldwork, the scarcity of and competition for nightly beds rendered a number of individuals unable to benefit from certain services, like the Los Angeles Community Action Network's free legal clinic, because they had to race to secure a place in line outside one of the mega-shelters.

107. Blasi (2007).

108. Ibid., 18. Other US cities, largely in response to inclement weather and the

threat of freezing deaths, have instituted "no questions asked" shelters, which relieve many of the obstacles to shelter that those in Skid Row continue to face.

109. Mungen (1997).

110. Hubler (1992).

111. Los Angeles Community Action Network (2005).

112. Catania (2003).

113. Ibid.

114. Perry (2005, M5).

115. Stewart (2003, 1).

116. Hayasaki (2000).

117. Decker (2000).

118. Ibid.

119. Wilson and Kelling (1982).

120. Ibid., 35. Unfortunately, the majority of discussion surrounding the broken windows thesis narrowly fixates on its soundness as a criminological theory, questioning the causal links between neighborhood disorder and crime (see Skogan 1990; Harcourt 2001). These debates too often miss the fact that Wilson and Kelling's (1982) work is, first and foremost, a critique of the twentieth-century shift away from preventive crime control toward a reactive, legalistic approach. Noting the police reforms described earlier, Wilson and Kelling (1982) emphatically state:

> Into the 1970s, attention shifted to the role of police as crime-fighters. Studies of police behavior ceased, by and large, to be accounts of the order maintenance function and became, instead, efforts to propose and test ways whereby the police could solve more crime, make more arrests, and gather better evidence.

As a result, "the link between order maintenance and crime-prevention, so obvious to earlier generations, was forgotten" (1982, 34). Evoking the rationale of August Vollmer and other police experts in the early 1900s, Wilson in particular advocates moving up the stream of criminality to dam its source, thereby reconstituting law enforcement as "a means to an end, not an end in itself." Extending the work of his mentor, Edward Banfield (1974), Wilson (1975) argues that urban ills, including poverty and crime, spring from a common origin: the cultural propensities, present-orientedness, and impulsivity of the poor (see Harcourt 2001). To be clear, Wilson is more pessimistic than Vollmer about wholesale corrections to the "ethos" of the "lower-class." As a result, he recommends aiming slightly lower on the stream of criminality to regulate the situational inducements that allow for cultural propensities to materialize. Despite this difference, Wilson and Vollmer similarly stress that preventing serious crime requires that the police regulate "behavior that is antisocial without being illegal" (Banfield 1991, 315), what Wilson and Kelling (1982) later came to refer to as "disorder."

121. Wilson and Kelling (1982); see Beckett and Herbert (2010).

122. Gowan (2010).

123. Wilson and Kelling (1982).

124. Los Angeles Police Department (2002).

125. Huey (2007, 30–31).

126. Blasi (2007).

127. Minutes, "LA Safer City Project—Central City East," August 6, 2003. Emphasis mine.

128. Minutes, "LA Safer City Initiative—Central City East," September 19, 2003; Minutes, "LA Safer City Initiative—Central City East," November 7, 2003.

129. McNott (2003, B24).

130. Blasi (2007).

131. Rivera (2003b, B1). In chapter 3, I provide an alternative perspective from several individuals who have absconded from SOS programs.

132. Coates (2006); DiMassa (2006).

133. Coates (2006, 8).

134. DiMassa and Winton (2005); Rivera (2006).

135. Intradepartmental Correspondence, "Central Area 2004 Strategic Plan to Address Encampments," January 13, 2004.

136. Internal Memorandum, "L.A. Safer City Initiative: Training and Deployment Plan, Central Area," October 13, 2003.

137. "Do Gang Injunctions Work?" *Airtalk*, 89.3 KPCC. April 8, 2010.

138. Complaint to Enjoin, Abate, and Prevent Public Nuisance Activity, pages 8–9.

139. Ibid.

140. Wacquant (2009).

141. Blasi (2007).

142. See Smith (1996); Mitchell (1997, 2003).

143. Oxsen (2013).

144. Beckett and Herbert (2010).

145. Lipsky (1980).

Chapter Two

1. LAMC 41.59 was signed into law in 1997.

2. While the historical analysis in the previous chapter strongly supports Officer Morgan's description of his own patrol experiences in the early 1990s, I was unable to definitively confirm his account. Indeed, I encountered a number of stories and narratives, retold throughout this book, whose factual accuracy I was similarly unable to definitively verify. This problem is hardly unique to my project. *All* qualitative, ethnographic, and interview-based studies rely heavily on the recollections of informants and respondents. I followed ethnographic convention and made a concerted effort to "check stuff out," usually by triangulating stories with multiple people (for a detailed discussion of this process, see Duneier 1999, 345–46). At the same time, as a researcher committed to the interactionist tradition of the Chicago School, I am ultimately less interested in ferreting out the "truth" of informants' stories than I am in how *they* interpret and perceive events. I direct attention to how and why individuals' *own* views, precisely because they are *always* partial, become meaningful and consequential. To paraphrase early Chicago School thinker William I. Thomas, if someone defines a situation as real, then it is real in its consequences. This principle forms the basis of my general approach.

3. For a review see Sousa (2010).

4. White (2010).

5. Ibid. Also see Muir (1977); Wilson (1978); Skolnick ([1966] 2011).

6. Wacquant (2009, 2); also see Feeley and Simon (1992) on the "new penology."

7. Throughout England and Wales, for instance, officers draw on the availability of anti-social behavior orders (ASBOs)—broad prohibitions against "actions that cause or

are likely to cause harassment, alarm, or distress"— to detain and investigate practically anyone in public space (Johnsen and Fitzpatrick 2010). Officers in Seattle, Washington, similarly rely on broad trespass laws to justify repeated contact with pedestrians (Beckett and Herbert 2010). Officers in Ottawa, Canada, also mobilize the city's collection of underspecified "nuisance laws" (Walby and Lippert 2012).

8. See Moskos (2008).

9. See Bittner (1967); Herbert (1997).

10. Brenner and Theodore (2002).

11. For a comprehensive bibliography see Bahr (1970).

12. Rumbaut and Bittner (1979).

13. Bittner (1967).

14. Burawoy (2003, 650).

15. Cresswell (1996); Herbert (1997).

16. Irwin (1985); Bogue (1963, 405–6).

17. Bittner (1967).

18. Ibid., 709; see Bahr (1973, 207).

19. Reporting on these imperatives, one officer professed to Bittner (1967, 709), "In the last analysis, I really never solve any problems. The best I can hope for is to keep things from getting worse."

20. Bittner (1967, 709). Throughout interviews conducted in the 1960s and 1970s, officers consistently asserted that they felt the population was beyond saving. As a result, they actively disavowed any transformative, social work role at all. When officers did grant assistance, it was instead based on "the recognition that the hungry, the sick, and the troubled are a potential source of problems" (Bittner 1967, 709).

21. Wiseman (1970); also see Muir (1977); Van Maanen (1978).

22. Bittner (1967).

23. Ibid.

24. Spradley (1970).

25. Bittner (1967).

26. Ibid.

27. Gesler (1992); Wilton and DeVerteuil (2006).

28. Even after moving to Chicago, I have continued to see television advertisements for Malibu drug rehabilitation clinics.

29. Moskos (2008).

30. See Rivera (2003b).

31. Federal Bureau of Investigation (2006).

32. Blasi (2007).

33. Moskos (2008).

34. Ibid., 143.

35. Bittner (1967, 711; emphasis in original).

36. See Desmond (2008); Jerolmack (2013).

37. Blasi (2007).

38. Central Division leadership presented this statistic at a Community Impact Team Meeting on March 8, 2010.

39. My presence may have increased officers' willingness to engage in these back-and-forths. However, I strongly suspect that some version of these interactions occurred even when I was not present. On a number of occasions, it was clear that officers'

banter and braggadocio regarding recent diversions was a continuation of an exchange initiated on a previous shift or on previous days when I had not been present. Officers referenced names and incidents that were unknown to me, and seemed to feel no real compulsion to pause their quips to explain the details to me.

40. Wieder (1974).

41. Paperman (2003).

42. Sugarman (1976).

43. Most LA residents, even native Angelenos, are unaware that this behavior is technically illegal and carries a fine of up to $250. I myself had been oblivious to the law until I began my research in Skid Row, where constant enforcement has made many residents *hyperaware* of the law. On my very first fieldwork visit to the neighborhood, I was about to step into an intersection during the flashing red hand; a man standing on the curb behind me grabbed my shirt and pulled me back onto the sidewalk just as a patrol car turned the corner in front of us. "You'll get a ticket for jaywalking if you do that down here," he scolded me as we waited for the walk signal to appear again. Officer Garcia was undoubtedly responsible for providing many residents with this expensive legal education.

44. See Gowan (2010); Wilton and DeVerteuil (2006).

45. DiMassa and Fausset (2005). Skid Row "dumping" gained national attention with the release of Michael Moore's 2007 documentary *Sicko*. The film shows closed-circuit camera footage of an elderly and disoriented woman in a hospital gown who had been abandoned by a local hospital on the doorsteps of the Union Rescue Mission.

46. Bittner (1967).

47. Ibid.

48. Los Angeles Community Action Network (2005).

49. See Zavis (2010).

50. Some officers advanced this practice as particularly effective for enticing mentally disabled individuals into programs. As one officer told me, "We've got a fair share of mentally handicapped down here, and they don't always respond to our instructions. But everyone needs to eat, right? Handicapped or not, we're all going to go wherever we can get food."

51. Irwin (1985).

52. Garland (1996, 2001).

Chapter Three

1. Garland (1985, 251).

2. Anderson (1999).

3. Vaillancourt (2010).

4. In the late 1990s, California enacted a series of laws to reduce, and in some cases ban, the use of weight-lifting equipment in prisons. Despite these mandates, many prisons still possess and maintain such equipment, which inmates continue to use. Where formal equipment is absent, prisoners frequently construct their own makeshift weight piles, lifting stacks of books or heavy kitchen equipment, using cell bars and bunk beds for pull-ups, and performing lengthy sessions of calisthenics. While proper weight piles may be on the decline, the term is used as a catchall to describe those locations within the prison where inmates gather to exercise.

5. O.G. stands for "original gangster." However, in its common usage, the title need

not denote gang affiliation. In Skid Row, as in many other impoverished communities of color, O.G. is a deferential term used to refer to one's elders or superiors. It operates much like the term "old head" as described in the work of Anderson (1990, 1999) and Duneier (1999).

6. Wolch and Dear (1993).

7. Ibid., 273.

8. Wacquant (1993, 2008).

9. Wacquant (2008).

10. Also see Anderson (1976); Newman (1999); Bourgois and Schonberg (2009).

11. Wacquant (1993, 371).

12. Tex had been convicted of trespassing after LAPD officers found him sleeping behind a trendy coffeehouse in Hollywood. A fellow jail inmate informed Tex about the city's "camping ordinance," which allows homeless individuals to legally sleep on the sidewalks of Skid Row between the hours of 9:00 p.m. and 6:00 a.m.

13. Anderson (1976, 1990, 1999).

14. Anderson (1990, 5).

15. Ibid., 231.

16. Tex was referring to LAPD's "Eastside Detail," discussed in chapters 1 and 2.

17. For an extended account of the lived experience of dopesickness, see Bourgois and Schonberg (2009, 80–88).

18. Several in the group spent an occasional night in emergency beds, and a few continued to attend meal services, particularly those whose drug felony convictions disqualified them from food stamps under California law.

19. I experienced many of these conditions firsthand. In the first two years of my fieldwork, I sometimes escaped the summer heat and ate my lunch at the Los Angeles Mission, where an hour-long religious sermon is mandatory before receiving food. Each day, mission staff members closely guard the rear of the procession from the chapel into the cafeteria, making sure that the "chow line" cannot be infiltrated by anyone who has not attended the sermon. As they stand watch, they often yell "last man walking" in a call-and-response fashion. Dante was among a number of the men who drew comparisons between this practice and an inmate's final march down death row—"dead man walking."

20. Scott (1990).

21. For a review of other examples of "verbal duels," see Lee (2009). For other examples of the role of "competitive sociability" in peer group formation and maintenance, see Anderson (1976); Desmond (2008); Jerolmack (2009).

22. Scott (1990, 137).

23. Goffman (1963, 44).

24. See Logan and Molotch (1987).

25. See Anderson (1990); Gotham and Brumley (2002); Merry (1981); Venkatesh (1997).

26. Venkatesh (1997, 104).

27. Gotham and Brumley (2002); Suttles (1968).

28. See Anderson (1976); Desmond (2012); Hunter (2010); Small (2004); Suttles (1968); Venkatesh (2000, 2006).

29. Goffman (2009).

30. Rios (2011).

31. Wacquant (2001, 116).

32. Scott (1985, 1990).

33. As detailed in the previous chapter, I observed officers granting additional leniency to those who could produce mega-shelter badges. I was not able to discern whether officers recognized that some individuals, like James, were merely feigning enrollment in mega-shelter programs. Only two of the officers I shadowed or spoke with indicated that they had any knowledge of this tactic of evasion. As with all of the tactics deployed by Steel and his crew, I made the conscious decision *not* to ask officers if they were aware that they were being fooled. This would have been a gross betrayal of the trust I had established with the men, and threatened to expose them to harsh consequences.

34. Unlike formal probation, in which an individual reports to a probation officer, summary probationers report directly to a judge. The unpredictability of the outcome in the wake of an additional violation clearly worried Demetrius.

35. Beyond the difference in exercises performed in the two settings, the park provided a natural buffer between the men and the street that was missing on San Julian Street. Officers seldom entered the park, which was patrolled by private security guards employed by the SRO Corporation.

36. When I share these findings with colleagues or in public forums, I am occasionally asked, "Don't Skid Row officers catch on to residents' cop wisdom? Don't they adapt? Surely officers are not oblivious. They are not dopes." I agree: Central Division officers are an incredibly perceptive and conscientious lot. This leads me to respond with questions of my own: What exactly does it mean to "catch on" to cop wisdom? How might such a clued-in officer behave? It is critical to underline the fact that, in developing and deploying cop wisdom, residents seek to alter their appearances, routines, and behaviors to more closely resemble types to whom officers pay less attention. For instance, residents avoid self-grooming to appear less like addicts, stick to relatively deserted streets to sidestep known drug spots, and sequester themselves in their SRO rooms to reduce the probability of police contact. How, exactly, might an officer "adapt" to such tactics? By more readily detaining those who do *not* appear to be involved in drug activity? By interrogating individuals who are walking alone? While I suppose that officers could undertake these adaptive measures, they did not. And why would they? They are on the hunt for individuals who appear suspicious and in need of criminal justice interventions.

With that said, I did encounter two officers who, over the course of my fieldwork, became increasingly suspicious of residents like James, who flashed their mega-shelter badges to gain leniency. Under certain circumstances, particularly if they encountered an individual far from the Top, these officers disregarded badges as proof of compliance and punished those who presented them more harshly than others. In these cases, officers continued to pursue the chief demands of therapeutic policing, punishing copwise tactics that violated the normative geography enforced by officers.

37. Wacquant (2008).

Chapter Four

1. Rose (1999); Garland (2001).

2. Buerger and Mazerolle (1998).

3. For a review see Desmond and Valdez (2012).

4. See Duneier (1999); Venkatesh (2006); Gowan (2010).
5. Duneier (1999, 60–80).
6. Ibid., 79.
7. Ibid., 63.
8. Duneier (1999).
9. Rivera (2006); Winton (2007).
10. Jacobs ([1961] 1993).
11. Ibid., 40.
12. Ibid.
13. Sampson and Groves (1989, 777).
14. Jacobs ([1961] 1993).
15. Ibid.; Wilson and Kelling (1982).
16. See Skogan (1990); Harcourt (2001); Hinkle and Weisburd (2008).
17. Wilson and Kelling (1982).
18. Bittner (1967, 703).
19. Bahr (1973); Huey and Kemple (2007). This assumption has become standard throughout the social disorganization tradition, which tends to conclude analysis at precisely this stage (see Sampson and Groves 1989; Bursik and Grasmick 1993; Silver and Miller 2004). Social disorganization researchers interpret any increase in residents' willingness to intervene—whether in the event of a street fight, vandalism, or the presence of troublesome street-corner groups—as straightforward evidence of an elevated propensity to support the "common good" of the community (Sampson 2012). However, in limiting inquiry to residents' willingness to intercede in response to a limited set of "problematic" behaviors—defined in advance by the researcher rather than the resident—social disorganization research risks overlooking a range of concomitant regulations, supplementary targets, and unanticipated consequences as informal control concretely unfolds on the ground.
20. Jacobs ([1961] 1993); Wilson and Kelling (1982).
21. Jacobs ([1961] 1993, 46).
22. Jacobs ([1961] 1993).
23. Ibid., 90–92.
24. Ibid., 90.
25. Jacobs ([1961] 1993).
26. Ibid.
27. Wilson and Kelling (1982).
28. Jacobs ([1961] 1993, 44).
29. Ibid., 48.
30. Wilson and Kelling (1982); Jacobs ([1961] 1993).
31. Los Angeles Community Action Network (2009).
32. I later received word that Sam had been arrested for being in possession of over a hundred pirated DVD movies, a felony under California Penal Code 350.
33. See von Mahs (2013).
34. For a detailed discussion of inner-city apartheid, see Bourgois (1996).

Chapter Five
1. Goffman (1974).
2. Small (2004).

3. In his ethnographic study of a Puerto Rican barrio, for instance, Small (2004) finds that variations in residents' neighborhood frames determined their divergent levels of participation in community affairs.

4. LACAN also differs from the mega-shelters in terms of funding. LACAN draws its funds primarily from philanthropic organizations specializing in public health, housing, legal aid, and community organizing. These include the Marguerite Casey Foundation, the California Endowment, and the Diane Middleton Foundation. The organization has also received funding from the US Department of Justice for its civil rights work, as well as a US Centers for Disease Control Community Transformation Grant.

5. Residents' participation and affiliation with LACAN reinforced this orientation. During various events and gatherings, I consistently observed residents correcting one another when someone uttered statements that derided or marginalized those unaffiliated with the organization. For instance, after returning from a Community Watch patrol, I stood chatting with a group of residents gathered in the lobby of the LACAN office. Recounting a police incident, a team member referred to an arrestee as "schizoid." Karl, another team member who had been standing nearby, responded with a brief lecture. "You mean 'schizophrenic,' right? You can't just go around calling people 'schizoid.' That makes them sound like they're some kind of maniac, when all they really need is medication. People down here can't afford medication. You know that. We all got our own problems we're dealing with. Some of us more than others." The first team member quickly apologized.

6. McAdam (1983).

7. Ibid., 735.

8. Throughout my fieldwork, LACAN made a number of efforts to distribute disposable cameras and even camera-equipped phones to various groups of neighborhood residents. The thought was that, since these individuals spent considerable time in public space, they would be able to observe police interactions from start to finish. While the few resulting photographs and videos did occasionally show officer misconduct in a manner that supported the organization's more general claims, these pictures and recordings generally did not adequately capture contextual information and precipitating events in a manner that would overcome the organization's crisis of credibility. The fact that evidence produced through serendipitous recordings was largely unusable speaks to the level of sophistication Malcolm and the rest of the Community Watch team had developed over the course of their daily patrols.

9. Irrespective of the Fitzgerald Injunction, these patrol behaviors violate pedestrians' constitutional protections against unlawful search and seizure.

10. Gooding-Williams (1993); Goodwin (1994); Lawrence (2000).

11. Lawrence (2000).

12. I often overheard officers discussing members of LACAN by name while in the station or out on patrol. Officers were not shy about sharing their negative opinions about the organization with me, particularly once they observed me shadowing the organization.

13. LACAN's leadership repeatedly lectured those on Community Watch to remain silent while the cameras were on. On several occasions, team members' quiet, but audible, derogatory comments toward the police rendered tapes unusable as evidence.

14. There are no shortage of public narratives claiming that homeless and other

poor populations attempt to get arrested to secure more stable living accommodations and meals. I never once encountered this during my fieldwork, either among homeless or housed Skid Row residents. Residents overwhelmingly described jail as somewhere they worked diligently to avoid.

15. The scene highlights the uphill battle that stigmatized populations face in making claims of injustice. Both the officer and Malcolm convey a shared recognition that, when their street-level contests move into court, it will not be enough for someone like Malcolm to reveal wrongdoing by officers. He must first prove his own moral worth for his claims to be seen as legitimate.

16. I took field notes throughout the court proceedings. To ensure the accuracy of the quotes used here, I double-checked my notes against the transcripts written by the court reporter.

17. LACAN feared that the city was punishing it for its legal action by refusing to pick up even items that city workers would remove from other neighborhoods.

18. *New York Times* (2012, 12).

19. *Los Angeles Times* (2014, A14); *Los Angeles Times* (2012).

20. Farrar (2013).

21. Decker (2000).

22. Holland (2014); *Los Angeles Times* (2014).

23. Gooding-Williams (1993); Goodwin (1994).

Conclusion

1. Pratt et al. (2005).

2. Pratt et al. (2005, xiii).

3. Wacquant (2009, 296).

4. Kohler-Hausmann (2013, 352).

5. Eith and Durose (2011).

6. See Bittner (1967); Wiseman (1970); Manning (1977); Herbert (2006); Huey (2007).

7. Lipsky (1980); Watkins-Hayes (2009).

8. Wacquant (2009).

9. See Valverde (2003); Moore and Hannah-Moffat (2005).

10. Wolch (1990).

11. Lofland (1973, 90).

12. Scroggin (2012).

13. Vaillancourt (2009); Green (2013).

14. In a study similarly concerned with the attitudes and actions of street-level bureaucrats, sociologist Celeste Watkins-Hayes (2009) finds that some minority welfare caseworkers identify more closely with their clients on race and class lines, which leads them to offer more tailored advice and guidance to fellow members of "the community."

15. Symbolic power, as French sociologist Pierre Bourdieu (1991, 170) writes, refers to the "power of constituting the given through utterances, of making people see and believe, of confirming or transforming the vision of the world and, thereby, action on the world and thus the world itself." As criminologist Ian Loader (1997, 3) notes, "The police's entitlement and capacity to speak about the world is seldom challenged. They start from a winning position."

16. See Wilson (2000).

17. See Duncan (1976); Anderson (1990); Wacquant (2008).

18. See Papachristos, Hureau, and Braga (2013).

19. See Brunson and Weitzer (2011); Amber (2013).

20. Tsemberis (2004).

21. Bourgois (1996).

22. For a more detailed discussion of the principles of harm reduction, see Marlatt (2002).

23. Given Project 50's commitment to noncoercive supports, the program has been subject to stinging, if unsurprising, criticism from Central Division and its mega-shelters partners. The program's unwillingness to allow the police unfettered access to its residences has prompted Central Division officers to accuse the program of facilitating (and even promoting) drug sales and abuse. Mega-shelter representatives similarly disseminate this message throughout their own facilities, during community meetings, and in the media.

24. Lopez (2009).

25. Zavis (2012).

Appendix

1. Duneier (1999); Gowan (2010); Goffman (2014).

2. See especially Duneier (1999); Desmond (2008); Orrico (2014).

3. Romero (2011).

4. Romero (2013).

5. In recent years, these "prison-style" workouts are popping up in the parks of low-income neighborhoods across the United States. They have been popularized in fitness blogs and major magazines (including *Esquire* and *Vice Magazine*) and now serve as a primary vehicle through which some community organizations, like New York City's Bartendaz, engage in youth empowerment, prisoner reentry, and violence prevention programs.

6. Black and Metzger (1965).

7. Ibid., 144.

8. Wiseman (1970, 10–14).

9. See Anderson (1976, 1999); Jones (2010).

10. Duneier (2011).

11. See Smith (1996); Mitchell (1997, 2001, 2003).

12. See Smith (1996); Mitchell (1997).

References

Amber, Jeannine. 2013. "The Talk." *Time*, July 29, 33.

Anderson, Elijah. 1978. *A Place on the Corner*. Chicago: University of Chicago Press.

———. 1990. *Streetwise: Race, Class, and Change in an Urban Community*. Chicago: University of Chicago Press.

———. 1999. *Code of the Street: Decency, Violence, and the Moral Life of the Inner City*. New York: W. W. Norton.

Anderson, Nels. 1923. *The Hobo: The Sociology of the Homeless Man*. Chicago: University of Chicago Press.

Ausubel, Herman. 1951. "General Booth's Scheme of Social Salvation." *American Historical Review* 56 (3): 519–25.

Bahr, Howard M. 1970. *Disaffiliated Man: Essays and Bibliography on Skid Row, Vagrancy, and Outsiders*. Toronto: University of Toronto Press.

———. 1973. *Skid Row: An Introduction to Disaffiliation*. New York: Oxford University Press.

Banfield, Edward C. 1974. *The Unheavenly City Revisited*. Boston: Little, Brown.

———, ed. 1991. *Here the People Rule: Selected Essays*. 2nd ed. Washington, DC: American Enterprise Institute.

Beauregard, Robert A. 1991. "Capital Restructuring and the New Built Environment of Global Cities: New York and Los Angeles." *International Journal of Urban and Regional Research* 15 (1): 90–105.

Becker, Howard S. 1963. *Outsiders*. New York: Macmillan.

Beckett, Katherine, and Steven Herbert. 2010. *Banished: The New Social Control in Urban America*. New York: Oxford University Press.

Beckett, Katherine, and Bruce Western. 2001. "Governing Social Marginality: Welfare, Incarceration, and the Transformation of State Policy." *Punishment & Society* 3 (1): 43–59.

Bittner, Egon. 1967. "The Police on Skid-Row: A Study of Peacekeeping." *American Sociological Review* 32 (5): 699–715.

Black, Mary, and Duane Metzger. 1965. "Ethnographic Description and the Study of Law." *American Anthropologist* 67 (6): 141–65.

Blasi, Gary. 2007. *Policing Our Way Out of Homelessness? The First Year of the Safer Cities Initiative on Skid Row*. Los Angeles: Inter-University Consortium on Homelessness.

Blasi, Gary, and Forrest Stuart. 2008. *Has the Safer Cities Initiative in Skid Row Reduced Serious Crime?* Los Angeles: UCLA School of Law.

Bogue, Donald. 1963. *Skid Row in American Cities*. Chicago: University of Chicago Press.

Booth, William. 1890. *In Darkest England, and the Way Out*. London: Sergel.

Boritch, Helen, and John Hagan. 1987. "Crime and the Changing Forms of Class Control: Policing Public Order in 'Toronto the Good,' 1859–1955." *Social Forces* 66 (2): 307–35.

Bourdieu, Pierre. 1984. *Distinction: A Social Critique of the Judgement of Taste*. Cambridge, MA: Harvard University Press.

———. 1991. *Knowledge and Symbolic Power*. Cambridge: Polity.

Bourgois, Philippe. 1996. *In Search of Respect: Selling Crack in El Barrio*. Cambridge: Cambridge University Press.

Bourgois, Philippe, and Jeffrey Schonberg. 2009. *Righteous Dopefiend*. Berkeley: University of California Press.

Boyarsky, Bill. 1987. "No Moratorium; Skid Row Sweeps on Again." *Los Angeles Times*, March 5, D1.

Boyer, Paul. 1978. *Urban Masses and Moral Order, 1820–1920*. Cambridge, MA: Harvard University Press.

Brenner, Neil, and Nik Theodore. 2002. "Cities and the Geographies of 'Actually Existing Neoliberalism.'" *Antipode* 34 (3): 349–79.

Brown, Wendy. 2003. "Neo-Liberalism and the End of Liberal Democracy." *Theory & Event* 7 (1).

Brunson, Rod K., and Ronald Weitzer. 2011. "Negotiating Unwelcome Police Encounters: The Intergenerational Transmission of Conduct Norms." *Journal of Contemporary Ethnography* 40 (4): 425–56.

Buerger, Michael E., and Lorraine Green Mazerolle. 1998. "Third-Party Policing: A Theoretical Analysis of an Emerging Trend." *Justice Quarterly* 15 (2): 301–27.

Burawoy, Michael. 2003. "Revisits: An Outline of a Theory of Reflexive Ethnography." *American Sociological Review* 68 (5): 645–79.

Bursik, Robert J., Jr., and Harold G. Grasmick. 1999. *Neighborhoods & Crime*: Lexington Books.

Catania, Sarah. 2003. "Bucking Skid Row." *LA Weekly*, March 7, 20.

Central City East Association. 2005. *Walk with Us: Reclaiming a Community*.

Citron, Alan. 1989. "Well, That's Just Skid Row." *Los Angeles Times*, November 15, B3.

Clark, Kenneth B. 1965. *Dark Ghetto: Dilemmas of Social Power*. New York: Harper and Rowe.

Clifford, Frank, and Penelope McMillan. 1987. "Raids Meant to Rid Skid Row of Its Homeless Encampments." *Los Angeles Times*, February 19, 1.

Coates, Chris. 2005. "Midnight Mission Accomplished." *Los Angeles Downtown News*, April 4, 4.

———. 2006. "State Senate Considers Homeless Legislation." *Los Angeles Downtown News*, February 27, 8.

Cohen, Cathy J. 1999. *The Boundaries of Blackness: AIDS and the Breakdown of Black Politics*. Chicago: University of Chicago Press.

Cohen, Stanley. 1985. *Visions of Social Control*. Cambridge: Polity.

Cresswell, Tim. 1996. *In Place–Out of Place: Geography, Ideology, and Transgression*. Minneapolis: University of Minnesota Press.

Cruikshank, Barbara. 1999. *The Will to Empower: Democratic Citizens and Other Subjects*. Ithaca, NY: Cornell University Press.

Davis, Mike. 1987. "'Chinatown,' Part Two? The 'Internationalization' of Downtown Los Angeles." *New Left Review* 1 (164): 65–86.

———. 1990. *City of Quartz: Excavating the Future in Los Angeles*. New York: Vintage.

de Certeau, Michel. 1984. *The Practice of Everyday Life*. Berkeley: University of California Press.

Dean, Mitchell. 1999. *Governmentality: Power and Rule in Modern Society*. Thousand Oaks, CA: Sage.

Decker, Twila. 2000. "Skid Row Streets Are Home No Longer." *Los Angeles TImes*, October 29, B1.

Desmond, Matthew. 2008. *On the Fireline: Living and Dying with Wildland Firefighters*. Chicago: University of Chicago Press.

———. 2012. "Disposable Ties and the Urban Poor." *American Journal of Sociology* 117 (5): 1295–1335.

Desmond, Matthew, and Nicol Valdez. 2012. "Unpolicing the Urban Poor: Consequences of Third-Party Policing for Inner-City Women." *American Sociological Review* 78 (1): 117–41.

DeVerteuil, Geoffrey. 2006. "The Local State and Homeless Shelters: Beyond Revanchism?" *Cities* 23 (2): 109–20.

DeVerteuil, Geoffrey, Heidi Sommer, Jennifer Wolch, and Lois Takahashi. 2003. "The Local Welfare State in Transition: Welfare Reform in Los Angeles County." In *New York and Los Angeles: Politics, Society, and Culture—A Comparative View*, edited by David Halle, 269–88. Chicago: University of Chicago Press.

DeVerteuil, Geoff, Jon May, and Jurgen von Mahs. 2009. "Complexity Not Collapse: Recasting the Geographies of Homelessness in a 'Punitive' Age." *Progress in Human Geography* 33 (5): 646–66.

Devine, Edward T. 1897. "The Shiftless and Floating City Population." *Annals of the American Academy of Political and Social Science* 10 (2): 1–16.

DiMaggio, Paul J., and Walter W. Powell. 1983. "The Iron Cage Revisited: Institutional Isomorphism and Collective Rationality in Organizational Fields." *American Sociological Review* 48 (2): 147–60.

DiMassa, Cara. 2006. "A Polished Big Apple Gives L.A. Ideas." *Los Angeles Times*, January 28, B1.

DiMassa, Cara, and Richard Fausset. 2005. "Mayor Orders Probe of Skid Row Dumping." *Los Angeles Times*, September 27, B1.

DiMassa, Cara, and Richard Winton. 2005. "Skid Row Strategy Hits First at Drugs." *Los Angeles Times*, November 23, A1.

Drake, St. Clair, and Horace R. Cayton. 1945. *Black Metropolis*. New York: Harcourt, Brace and Company.

Duncan, Burt L. 1976. "Differential Social Perception and Attribution of Intergroup Violence: Testing the Lower Limits of Stereotyping Blacks." *Journal of Personality and Social Psychology* 43 (4): 590–98.

Duneier, Mitchell. 1999. *Sidewalk*. New York: Farrar, Straus and Giroux.

———. 2011. "How Not to Lie with Ethnography." *Sociological Methodology* 41 (1): 1–11.

Eith, Christine, and Matthew R. Durose. 2011. "Contacts between the Police and the Public, 2008." *Bureau of Justice Statistics Special Report*, NCJ 234599, 1–28.

Esping-Andersen, Gøsta. 1990. *The Three Worlds of Welfare Capitalism*. Cambridge: Polity.

———. 2013. *The Three Worlds of Welfare Capitalism*. Princeton, NJ: Princeton University Press.

Fairbanks, Robert P. 2009. *How It Works: Recovering Citizens in Post-Welfare Philadelphia*. Chicago: University of Chicago Press.

Farrar, Tony. 2013. *Self-Awareness to Being Watched and Socially-Desirable Behavior: A Field Experiment on the Effect of Body-Worn Cameras and Police Use-of-Force*. Washington, DC: Police Foundation.

Federal Bureau of Investigation. 2006. "Arrest for Drug Abuse Violations, Percent Distribution by Region." https://www2.fbi.gov/ucr/cius2006/arrests/.

Feeley, Malcolm M., and Jonathan Simon. 1992. "The New Penology: Notes on the Emerging Strategy of Corrections and Its Implications." *Criminology* 30 (4): 449–74.

Ferdinand, Theodore N. 1976. "From a Service to a Legalistic Style Police Department: A Case Study." *Journal of Police Science and Administration* 4 (3): 302–19.

Foucault, Michel. 1977. *Discipline and Punish: The Birth of the Prison*. New York: Vintage.

———. 1991. "Governmentality." In *The Foucault Effect: Studies in Governmentality*, edited by Graham Burchell, Colin Gordon, and Peter Miller. Chicago: University of Chicago Press.

Garland, David. 1985. *Punishment and Welfare: A History of Penal Strategies*. Chicago: University of Chicago Press.

———. 1990. *Punishment and Modern Society: A Study in Social Theory*. Chicago: University of Chicago Press.

———. 1996. "The Limits of the Sovereign State: Strategies of Crime Control in Contemporary Society." *British Journal of Criminology* 36 (4): 445–71.

———. 2001. *The Culture of Control: Crime and Social Order in Contemporary Society*. Chicago: University of Chicago Press.

Gesler, Wilbert M. 1992. "Therapeutic Landscapes: Medical Issues in Light of the New Cultural Geography." *Social Science & Medicine* 34 (7): 735–46.

Gilliom, John. 2001. *Overseers of the Poor: Surveillance, Resistance, and the Limits of Privacy*. Chicago: University of Chicago Press.

Goetz, Edward G. 1992. "Land Use and Homeless Policy in Los Angeles." *International Journal of Urban and Regional Research* 16 (4): 540–54.

Goffman, Alice. 2009. "On the Run: Wanted Men in a Philadelphia Ghetto." *American Sociological Review* 74: 339–57.

———. 2014. *On the Run: Fugitive Life in an American City*. Chicago: University of Chicago Press.

Goffman, Erving. 1963. *Stigma: Notes on the Management of Spoiled Identity*. New York: Touchstone.

———. 1974. *Frame Analysis: An Essay on the Organization of Experience*. Boston: Northeastern University Press.

Gooding-Williams, Robert, ed. 1993. *Reading Rodney King/Reading Urban Uprising*. New York: Routledge.

Goodwin, Charles. 1994. "Professional Vision." *American Anthropologist* 96 (3): 606–33.

Gordon, Larry. 1994. "A New Home for the City's Homeless in Skid Row." *Los Angeles Times*, September 15, A1.

Gotham, Kevin Fox, and Krista Brumley. 2002. "Using Space: Agency and Identity in a Public-Housing Development." *City & Community* 1 (3): 267–89.

Gowan, Teresa. 2010. *Hobos, Hustlers, and Backsliders: Homeless in San Francisco*. Minneapolis: University of Minnesota Press.

Gowan, Teresa, and Sarah Whetstone. 2012. "Making the Criminal Addict: Subjectivity and Social Control in a Strong-Arm Rehab." *Punishment & Society* 14 (1): 69–93.

Green, Sarah Jean. 2013. "Lead Program Turns Drug Bust into Help, Not Jail." *Seattle Times*, January 3, 1B.

Haas, Gilda, and Allan David Heskin. 1981. "Community Struggles in Los Angeles." *International Journal of Urban and Regional Research* 5 (4): 546–63.

Harcourt, Bernard. 2001. *Illusion of Order: The False Promises of Broken Windows Policing*. Cambridge, MA: Harvard University Press.

———. 2005. *Policing L.A.'s Skid Row: Crime and Real Estate Development in Downtown Los Angeles (an Experiment in Real Time)*. Chicago: University of Chicago Law School.

Harding, David J. 2010. *Living the Drama: Community, Conflict, and Culture among Inner-City Boys*. Chicago: University of Chicago Press.

Harvey, David. 2005. *A Brief History of Neoliberalism*. Oxford: Oxford University Press.

Hayasaki, Erika. 2000. "Shelter Beds Stay Empty as Homeless Resist Confinement." *Los Angeles Times*, December 27, B1.

Herbert, Ray. 1971. "Plans to Rebuild Skid Row Section Revived by Yorty." *Los Angeles Times*, November 15, B1.

Herbert, Steve. 1997. *Policing Space: Territoriality and the Los Angeles Police Department*. Minneapolis: University of Minnesota Press.

———. 2006. *Citizens, Cops, and Power: Recognizing the Limits of Community*. Chicago: University of Chicago Press.

Herbert, Steve, and Katherine Beckett. 2010. "'This Is Home for Us': Questioning Banishment from the Ground Up." *Social and Cultural Geography* 11 (3): 231–45.

Hinkle, Joshua C., and David Weisburd. 2008. "The Irony of Broken Windows Policing: A Micro-Place Study of the Relationship between Disorder, Focused Police Crackdowns and Fear of Crime." *Journal of Criminal Justice* 36 (6): 503–12.

Hoch, Charles, and Robert A. Slayton. 1989. *New Homeless and Old: Community and the Skid Row Hotel*. Philadelphia: Temple University Press.

Holland, Gale. 2014. "Skid Row Cleanup Funding is OKd." *Los Angeles Times*, May 14, AA3.

Hopper, Kim. 1990. "Public Shelter as Hybrid Institutions: Homeless Men in Historical Perspective." *Journal of Social Issues* 46 (4): 13–29.

Hubler, Shawn. 1992. "Homeless Tell Need for Job Skills, Programs." *Los Angeles Times*, December 15, 1.

Huey, Laura. 2007. *Negotiating Demands: The Politics of Skid Row Policing in Edinburgh, San Francisco, and Vancouver*. Toronto: University of Toronto Press.

Huey, Laura, and Thomas Kemple. 2007. "'Let the Streets Take Care of Themselves': Making Sociological and Common Sense of Skid Row." *Urban Studies* 44 (12): 2305–19.

Hunter, Marcus A. 2010. "The Nightly Round: Space, Social Capital, and Urban Black Nightlife." *City & Community* 9 (2): 165–86.

Inter-University Consortium against Homelessness. 2007. *Ending Homelessness in Los Angeles*. Los Angeles.

Irwin, John. 1985. *The Jail: Managing the Underclass in American Society*. Berkeley: University of California Press.

Jacobs, Jane. (1961) 1993. *The Death and Life of Great American Cities*. New York: Random House.

Jencks, Christopher. 1995. *The Homeless*. Cambridge, MA: Harvard University Press.

Jerolmack, Colin. 2009. "Primary Groups and Cosmopolitan Ties: The Rooftop Pigeon Flyers of New York City." *Ethnography* 10 (4): 435–57.

———. 2013. *The Global Pigeon*. Chicago: University of Chicago Press.

Johnsen, Sarah, and Suzanne Fitzpatrick. 2010. "Revanchist Sanitisation or Coercive Care? The Use of Enforcement to Combat Begging, Street Drinking and Sleeping in England." *Urban Studies* 47 (8): 1703–23.

Jones, Nikki. 2010. *Between Good and Ghetto: African American Girls and Inner-City Violence*. Piscataway, NJ: Rutgers University Press.

Katz, Michael B. 1995. *Improving Poor People: The Welfare State, the "Underclass," and Urban Schools as History*. Princeton, NJ: Princeton University Press.

———. 1996. *In the Shadow of the Poorhouse: A Social History of Welfare in America*. New York: Basic Books.

———. 2002. *The Price of Citizenship: Redefining the American Welfare State*. New York: Macmillan.

Kelling, George L., and Katherine M. Coles. 1996. *Fixing Broken Windows: Restoring Order and Reducing Crime in Our Communities*. New York: Touchstone.

Kohler-Hausmann, Issa. 2013. "Misdemeanor Justice: Control without Conviction." *American Journal of Sociology* 119 (2): 351–93.

Lawrence, Regina G. 2000. *The Politics of Force: Media and the Construction of Police Brutality*. Berkeley: University of California Press.

Lee, Jooyoung. 2009. "Battlin' on the Corner: Techniques for Sustaining Play." *Social Problems* 56 (3): 578–98.

Levine, Lawrence W. 1977. *Black Culture and Black Consciousness*. New York: Oxford University Press.

Liddick, Betty. 1976. "Rehabilitation or Jail for Drunkenness?" *Los Angeles Times*, March 10, F1.

Liebow, Elliot. 1967. *Tally's Corner*. Boston: Little Brown.

Lipsky, Michael. 1980. *Street-Level Bureaucracy: Dilemmas of the Individual in Public Services*. New York: Russell Sage Foundation.

Loader, Ian. 1997. "Policing and the Social: Questions of Symbolic Power." *British Journal of Sociology* 48 (1): 1–18.

Lofland, Lyn H. 1973. *A World of Strangers: Order and Action in Public Space*. Prospect Heights: Waveland Press.

Logan, John R., and Harvey L. Molotch. 1987. *Urban Fortunes: The Political Economy of Place*. Berkeley: University of California Press.

Lopez, Steve. 2009. "Saving Lives, Saving Money." *Los Angeles Times*, February 11, B1.

Los Angeles Community Action Network. 2005. *Taken for Granted: Ignoring Downtown Food-Insecurity*.

———. 2009. *Demographics and Skid Row Los Angeles*.

———. 2010. *Community-Based Human Rights Assessment: Skid Row's Safer Cities Initiative*.

Los Angeles Community Design Center. 1976a. *Skid Row: Recommendations to Citizens Advisory Committee on the Central Business District Plan for the City of Los Angeles*. Part 1, *Conceptual Analysis*.

———. 1976b. *Skid Row: Recommendations to Citizens Advisory Committee on the Central Business District Plan for the City of Los Angeles*. Part 2, *Social Programs*.

———. 1976c. *Skid Row: Recommendations to Citizens Advisory Committee on the Central Business District Plan for the City of Los Angeles*. Part 4, *Physical Containment*.

Los Angeles Community Redevelopment Agency. 1975. *Redevelopment Plan: Central Business District Redevelopment Project*.

Los Angeles Homeless Services Authority. 2006. *2005 Greater Los Angeles Homeless Count*.

Los Angeles Times. 1901a. "Too Many Beggars on Our City Streets." November 14, 8.

———. 1901b. "Police Begin Clearing out the Begging Evil." November 14, 12.

———. 1901c. "Activity of Police Checks Begging Evil." November 15, 15.

———. 1905. "Eyesores to Be Banished." November 12, 1, 2.

———. 2012. "Cleaning Skid Row, Carefully." June 21, A14.

———. 2014. "A Welcome New Approach to Skid Row." April 4, A14.

Lyon-Callo, Vincent. 2008. *Inequality, Poverty, and Neoliberal Governance: Activist Ethnography in the Homeless Sheltering Industry*. Toronto: University of Toronto Press.

Manning, Peter. 1977. *Police Work: The Social Organization of Policing*. Prospect Heights, IL: Waveland Press.

Marlatt, G. Alan. 2002. *Harm Reduction: Pragmatic Strategies for Managing High Risk Behaviors*. New York: Guilford Press.

Marquis, Greg. 1992. "The Police as a Social Service in Early Twentieth-Century Toronto." *Histoire sociale/Social History* 25 (50): 335–58.

Martinez, Marilyn. 1995. "A Man with a Mission." *Los Angeles Times*, February 19, A3.

Marwell, Nicole P. 2009. *Bargaining for Brooklyn: Community Organizations in the Entrepreneurial City*. Chicago: University of Chicago Press.

McAdam, Doug. 1983. "Tactical Innovation and the Pace of Insurgency." *American Sociological Review* 48 (6): 735–54.

McLean, Albert F. 1965. *American Vaudeville as Ritual*. Lexington: University of Kentucky Press.

McMillan, Penelope. 1992. "Super Shelter Size of New Mission on Skid Row Draws Applause, Criticism." *Los Angeles Times*, January 22, A1.

McNott, Marshall. 2003. "A New Perspective along Skid Row." *Los Angeles Times*, March 15, B24.

Meek, Jack W., and Paul Hubler. 2006. "Business Improvement Districts in Southern California: Implications for Local Governance." *International Journal of Public Administration* 29 (1–3): 31–52.

Merry, Sally Engle. 1981. *Urban Danger: Life in a Neighborhood of Strangers*. Philadelphia: Temple University Press.

Mitchell, Don. 1997. "The Annihilation of Space by Law: The Roots and Implications of Anti-Homeless Laws in the United States." *Antipode* 29 (3): 303–35.

———. 2001. "Postmodern Geographical Praxis? The Postmodern Impulse and the War against Homeless People in the 'Post-Justice' City." In *Postmodern Geography: Theory and Praxis*, edited by Claudio Minca, 57–92. Oxford: Blackwell.

———. 2003. *The Right to the City: Social Justice and the Fight for Public Space*. London: Guilford.

Moffitt, Robert A. 2014. "Presidential Address: The Deserving Poor, the Family, and the U.S. Welfare System." Population Association of America, Boston, MA, May 2.

Monkkonen, Eric H. 1981. *Police in Urban America, 1860–1920*. Cambridge: Cambridge University Press.

———. 1982. "From Cop History to Social History: The Significance of the Police in American History." *Journal of Social History* 15 (4): 575–91.

Moore, Dawn, and Kelly Hannah-Moffat. 2005. "The Liberal Veil: Revisiting Canadian Penality." In *The New Punitiveness: Trends, Theories, Perspectives*, edited by John Pratt, David Brown, Mark Brown, Simon Hallsworth, and Wayne Morrison, 85–100. London: Routledge.

Morris, Andrew J.F. 2009. *The Limits of Voluntarism: Charity and Welfare from the New Deal through the Great Society*. Cambridge: Cambridge University Press.

Moskos, Peter. 2008. *Cop in the Hood: My Year Policing Baltimore's Eastern District*. Princeton, NJ: Princeton University Press.

Muir, William K. 1977. *Police: Streetcorner Politicians*. Chicago: University of Chicago Press.

Mungen, Donna. 1997. "Warren Currie, Tackling the Spiritual Side of the Homeless Problem." *Los Angeles Times*, October 5.

New York Times. 2012. "The Constitution on Skid Row." September 9, SR 12.

Newman, Katherine S. 1999. *No Shame in My Game: The Working Poor in the Inner City*. New York: Random House.

Orrico, Laura A. 2014. "'Doing Intimacy' in a Public Market: How the Gendered Experience of Ethnography Reveals Situated Social Dynamics." *Qualitative Research*. doi: 10.1177/1468794114543403.

Oxsen, Courtney. 2014. "Embracing 'Choice' and Abandoning the Ballot: Lessons from Berkeley's Popular Defeat of Sit-Lie." *Hastings Women's LJ* 25 (1): 135–35.

Papachristos, Andrew V., David M. Hureau, and Anthony A. Braga. 2013. "The Corner and the Crew: The Influence of Geography and Social Networks on Gang Violence." *American Sociological Review* 78 (3): 417–47.

Paperman, Patricia. 2003. "Surveillance Underground: The Uniform as an Interaction Device." *Ethnography* 4 (3): 397–419.

Park, Robert E., and Ernest W. Burgess. 1925. *The City: Suggestions for Investigation of Human Behavior in the Urban Environment*. Chicago: University of Chicago Press.

Perry, Jan. 2005. "Homeless Need Help, Not ACLU." *Los Angeles Times*, October 30, M5.

Polsky, Andrew J. 1991. *The Rise of the Therapeutic State*. Princeton, NJ: Princeton University Press.

Pratt, John, David Brown, Mark Brown, Simon Hallsworth, and Wayne Morrison, eds. 2005. *The New Punitiveness: Trends, Theories, Pespectives*. London: Routledge.

Reich, Jennifer A. 2005. *Fixing Families: Parents, Power, and the Child Welfare System*. New York: Routledge.

Rice, Stuart A. 1918. "The Homeless." *Annals of the American Academy of Political Science* 77:140–53.

Riis, Jacob A. (1890) 1957. *How the Other Half Lives: Studies among the Tenements of New York*. New York: Hill and Wang.

Rios, Victor. 2011. *Punished: Policing the Lives of Black and Latino Boys*. New York: New York University Press.

Rivera, Carla. 2003a. "Midnight Mission Growing Even as Downtown Gentrifies." *Los Angeles Times*, December 15, B1.

———. 2003b. "Program Offers a Way Off the Street." *Los Angeles Times*, December 26, B1.

——. 2006. "Ambush on Path to Recovery." *Los Angeles Times*, August 9, A1.

Romero, Dennis. 2011. "America's Second Poorest Big City Is Right Here in Southern California: San Bernardino." *LA Weekly*, October 17. http://www.laweekly.com (accessed January 5, 2012).

——. 2013. "LAPD Command Is Majority White Even as the Department Has Diversified." *LA Weekly*, May 31. http://www.laweekly.com (accessed February 12, 2014).

Rose, Nikolas. 1999. *Powers of Freedom: Reframing Political Thought*. Cambridge: Cambridge University Press.

Rosenzweig, David. 2004. "Harry L. Hupp, 74: Judge Changed the Treatment of Homeless Drunks in L.A." *Los Angeles Times*, January 29, B13.

Rumbaut, Ruben G., and Egon Bittner. 1979. "Changing Conceptions of the Police Role: A Sociological Review." *Crime and Justice* 1:239–88.

Ruswick, Brent. 2013. *Almost Worthy: The Poor, Paupers, and the Science of Charity in America, 1877–1917*. Bloomington: Indiana University Press.

Sampson, Robert J. 2012. *Great American City: Chicago and the Enduring Neighborhood Effect*. Chicago: University of Chicago Press.

Sampson, Robert J., and W. Byron Groves. 1989. "Community Structure and Crime: Testing Social-Disorganization Theory." *American Journal of Sociology* 94 (4): 774–802.

Scheper-Hughes, Nancy. 1992. *Death without Weeping: The Violence of Everyday Life in Brazil*. Berkeley: University of California Press.

Scott, James C. 1985. *Weapons of the Weak: Everyday Forms of Peasant Resistance*. New Haven, CT: Yale University Press.

——. 1990. *Domination and the Arts of Resistance: Hidden Transcripts*. New Haven, CT: Yale University Press.

Scroggin, Samantha Yale. 2012. "Attorneys Welcome Misdemeanor Diversion Program." *Santa Maria Times*, October 29, 1.

Shaw, Clifford R., and Henry D. McKay. 1942. *Juvenile Delinquency and Urban Areas*. Chicago: University of Chicago Press.

Silver, Eric, and Lisa L. Miller. 2004. "Sources of Informal Social Control in Chicago Neighborhoods." *Criminology* 42 (3): 551–84.

Skogan, Wesley G. 1990. *Disorder and Decline: Crime and the Spiral of Decay in American Neighborhoods*. Berkeley: University of California Press.

Skolnick, Jerome H. (1966) 2011. *Justice without Trial: Law Enforcement in Democratic Society*. New Orleans: Quid Pro Books.

Small, Mario L. 2004. *Villa Victoria: The Transformation of Social Capital in a Boston Barrio*. Chicago: University of Chicago Press.

——. 2007. "Is There Such a Thing as 'the Ghetto'? The Perils of Assuming That the South Side of Chicago Represents Poor Black Neighborhoods." *City* 11 (3): 413–21.

——. 2008. "Four Reasons to Abandon the Idea of 'the Ghetto.'" *City & Community* 7 (4): 389–98.

Smith, Neil. 1996. *The New Urban Frontier: Gentrification and the Revanchist City*. London: Routledge.

Snow, David A., and Leon Anderson. 1987. "Identity Work among the Homeless: The Verbal Construction and Avowal of Personal Identities." *American Journal of Sociology* 92 (6): 1336–71.

——. 1993. *Down on Their Luck: A Study of Homeless Street People*. Berkeley: University of California Press.

Soja, Edward W. 1989. *Postmodern Geographies: The Reassertion of Space in Critical Social Theory*. London: Verso.

Soss, Joe, Richard C. Fording, and Sanford Schram. 2011. *Disciplining the Poor: Neoliberal Paternalism and the Persistent Power of Race*. Chicago: University of Chicago Press.

Sousa, William H. 2010. "Paying Attention to Minor Offenses: Order Maintenance Policing in Practice." *Police Practice and Research: An International Journal* 11 (1): 45–59.

Sparks, Tony. 2012. "Governing the Homeless in an Age of Compassion: Homelessness, Citizenship, and the 10-Year Plan to End Homelessness in King County Washington." *Antipode* 44 (4): 1510–31.

Spradley, James P. 1970. *You Owe Yourself a Drunk: An Ethnography of Urban Nomads*. Boston: Little Brown.

Stewart, Jocelyn Y. 2003. "ACLU Sues to Block Enforcement of LA Ordinance against Homeless." *Los Angeles Times*, February 20, B3.

Sugarman, Barry. 1976. *Daytop Village: A Therapeutic Community*. New York: Holt, Rinehart, and Winston.

Suttles, Gerald D. 1968. *The Social Order of the Slum: Ethnicity and Territory in the Inner City*. Chicago: University of Chicago Press.

Swidler, Ann. 2001. *Talk of Love: How Culture Matters*. Chicago: University of Chicago Press.

Thompson, William E. 1983. "Hanging Tongues: A Sociological Encounter with the Assembly Line." *Qualitative Sociology* 6:215–37.

Tsemberis, Stanley. 2004. "Housing First." In *Encyclopedia of Homelessness*, edited by David Levinson, 277–80. Thousand Oaks, CA: Sage.

Vaillancourt, Ryan. 2009. "The Halo Effect: New Program Steers Homeless Offenders to Social Services Instead of Jail." *Los Angeles Downtown News*, June 11, 1.

———. 2010. "Police Brace for Unsupervised Parolees." *Los Angeles Downtown News*, February 26, 6.

Valverde, Mariana. 2003. "Targeted Governance and the Problem of Desire." In *Risk and Morality*, edited by Richard V. Ericson and Aaron Doyle, 438–58. Toronto: University of Toronto Press.

Van Maanen, John. 1978. "The Asshole." In *Policing: A View from the Street*, edited by Peter K. Manning and John Van Maanen, 221–38. Santa Monica, CA: Goodyear Publishing.

Venkatesh, Sudhir. 1997. "The Social Organization of Street Gang Activity in an Urban Ghetto." *American Journal of Sociology* 103 (1): 82–111.

———. 2000. *American Project: The Rise and Fall of a Modern Ghetto*. Cambridge, MA: Harvard University Press.

———. 2006. *Off the Books: The Underground Economy of the Urban Poor*. Cambridge, MA: Harvard University Press.

von Mahs, Jürgen. 2013. *The Sociospatial Exclusion of Homeless People*. Philadelphia: Temple University Press.

Wacquant, Loïc. 1993. "Urban Outcasts: Stigma and Division in the Black American Ghetto and the French Urban Periphery." *International Journal of Urban and Regional Research* 17 (3): 366–83.

———. 1998. "Negative Social Capital: State Breakdown and Social Destitution in

America's Urban Core." *Netherlands Journal of Housing and the Built Environment* 13 (1): 25–40.

———. 2001. "Deadly Symbiosis: When Ghetto and Prison Meet and Mesh." *Punishment and Society* 3 (1): 95–133.

———. 2003. "Ethnografeast: A Progress Report on the Practice and Promise of Ethnography." *Ethnography* 4 (1): 5–14.

———. 2008. *Urban Outcasts: A Comparative Study in Urban Marginality*. Cambridge: Polity.

———. 2009. *Punishing the Poor: The Neoliberal Government of Social Insecurity*. Durham, NC: Duke University Press.

Walby, Kevin, and Randy Lippert. 2012. "Spatial Regulation, Dispersal, and the Aesthetics of the City: Conservation Officer Policing of Homeless People in Ottawa, Canada." *Antipode* 44 (3): 1015–33.

Walker, Richard A., and Gray Brechin. 2010. *The Living New Deal: The Unsung Benefits of the New Deal for the United States and California*. Institute for Research on Labor and Employment.

Walker, Samuel. 1977. *A Critical History of Police Reform*. Lexington, MA: Lexington Books.

Watkins-Hayes, Celeste. 2009. *The New Welfare Bureaucrats: Entanglements of Race, Class, and Policy Reform*. Chicago: University of Chicago Press.

Whetstone, Sarah, and Teresa Gowan. 2011. "Diagnosing the Criminal Addict: Biochemistry in the Service of the State." *Advances in Medical Sociology* 12:309–30.

White, Michael D. 2010. "Jim Longstreet, Mike Marshall, and the Lost Art of Policing Skid Row." *Criminology & Public Policy* 9 (4): 883–96.

Wieder, D. Lawrence 1974. *Language and Social Reality: The Case of Telling the Convict Code*. Lanham, MD: University Press of America.

Williams, Terry M. 1992. *Crackhouse: Notes from the End of the Line*. Reading, MA: Addison-Wesley.

Wilson, Christopher P. 2000. *Cop Knowledge: Police Power and Cultural Narrative in Twentieth-Century America*. Chicago: University of Chicago Press.

Wilson, James Q. 1975. *Thinking about Crime*. New York: Basic Books.

———. 1978. *Varieties of Police Behavior*. Cambridge, MA: Harvard University Press.

———. 1997. "Paternalism, Democracy, and Bureaucracy." In *The New Paternalism: Supervisory Approaches to Poverty*, edited by Lawrence M. Mead, 330–43. Washington, DC: Brookings Institution.

Wilson, James Q., and George L. Kelling. 1982. "Broken Windows: The Police and Neighborhood Safety." *Atlantic Monthly*, March, 29–38.

Wilson, William Julius. 2010. "Why Both Social Structure and Culture Matter in a Holistic Analysis of Inner-City Poverty." *Annals of the American Academy of Political and Social Science* 629 (1): 200–219.

Wilton, Robert, and Geoffrey DeVerteuil. 2006. "Spaces of Sobriety/Sites of Power: Examining Social Model Alcohol Recovery Programs as Therapeutic Landscapes." *Social Science & Medicine* 63 (3): 649–61.

Winton, Richard. 2007. "Beefed-up LAPD Presence on Skid Row Begins Paying Off." *Los Angeles Times*, January 27, B1.

Wiseman, Jacqueline P. 1970. *Stations of the Lost: The Treatment of Skid Row Alcoholics*. Chicago: University of Chicago Press.

Wolch, Jennifer. 1990. *The Shadow State: Government and Voluntary Sector in Transition*. Ann Arbor: University of Michigan Press.

Wolch, Jennifer, and Michael Dear. 1993. *Malign Neglect: Homelessness in an American City*. San Francisco: Jossey-Bass.

Wolch, Jennifer R., Michael Dear, and Andrea Akita. 1988. "Explaining Homelessness." *Journal of the American Planning Association* 54 (4): 443–53.

Zavis, Alexandra. 2010. "Not All Welcome Skid Row Charity." *Los Angeles Times*, September 12, A39.

———. 2012. "Housing for Homeless Pays Off." *Los Angeles Times*, June 8, AA1.

Zussman, Robert. 2004. "People in Places." *Qualitative Sociology* 27 (4): 351–63.

Index